# Wildlife & Warfare

At the beginning everything seems simple: from the experience of a few years every problem of animal behaviour appears to have been solved. A few more years pass, and this mental complacency becomes shaken... Nowhere is the truth of the proverb about a little knowledge being a dangerous thing more obvious than in matters connected with wild life. Man, today, has such absolute power over the existences of other creatures of the earth, that any action taken as the result of inaccurate observation, or faulty deduction, may not only cause irreparable mischief, but may defeat the very interests which it is intended to serve.

From James Stevenson-Hamilton's Foreword to his book
*Wild Life in South Africa* (London, 1947).

# Wildlife & Warfare

## The Life of James Stevenson-Hamilton

Jane Carruthers

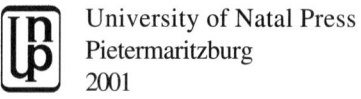

University of Natal Press
Pietermaritzburg
2001

Wildlife & Warfare: The Life of James Stevenson-Hamilton

ISBN 0 86980 986 5

© Jane Carruthers
First published in 2001

All rights reserved. No part of this publication may be reproduced or transmitted in any form or by any means, electronic or mechanical, including photocopying, recording or any information storage and retrieval system, without prior permission in writing from University of Natal Press.

Published by University of Natal Press
Private Bag X01
Scottsville 3209
South Africa
E-mail: books@nu.ac.za

Editor: Andrea Nattrass
Cover designer: Brett Armstrong

Printed and bound by Interpak Books, Pietermaritzburg

# Contents

List of Illustrations .................................... vi
List of Maps ........................................... vii
Acknowledgements ..................................... ix
Foreword .............................................. xi

Introduction ........................................... 1

1 'A Good Family': Family Background and School Days
  (1867–1883) ......................................... 5
2 'Brought up with Military Ideas': Army Training and
  First Commission in Pietermaritzburg (1883–1890) ...... 15
3 'No Goal or Object': Regimental Life in Britain (1890–1898) .... 33
4 'This Life Just Suits Me': Barotseland (1898–1899) .......... 47
5 'My Regiment was in South Africa': The South African War
  (1899–1902) ......................................... 65
6 'My Own Creation': Sabi Game Reserve (1902–1914) ......... 81
7 'Puzzling are the Ways of Wild Animals': Sabi Game Reserve
  (1902–1914) ......................................... 97
8 'Biggest War in 100 Years': England and Gallipoli (1914–1917) ... 119
9 'Truculent Dinka Clans': The Sudan (1917–1919) ............ 131
10 'An Imperishable Monument': Founding the Kruger National Park
   (1920–1930) ........................................ 147
11 'The Guardian Spirit of the Low-veld': The Kruger National Park
   and Retirement (1930–1946) .......................... 175
12 'Little Benefit to Living after One's Work is Done':
   After Retirement (1946–1957) ........................ 199

Notes ................................................. 211
Selected Sources ....................................... 223
Index ................................................. 235

# List of Illustrations

1. Father and James (at right), attended by Joe (at left), with Fairholm in the background (1887) .................................................. 6
2. The newly born James with his parents (1867) ....................... 9
3. Olmar, James, Cissy and Father at Fairholm (1887). Lying in front is Val ..... 21
4. Table Mountain from Pietermaritzburg ............................. 26
5. Stevenson-Hamilton (wearing straw boater) with companions from the garrison (1889) ................................................. 28
6. Listening through augur holes .................................... 43
7. Lialui .......................................................... 56
8. The Kafue Falls ................................................. 59
9. 'C' Squadron, Heilbron (1902) ................................... 78
10. View of Sabi Game Reserve looking east from Legogote ............... 85
11. View up Sabi River from the warden's quarters ..................... 89
12. The warden's annual tour ........................................ 98
13. Tshokwane ..................................................... 100
14. Lion skulls at Sabi Bridge (1924) ................................ 107
15. Early game photo (taken by Paul Selby) ........................... 114
16. General view of Cape Helles ..................................... 124
17. Stevenson-Hamilton's dug-out ................................... 128
18. View from terrace, Kajo Kaji .................................... 135
19. A Nuer dance ................................................... 138
20. In this posed portrait Sergeant Judas Ndlovu apprehends an armed poacher .. 153
21. Advertising poster for the Kruger National Park designed by Harry Stratford Caldecott ....................................... 164
22. Unveiling the plaque to Paul Kruger (1933). Piet Grobler is speaking and Hilda Stevenson-Hamilton (who married James in 1930) stands in front of the South African flag ...................................... 167
23. Skukuza rest camp (c.1929) ..................................... 176
24. Stevenson-Hamilton with Wolhuter at the Lindanda tree – site of the latter's escape from being killed by a lion (in 1903). Wolhuter was seriously mauled but managed to kill the lion with his sheath knife ................... 181
25. Tourists camping out in the Kruger National Park (c.1930) .......... 182
26. James with his children, Jamie and Anne .......................... 193
27. A sketch of Gibraltar by Hilda Stevenson-Hamilton ................. 202
28. James Stevenson-Hamilton next to the trophy of his first lion in the hall at Fairholm .................................................. 205

# List of Maps

1. Stevenson-Hamilton in Barotseland .................................. 48
2. Stevenson-Hamilton's involvement in the South African War .............. 66
3. Sabi and Singwitsi Game Reserves (showing modern Kruger National Park camps) ................................................................ 82
4. Gallipoli ............................................................. 120
5. Stevenson-Hamilton in the southern Sudan (based on his own 'Sketch-map of the Dinka country', 1920) ........................................... 132

# Acknowledgements

In the course of researching and writing this book I received help and advice from many people and I welcome the opportunity to thank them for their contributions.

The first and most important acknowledgment is to James Stevenson-Hamilton, son of the subject of this biography, and his wife Jennifer. The extensive Stevenson-Hamilton collection is housed at 'Fairholm', the estate near Larkhall, Lanarkshire, that has been in the family for more than five hundred years. Over the many years we discussed and planned this book the Stevenson-Hamiltons allowed me full use of these archives and assisted me to discover and examine the manuscript material on which this work is based. I am extremely grateful for their hospitality during long working visits to Scotland, and also for their thoughtful ideas, suggestions and criticisms, and for their assistance in very many other ways. It is a rare privilege for a stranger to be allowed such unimpeded access to private family documentation of this kind. The house, with its remarkable library and papers, is one to touch the imagination, and the Stevenson-Hamiltons could not have been more hospitable and generous.

James's sister, Mrs Anne Roupell (formerly Doyle), was also enthusiastic, as were Hamish and Jo Stevenson-Hamilton, John Stevenson-Hamilton and Andrew Stevenson-Hamilton. My thanks go in addition to Mrs Ethel Godfrey and Miss Lettice Cholmondeley, the sisters of Hilda Stevenson-Hamilton.

On numerous visits to Britain my husband's family were extraordinarily supportive and kind, providing accommodation, entertainment and assistance with complex travel arrangements. For the help of Tom and Felicity Crawley and Mary Rose and the late Richard Farley I am very grateful. My gratitude must go also to my own patient South African family – my mother, Mary Swingler, sister Sally Haden-Smith and brothers Robert and John Swingler – and my housekeeper, Mabel Ngqame, who were all extremely forbearing about my obsessive research agenda.

In Britain, I was helped by many people associated with the places and institutions which featured in the life of James Stevenson-Hamilton. I would like to thank: the Alston family and Mrs Shand at Usan; the Librarian, Helensburgh; Mrs Ruth Barden and the staff of Lockers Park School, Hemel Hempstead; Mr Warren of Lomond School, Helensburgh; Mrs Claire Morton and the Museum Curator, Rugby School; Major Park-Weir, Sandhurst Military Academy; and the staff of South Lodge.

In South Africa, a number of people and institutions gave me invaluable assistance: Ms Mary-Lynn Suttie, University of South Africa Library; Miss Carol Lee, Johannesburg Public Library; Archivists and staff of the State Archives, Pretoria; Dr U. de V. Pienaar (former Warden) and staff, Skukuza Archives, Kruger National Park; Mrs Irene Grobler,

Stevenson-Hamilton Library, Skukuza; Manuscript Library, University of the Witwatersrand; and Dr J.A. Dunn, Chief Psychiatrist, Fort Napier Hospital, Pietermaritzburg.

Colleagues in the History Department at the University of South Africa appraised drafts of this work. For valuable observations and insights, I am grateful to: Professor Greg Cuthbertson, Dr Tilman Dedering, Dr Phil Eidelberg, Professor Albert Grundlingh, and Dr Alex Mouton. Over the last few years, colleagues at other universities have also helped me to refine my ideas or to locate appropriate sources, and I would like to thank Professor William Beinart, Dr Tom Griffiths, Dr Douglas Johnson, Professor Basil le Cordeur, Dr Libby Robin and Professor Christopher Saunders.

I have always greatly admired the work of imperial historian Professor John MacKenzie and I am honoured that he agreed to write the foreword to this book.

I would also like to extend my appreciation to Roger Loveday for editing my unwieldy draft manuscript into manageable form and to Andrea Nattrass, editor at University of Natal Press, who together with Glenn Cowley and his professional staff at the Press expertly prepared the manuscript for publication. I am also grateful to Olive Anderson, cartographer, and Margie Ramsay, indexer, for their contributions to this book.

For the various photographs and illustrations thanks are due to: the KwaZulu-Natal Provincial Museum Services; the South African National Parks who hold many photographs on loan from James Stevenson-Hamilton; Ian Davidson at Edinburgh University Press and Raymond Ashworth at Alexander Ritchie & Son who organised for the scanning of the Scotland-based photographs, sketches and water-colours; and James Stevenson-Hamilton who generously allowed and helped to organise the use of material from the Fairholm archives.

Above all, I would like to acknowledge with very deep gratitude the support of my husband, Vincent, who has always encouraged and assisted me in all my endeavours.

# Foreword

*Wildlife & Warfare: The Life of James Stevenson-Hamilton* is a book about complex and multi-layered identities. On the face of it, it is the story of a Scot who, through his love of African landscape and wildlife, becomes an honorary African. But it goes much further than this. The life of the remarkable James Stevenson-Hamilton offers insights into what it meant to be an upper class land-owning Scot in the late nineteenth century, how his Scottishness interacted with his sense of also being English in culture and language, British in nationality, and a citizen of the British Empire at the height of its power. It also reflects his educational and social milieux, his relationship with and experience of the army, particularly in times of crises, as well as his opportunities for adventure and travel in little-known parts of Africa. But Stevenson-Hamilton marked himself out for experiences and achievements which raised him far above the normal run of subalterns. Like David Livingstone, a compatriot from the same county of Lanarkshire, Stevenson-Hamilton developed a remarkable sympathy for Africa and Africans, for the African environment and its wildlife.

Thus Stevenson-Hamilton's identities as soldier, adventurer and administrator were soon overlaid with his achievements as writer, propagandist, draughtsman of game law, zoologist, game warden and national park superintendent. On several occasions his life and career seemed to be becalmed, but he always discovered a fresh wind and new inspiration from his love of the African environment. However, his love was not a misty-eyed romantic thing. It was something much more hard-headed, as his constant questing for knowledge and information, and his willingness to change his mind on key issues (like the status of lions or the presence of African settlements within a game reserve) indicated. Before him game rangers had been rough and ready, hunting freebooters. He, almost single-handedly, created a new profession, that of game warden and conservationist, combining intelligent observation and practical science with a desire to make the great and small game of Africa a source of fascination and recreation to a wider public. In this, he recognised the revolutionary power of the internal combustion engine and the key tendency of African game almost to ignore the presence of vehicles. If at first that public was likely to be white and middle class, still his labours in the Sabi Game Reserve and later the Kruger National Park would ultimately preserve aspects of the environment and of wildlife for others in the modern republic of South Africa.

In all of these activities, Stevenson-Hamilton became almost larger than life. Although he never forgot his Scottish origins and frequently yearned to return to his roots, he continued to find Africa irresistible. He mixed with the so-called 'great and the good'. His writings gave him international fame. His late marriage and family brought him personal happiness and the knowledge that the Lanarkshire house and lands might also be preserved. In his lifespan, he exploited to the full all the opportunities and obligations which Empire placed upon an individual of his standing and predilections.

Jane Carruthers's work on the history of the Kruger National Park and on many other aspects of environmental history is well known. Here she brings both a critical and a sympathetic understanding to bear upon the life of James Stevenson-Hamilton. As she rightly points out, it is both ahistorical and not particularly sensible to apply modern standards to people who lived in somewhat different pasts. And yet, even when that has been said, one of the striking things about her subject is that, despite the inevitable social and other attitudes of the day which Stevenson-Hamilton represented, so much of his work remains both acceptable and admirable to modern eyes, hopefully even to those of his African compatriots and successors. Hence, this is a timely book. In exploring an extraordinary life, it tells us a great deal about many issues which remain very much alive and significant in the here and now. By interrogating Stevenson-Hamilton's life, we are persuaded to think harder about our modern concerns for the environment, for wildlife, and for human contexts of all sorts. *Wildlife & Warfare* should be read by everyone who regards the natural world as the vital context for all our lives, actions and thoughts.

John M. MacKenzie

# Introduction

MORE THAN ANY OTHER individual, James Stevenson-Hamilton can be credited with the creation of the Kruger National Park, spanning some nineteen thousand square kilometres across the Northern Province and Mpumalanga in South Africa. In 1902, when the South African War ended, he left his military career for the more uncertain calling of 'game warden'. Under his supervision the small, neglected and war-ravaged Sabi Game Reserve expanded in stature and size so that by the time he retired, in 1946, it had become one of the great national parks of the world.

In addition, he was an observant naturalist and accomplished writer who published widely on South African wildlife biology, doing much to coax it away from nineteenth-century amateur natural history towards what is now recognised as modern ecology and wildlife management science.

Stevenson-Hamilton's wildlife accomplishments have been well documented and appreciated, especially in South Africa, but the rest of his long and varied life has remained obscure. This biography examines the diversity of the entire ninety-year lifespan of James Stevenson-Hamilton, a task made possible by his meticulous journal which – like many Victorians – he maintained almost every day from the age of 13 in 1880 until just a week before his death in 1957.

James Stevenson-Hamilton was born in Dublin while his father was in Ireland on military duty. Around the time of his birth his mother inherited Fairholm, a large family estate within easy reach of Glasgow. No large income came with the property so James continued in the family tradition of a military career. With his cavalry regiment he was stationed in Natal in South Africa between 1888 and 1890 and developed a deep love of Africa. He explored Barotseland in 1898 as part of a small expedition partly funded by the Royal Geographical Society. As this venture was coming to an end in 1899 war was declared in South Africa and Stevenson-Hamilton joined his regiment in the field. When war was over he left the army and became warden of the Sabi Game Reserve.

Although the evolution of the Kruger National Park was his life's work he kept his other interests alive, including his involvement with the family property in Scotland. During the First World War he saw action in Gallipoli and Egypt. In 1917 he was seconded to a civilian administrative post in the southern Sudan and he remained there until 1921. During the late 1920s and 30s he consolidated the development of the Kruger National Park. After his retirement in 1946 he remained in South Africa and lived with his wife and family near White River in Mpumalanga. During these last years he was forced to adopt a slightly slower pace, but the clarity of his mental faculties continued and his remarks about the onset of infirmity and the tribulations of old age are both poignant and interesting.

Together with the Kruger National Park, Stevenson-Hamilton's great legacy is his consistent, critical and honest record of the details of his long life. Little escaped his shrewd eye and his comments are those of an astute and analytical man. His diary not only relates to his daily activities; it also includes context, background and reflections about personal concerns and current opinions. His journal style is economical and concise, and he has the gift of conveying in a few terse words the essence of a person or situation.

Aspiring historians are warned against the uncritical use of their source materials. As primary documents private journals have to be treated with particular caution because, although they appear to have been written with only the writer in mind, the very fact that thoughts have been committed to paper indicates that other readers may also have been envisaged. Stevenson-Hamilton came from a long line of men who recorded the events of their lives to explain their actions to their descendants, and James followed in this tradition. Thus, from the outset he knew his audience: he wrote for himself and for his family. Occasionally there were happenings or actions that he did not wish even his closest relatives to know about. To keep them confidential he judiciously tore out the appropriate pages or crossed out certain lines in thick black ink so that they would be illegible.

For most years of his adult life Stevenson-Hamilton wrote in a Letts Diary, which allowed space for a daily paragraph. But there are also special journals, written without the constraints of a daily allocation. Most of these relate to a period (such as Barotseland or Gallipoli) or highlights which he thought would be particularly interesting. When he had the time he typed out some of these journals, as he did with many of those of his later years. A few are illustrated with pen or pencil sketches of places, companions, or events, or have press cuttings, letters and other documents placed between the leaves. Since James was a competent water-colourist, there are a number of paintings of places which took his fancy. He took many photographs and some of them – like those of the eastern Transvaal at the turn of the century – were the first photographs of the area ever taken and are therefore of considerable historical significance. He was also an inveterate hoarder of many objects. He thus kept some of his clothes (especially uniforms), games which he played, photographs of friends, and press cuttings, all of which, taken with the written record, enable one to gain a better measure of the man.

Faced with such an overwhelmingly large body of primary material, the process of selection becomes difficult. While a publication consisting of all the journals would be desirable, there is inevitably much in them that is routine and would detract from or weigh down the more important events. I have attempted to avoid focussing on minutiae and have treated the journals and other archival matter as raw material for the preparation of this biography. I have used appropriate inverted commas when quoting James's exact words. In accordance with normal scholarly practice I have acknowledged my sources in the form of endnotes. However, because most of this book is based on evidence in the daily journals, these are not always acknowledged where it is quite clear that they are the source.

The sheer scope of James's life presented me with another problem: how to do justice to the length and complexity of his life, while at the same time adopting an orderly approach to the main periods and themes. Any life needs to be balanced against its historical context and, as all biographers know, this is not an easy task. Because the British imperial era and its values are now largely discredited, it would be easy but facile to reject the people and situations which were embedded in the imperial and colonial matrix. From this vantage point we may, instead, take a more nuanced look at some of those who participated in the dramatic social and political changes at the turn of the twentieth century. Although he certainly could have been described as conservative, Stevenson-Hamilton himself was not always in harmony with the trends of imperial politics, and some of his values were decidedly unconventional. It is futile for a historian to impose modern standards on those who could not share them.

Stevenson-Hamilton's motivations throughout his long life were frequently unclear, but that is probably true of most human beings. There were, in addition, great contradictions. Thus, while he was well-connected and longed for the honours, wealth and other benefits which this might have brought, he consistently hoped and felt that he might make a difference with his time on earth. He also straddled two worlds – Britain and South Africa – and, in the beginning, he did not think of them as essentially different. He also never imagined that one day he would have to choose between them.

# 1

# 'A Good Family'[1]
## Family Background and School Days
## (1867–1883)

THE LIFE OF James Stevenson-Hamilton is inseparable from Fairholm, his family estate near Larkhall in Lanarkshire, Scotland. The grey stone house is quintessentially Scottish in that it is sturdy and functional rather than opulent. The exterior is severe and unadorned by creepers, and its high tower lends a military air. But Fairholm is softened by its long lawns, tall trees and shrubbery, as well as by its position on the Avon River. In the mid-nineteenth century, the house was described as 'situated on a fertile haugh or holm, round which the Avon winds. It is embosomed by the most romantic scenery, by swelling braes and uplands, clothed with fine copsewood, forming quite a natural amphitheatre, so that it well merits the appellation of "the Fair-Holm".'[2]

Stevenson-Hamilton was intimately attached to this property throughout his life. There were times when he wanted nothing more than to immerse himself in the heritage which Fairholm represented, but there were other times when he became painfully aware of the enormous financial, administrative and emotional responsibilities which he had inherited with the ownership of the estate. In spite of this, and whatever his passing moods and resolutions, Fairholm was seldom far from his thoughts. His whole nature was enlivened and refined by the profound sense of continuity. Over the centuries the Hamiltons of Fairholm made it a part of their family tradition to accumulate and keep valuable documents and records, as did other well-established families of the time. What is unusual about the Fairholm papers is that they have survived to this day in the very place to which they have been tied by history. The house, the family and their accumulated artefacts still maintain their ancient connection with the landscape, the people and the region. They are closely interwoven with the fabric of Lanarkshire society but, unlike many rich and powerful families of the realm, the Hamiltons of Fairholm did not patronise their fellows and neighbours. Rather, they kept in the background and remained 'a good family'. Consequently, their documents, portraits, photographs and correspondence are in many ways unique and extremely valuable.

*Father and James (at right), attended by Joe (at left), with Fairholm in the background (1887).*

James Stevenson-Hamilton was proud of his position as one of the landed gentry of Scotland. That he was the sixteenth Laird of Fairholm and the head of an armigerous family with a recorded pedigree meant a great deal to him. In his youth, Stevenson-Hamilton relished the importance of his lineage, but his pride was not born of idle fantasy. It was rooted in the fact that he could trace his ancestors over many centuries, and that he could demonstrate their connection with Fairholm from 1492. He knew that he belonged intrinsically to this part of the world.

In the latter part of the nineteenth century the Stevenson-Hamiltons were one of many landed families in the neighbourhood. Numerous houses were better than theirs and other estates were both larger and grander. Indeed, the magnificently extravagant palace of the Dukes of Hamilton lay not far from Fairholm. Also close by was the Duke's chateau or shooting lodge, built in about 1732.[3] Recently restored, Chatelherault now houses a museum and is one of the sights of the district. It says much for the tenacity of the Fairholm branch of the Hamiltons that their establishment has survived while the glories of Hamilton Palace and the houses of most of the other landed families have vanished.

James Stevenson-Hamilton was born in 1867 just as Britain was reaching the zenith of its imperial power. This was a society characterised by immense wealth and privilege, a society divided by class distinctions and by social and economic inequalities. The country's landed gentry formed the backbone of the nation and were the arbiters of taste, custom and manners. But James lived through a time when power was shifting into the hands of a nascent working class, a development which marked the end of political dominance by the gentry. In the Scottish context Fairholm was extremely close to these changes because of its situation on the outskirts of the mining village of Larkhall, then a hotbed of early socialist political activity.

In the nineteenth century the coal fields of the west of Scotland contributed greatly to Glasgow's second wave of prosperity. Lanarkshire attracted workers from other parts of Scotland, together with many thousands of Irish immigrants and their families. The predominantly agricultural communities became outnumbered by the people seeking work in the developing industrial area. Unsatisfactory working conditions in the textile and mining industries nurtured the development of trade unions and this led to the emergence into political prominence of socialist leaders such as Keir Hardie and Robert Smillie who were both active in the Larkhall district in the latter part of the nineteenth and the early twentieth centuries. The labour movement has always attracted strong support in this part of Scotland and it continues to do so.

James's Hamilton ancestors had been involved in many of the political machinations of Scotland. One, Thomas Hamilton, was a prisoner-of-war of the English in the early 1400s. The Hamilton family, and with them the Hamiltons of Fairholm, had been supporters of Mary Queen of Scots and had suffered for their allegiance, being banished and stripped of their estates during the minority of King James VI, and Fairholm and other Hamilton houses being razed to the ground. The motto of the Hamiltons of Fairholm, 'Thankful', records their later gratitude when having returned to Scotland in 1585 with the army of the Banished Lords, they obtained restitution of their lands. The twelfth Laird, Charles, held a commission in the British army and fought against Bonnie Prince Charlie's rebels at Culloden in 1746. Thereafter he served in France, Gibraltar and Guadeloupe. His grandson, John Hamilton (1804–1867), extended the house at Fairholm and effected many of the changes and improvements which exist today. His younger brother James, born in 1807, was the grandfather of James Stevenson-Hamilton. As a younger son James saw few prospects in Scotland. Consequently, after his marriage he emigrated to Australia. He had two daughters, Eliza (born in November 1839 in New South Wales, Australia), later to be the mother of James Stevenson-Hamilton, and Anne, born a year later in New Zealand.[4]

When James Hamilton died in 1842 John arranged for the family to return to Scotland where they took up residence at Fairholm. Disputes arose between the two Mrs Hamiltons, leading to the eventual departure of Mrs James. The girls remained at Fairholm and were brought up under rather spartan conditions by the Laird (their uncle) and his wife, who was always known as Aunt Hamie. Eliza possessed artistic talent and was later sent to art school in Edinburgh.

In 1866, at the age of 27, Eliza Hamilton married James Stevenson, who was then 28, of Braidwood.[5] James was the eldest son of Nathaniel Stevenson who had built the nearby mansion house of Braidwood some forty years previously. Good-looking and athletic, James had begun his career as a shipping clerk, but had been commissioned into the 12th Royal Lancers with the rank of Captain in 1860.

James Stevenson-Hamilton – called Jasie to distinguish him from his father – was born in Dublin at the height of what were called the 'Fenian disturbances'. His father's regiment was there as part of the British military presence in Ireland, deployed to contain an upsurge of Irish nationalism.[6] At the time of the child's birth, at three in the afternoon on 2 October 1867 at 7 Cumberland Place, his mother and the midwife were in a state of fear and apprehension. James was away from Dublin at the time and Eliza and her servants had barricaded the doors of the house against nationalist rioters with the boxes that contained the as-yet-unpacked wedding presents from ten months earlier. Given these troubled circumstances in which promotion came rapidly to competent soldiers, a distinguished military career might have been envisaged for Stevenson-Hamilton's father. However, his active soldiering came to an abrupt end when, just a month before Jasie was born, Eliza's uncle, John, died. As heiress of entail to the estates of Fairholm and Kirkton Eliza returned to Scotland at the beginning of 1868. Her husband sold his commission and followed her a few months later. The terms of the entail with which the estate was burdened by Eliza's great-grandfather, Major Charles Hamilton, obliged his successors 'in all time coming to bear the surname, arms and title of Hamilton of Fairholm'. Thus on Eliza succeeding to the Scottish estates in 1867, the family assumed the name of Stevenson-Hamilton of Fairholm.

The marriage between Eliza and James seems to have been a happy one. Together they made the most of living at Fairholm and participated in the social activities of the county. Another baby was born in 1868, a son named John who did not survive the year. The next child, a daughter, Eliza, named after her mother but always called 'Cissy', was born in 1871. Two other daughters died in infancy.

'A Good Family'

*The newly born James with his parents (1867).*

When his mother was available Jasie spent the grey days at Fairholm sketching and drawing under her keen supervision. His sketchbooks of December 1873 show an interest in exotic animals – a kangaroo, and a hyaena eating a sheep. He was, as many little boys are, keen on action, and he drew battle scenes from books as well as fearsome 'Red Indians'. Despite the industrial progress which was sweeping relentlessly over the lowlands, Fairholm was still very rural. Jasie thus grew up in idyllic surroundings. According to records of the time the district was rich in flora and fauna – including otters, badgers, hedgehogs, and even the occasional roe-deer. The extensive woodlands around Fairholm and on the banks of the Avon harboured a wealth of birdlife and the river provided Jasie, a keen angler, with unlimited opportunities to fish for trout.

James and Eliza's youngest child was born on 15 September 1875. This was a boy whom they named Olmar after a remote Hamilton ancestor. Just a week later, at the age of 36, Eliza died from the effects of puerperal fever.

Her death, like that of so many other Victorian mothers, was caused by a failure to understand the virulently contagious nature of the disease.[7] Jasie later wrote that the 'sepsis [was] conveyed to her by the family doctor, Lennox, who came to her direct from a similar case'. James's journal records that Eliza's coffin was 'filled with roses and the choicest flowers we could find before the lid was soldered closed'.

The death of his mother affected young Jasie more profoundly than anything that happened to him in the rest of his life. He often referred to her in his journals in later years and her memory was one of his most emotional and enduring. After she had died Jasie became, if anything, even more solitary, but while he suffered alone, his father had other things on his mind. Fairholm and Kirkton now belonged to his oldest son and had to be taken care of. Money was not plentiful. There were three children to look after: Jasie was seven, Cissy was four, and Olmar just a week old.

At the time of his mother's death Jasie was under a private tutor who came to Fairholm every day, but in January 1877, at the age of nine, he was sent to a small boarding school of about 12 boys, some forty miles distant, where the teaching was good, but the discipline strict. Even in old age Stevenson-Hamilton remembered the event vividly, 'This day eighty years ago I was taken to school for the first time at Ardenlee, Helensburgh. I remember it as if it were yesterday. The boys were out for a walk with old Wilkins [the Headmaster] and my father... and I sat by the fire in the sitting room until they came back.'[8] Trouble was only a fortnight away. At two in the morning, Jasie was discovered with his nightshirt over his clothes, attempting to get out of his room. His father reacted as any good Victorian father would have done: he gave Jasie 'a lecture and a birching with Mr Wilkins's new birch which I hope will put such nonsense out of his head, poor boy'.

At this time Jasie's father was actively looking for a new wife. He found her in an agreeable twenty-year-old woman named Frances Leyland. Her father, Frederick Leyland, was one of the new breed of industrial entrepreneurs, and an extremely wealthy man. From humble beginnings Leyland had come to own a fleet of steamers and had other extensive business interests. Typically of the *nouveau riche*, Leyland loved ornamentation and was, according to one report, 'overfond of what is garish'. His London home, at 49 Prince's Gate, was the talk of London society and often featured in the newspapers. Its famous 'Peacock Room' had been painted by James Whistler, the controversial but fashionable Irish-American artist.[9]

Jasie's father married Frances Leyland in London on 2 July 1879 and the reception was held in the magnificent Peacock Room. A son, Leyland, was born prematurely on 29 February 1880, but Frances had contracted jaundice and died two days later, leaving James a sorrowing widower for the second time.

One of James's many problems was to find a suitable school to which to send Jasie after Ardenlee. The boy, in the conventional wisdom of the day, needed to make good connections, and the Stevenson-Hamilton ties with London were now stronger with another baby and in-laws in London. In 1879 Jasie was therefore sent to school at Lockers Park at Hemel Hempstead where he remained until the end of 1880. During these years he began to keep a regular diary and he recorded his friends and their activities: there was the pet fieldmouse, the minor squabbles over dormitory rights, and the friendships made and broken. Jasie maintained his many outdoor interests and hobbies. He enjoyed his favourite solitary pursuit of fishing, spending a lot of time at the Bury, the little stream nearby, with a rod in hand. There was the occasional party, replete with treats such as 'sardines, potted meats, jam, marmalade, walnuts, cake and biscuits'. On the curriculum were organised games in which Jasie participated, but without distinction.

The teaching staff and the discipline at the school were stereotypically Victorian. 'Cuts' were given for petty offences, and Jasie's diary describes the gruesome details. MacInnes had 'blood . . . coming through the black parts; [and had been] tied to a bedpost. Didn't blub. Can't sit down. Will bear the marks for 6 months or more. This will do him no end of good,' he ended his journal entry almost gleefully. Such schools were designed not only to educate, but also to instil the values of Victorian gentlemen.

Jasie was not a dedicated scholar but he did well enough, particularly when he tried hard. At the end of his school career at Lockers Park, on 20 December 1880, he came top of his class and was justifiably pleased, not least because the next best pupil was MacInnes. As a reward for this achievement he was presented with a copy of Lamb's *Tales of Shakespeare* bound in red and gold leather: 'Glad to have got to the top. Remember this time last year I was bottom of the class by far by over 100 marks. I like my prize awfully.'

In January 1881, when Jasie was 14, Rugby was the obvious choice as both his father and his Uncle Nathaniel had been there. Jasie's stay, from 1881 to 1883, was spent under the famous headmaster of the time, Dr Jex-Blake, the Oxford educated cleric and scholar – a man of 'striking beauty and grace of person [with] great dignity in address and a kind disposition'.[10] This type of school served many increasingly important functions in Victorian society. In them the sons of gentlemen received a classical education and were also able to consolidate long-term friendships and a network of professional contacts. These provided the future soldiers and administrators of Britain with the kind of common language and bonds of obligation which enabled them to rule the Empire effectively.

Jasie was unhappy at Rugby. He made few friends, and if he ever went back there he did not mention it in his diary. The most important part of the school for Jasie was the Temple Reading Room – a good place to draw and read on one's own, especially since he was neither a good games-player nor an outstanding scholar. He did not think much of the education (extolled by others) which the school provided. 'I learned very little at Rugby [other] than what was required for army examinations,' he recalled. In addition, Jasie considered that the victimisation and bullying prevalent at the school affected him for the rest of his life. He really dreaded going back to 'horrid old Rugby' after holidays at home. His diary of the time recalls his deep unhappiness: 'I don't know how I shall get through this week.'

School holidays were the highlight of his school days. They usually began with meeting his father in London: 'met Papa at the club, match at Lords, got a tall hat'. Jasie spent most of his holidays at Fairholm but he also visited his Uncle Tom Stevenson and his family in Ireland. The nephew noted that Uncle Tom was good fun: 'he will stand any amount of chaff with the most placid good nature'. There were also happy times with his eccentric Aunt Margaret and her husband, George Keith, at Usan near Montrose, on Scotland's east coast. Still rural and with a magnificent coastline Usan was a delightful place for children. Jasie spent many hours exploring the area: walking to the lime kiln at Boddin Point, watching the fishermen spread their large nets to dry, and fishing to his heart's content from a particular favourite rock on the beach. Occasionally, when the sea was calm, the family, including even the baby, Leyland, went out in a cobble.

However happy Jasie was away from home, Fairholm held his heart as no other place could. He always looked forward with joy to returning to the house and its incomparable setting. He kept pets, he fished, played lawn tennis, went out shooting with his father, and shared activities with his brother and sister. There were Christmas parties and gifts, pantomimes in Glasgow, and family visits. Still a solitary person, he often walked alone along the Avon River to Chatelherault, played games which he had himself invented, or immersed himself in the library of 'yellow backs' with which his father had stocked his study at Fairholm.

As he reached his teenage years Jasie was beginning to think like a Laird of Fairholm: 'Papa found a lot of whisky bottles in the kitchen today but never said anything. If I had been him I would have.' He was very proud of his father's military accomplishments and attended his father's regimental review, where, he noted, 'Papa's regiment did best. They marched right through the pools of water. Papa got a telegram from the Queen in the morning, complimenting him on the bearing of his men.' Jasie was too young to have been aware of the fact that the decade of the 1880s was a watershed for many wealthy families who were unable to keep up their estates in the face of low agricultural yields and high tenant expenses. Many sold off heirlooms to finance running costs.[11] Jasie's father, who at this period had to make some long-needed improvements to Fairholm (including the installation of gaslight), found himself hampered by the terms of the entail, which prevented him from raising money on his son's behalf from the sale of property. It was only very much later that Jasie appreciated the financial difficulties which his father had suffered at this time.

# 2

# 'Brought up with Military Ideas'[1]
## Army Training and First Commission in Pietermaritzburg
## (1883–1890)

JAMES LEFT RUGBY at the end of 1883 without any regrets. It was, until then, the most unhappy year of his life. Not surprisingly, his academic performance had been poor. His lack of academic achievement fortunately did not affect his chosen career path because there had never been any question but that, following the family tradition, his future lay with the army. Consequently, in common with many other young men intended for a similar profession, he abandoned the public school system to focus his energies on preparing for the military. If Rugby had dented his confidence James could look back on a long line of distinguished ancestors to bolster his decision to enter the army, and the recent careers of his father and four uncles provided him with good examples of success. His father, after leaving his regiment in 1868, commanded the prestigious local militia. His Uncle Nathaniel had joined the Royal Scots, and his marriage to a woman of some wealth enabled him to purchase an important command. Uncle Tom, with whom James had holidayed in Ireland, had joined the 67th Regiment in 1861 and later commanded the Royal Irish Fusiliers, serving with distinction in the Egyptian Campaign of 1882. Uncle Robert was also a distinguished soldier, but apparently of a different stamp. In 1885, James then aged 18 and a cynical, but observant, young man wrote thumbnail sketches of his entire family. In these notes James described Robert as

> the most agreeable, affable and pleasant companion as well as the biggest blackguard in the family . . . Entering without a penny a crack cavalry regiment of the 18th Hussars, he speedily commenced his career with the money lenders among whose numerous clients he still continues to be at once an ornament and a pillar. He has been three times bankrupt . . .

Although James looked on his uncle with sarcasm, Robert was in 1884 Equerry to the Duke of Connaught, and would later command the 6th Dragoon Guards, rising to the rank of full Colonel. He was also destined to be mentioned in dispatches on several occasions and to be awarded the CMG [Companion of (the order of) St Michael and St George]. James regarded his youngest uncle, Andrew, as tactless and stupid and dominated by a 'disagreeable' and flirtatious wife. 'I wish I could bring myself to like him, he is such a fine fellow,' he wrote, 'but I can't and never could.' Andrew was Colonel of the Black Watch, he fought in the Ashanti War, in Egypt, and in the Sudan. Renowned for his immense physical strength and boxing prowess, Andrew had earned the nickname 'The Jem Mace of the British Army'.[2]

But much had changed since the days when his father and uncles had entered the army. Cardwell, Secretary of State for War from 1868 to 1874, had radically reformed Britain's entire military system, and the army which James now sought to enter required officers to be far more professionally qualified than before. But despite the many changes which were to impact on him, there was no immediate alteration in the composition of the upper echelons of military personnel. The life of an officer – especially a cavalry officer – remained expensive and thus the officer class remained confined to those who could afford to maintain a relatively costly lifestyle.[3]

Because officers were drawn from the sons of the upper classes, their selection and advancement were often facilitated by family traditions and social influence. Here James enjoyed something of an advantage for the distinguished record of the Stevensons was well known in military circles, but he could not rely solely on his connections. The far-reaching army reforms predicated entrance to any of the prestigious military colleges – the Royal Military Academy at Sandhurst (specifically for infantry, cavalry and the guards), or Woolwich (for artillery and engineers) – on well-regulated, standardised and highly competitive examinations.[4] In order to ensure success in the entrance examinations many young men were sent to 'army crammers' to prepare them for either of the two academies. Since James was intended for Woolwich this was the route his father decided to take.

Between January and April 1884 Stevenson-Hamilton attended a small crammer in Richmond, called the 'Homestead', under the direction of the Reverend C. Coutts. Here he studied hard, often working late into the night. When he was motivated to study James did well and his high marks gained him acceptance by the most sought-after army crammer in London – James and Lynch – the mecca for aspiring young officers. James knew he was privileged to be studying under 'the best known army tutor in England'. There was no question of any kind of broad general education: only subjects and studies designed specifically to get young men into military life were pursued. The young army men felt themselves to be superior to those who were more academically inclined, and James commented on the behaviour of the 'varsity men' whom he met, regarding them in much the same way as did Winston Churchill in his memoirs, 'mere bookworms, quite undisciplined and irresponsible . . .'[5] In fact, he should not have been quite so dismissive for he failed the preliminary examination for Woolwich twice before returning to Coutts's crammer and trying for Sandhurst. He was eventually successful and was admitted early in 1887.

After James had left school he and his father established a closer relationship with one another. Instead of referring to him as 'papa' or 'my governor', James now called his father 'the Colonel'. His father gave him a pipe and together they dined at exclusive men's clubs or went shopping, purchasing smart clothes, cuff-links and the like. The Colonel began to induct his son into the duties which were incumbent upon a Laird. In August 1884, on a visit back to Scotland from London, he and his father spent time looking through old papers in the library, an exercise which initiated young James into his ancient family heritage and the requirements of administration of the estate.

A 16-year-old boy with aristocratic connections might have regarded himself in late Victorian London as something of a man. London, the hub of Empire, was almost ten times larger than Glasgow, and there was much to see and do. James began to learn about British political life from his father who, for example, took him to lunch at the House of Commons in May 1884. With hindsight we may appreciate the irony that much of the training which James was receiving would soon be of little help in adapting to the great changes that would sweep over the British Empire; changes that would profoundly affect the political and economic power of the class to which James and his father belonged. The years of young adulthood that James lived in London marked a watershed in Victorian politics. This could already be seen in the recently reformed army which James was to join: ability, and not merely title and influence, played a decisive role. The rise of technology, the age of democracy, and the power of the popular press made a new breed of professional politicians indispensable. These talented men soon replaced the amateur aristocratic political figures of the past.

Urban development went hand-in-hand with industrial growth and a new city ethos of strikes and riots, socialists and anarchists. The extension of the franchise meant that population numbers began to matter. The Third Reform Act, and various other measures, increased the voting public from three million in 1883 to six million in 1885. Many people, hitherto ignored, thus found themselves being courted by politicians. Socialism was becoming a force to be reckoned with. People like James and his father thought that

Gladstone was a villain: the duplicitous stage manager and instigator of the mobs, responsible for undermining the power of the landowners who had effectively ruled Britain since time immemorial. But although Stevenson-Hamilton hated Gladstone until well into his old age, it was really access to wealth by an entirely new class, rather than Gladstone's personal politics, which brought about the decline in landowners' power.

There were other changes also happening in society. A hierarchy based on professionalism was coming into being. It was not, as David Cannadine explains, merely that the old ruling class acquired fresh membership from the *nouveau riche*. There was a new structure to society: the organising principle being a vertical career hierarchy rather than the horizontal connection of class.[6] While landowners and millionaire capitalists were drawing together into a new plutocracy, the middle class, and even the working classes, were coalescing and seeking new avenues to power. A real change was appearing in political structures. In 1886, the Liberal Party split permanently. Landlords and capitalists began to support the new Conservative Party, while the proletariat contributed to the rise of the Labour Party. Home Rule for Ireland was another dominating concern of the decade, and the period from June 1885 to June 1886 – when James was in London – saw this question escalate into an ominous national crisis.[7] After the elections of January 1886 Gladstone was converted to Home Rule for Ireland, something to which James's father was adamantly opposed.

Although much that was happening in London in the 1880s only later affected him directly, James was percipient enough to realise that this life in London as a candidate for the army constituted a new chapter for him and he was duly excited. Only at examination time were his studies onerous and he was able to explore the London scene: there seemed no end to the entertainment and possibilities on hand. Like other young men in his position, James frequented Richmond Park, Kew Gardens, the Crystal Palace, Bushy Park, the Hampton Court maze, cricket matches, and the zoological gardens. He began to affect the grand manner and to show off, even to himself, writing, for example about how he 'knocked about the town in the evening'. He became a theatre *habitué* and relished the entertainment provided by Victorian melodrama, then at the height of its popularity.

In spite of all the enjoyment and interest of these years, his time in London was to be one of considerable trauma for James. He could see that his father was handsome and, aged only 47 in 1885, technically an eligible man. In spite of all his best efforts to keep everything running, and in spite of being a 'capital business man' (according to his son) desperation finally overtook the Colonel in 1884.

## 'Brought up with Military Ideas'

Against a background of rising costs and diminishing income the Colonel dropped a bombshell into James's life. The entry for that day in James's diary told it graphically enough:

12 July 1884. Papa came to my rooms and knocked me up about 8 o'clock. Breakfasted at the Club. Here I heard an astounding confession. He tells me that he got engaged to be married to a Miss Gibbs yesterday. She has about £10 000 a year. He doesn't care a [bit] for her and her father is against it.

Although his motives were informed by a desire to save Fairholm from ruination, the Colonel could hardly have been proud of his brutally mercenary decision, nor of his obtaining his impressionable son's collusion in it by telling him the entire truth quite so callously. However, if the Colonel and Fairholm benefited from £10 000 per annum, Florence Gibbs, the daughter of a successful Australian sheep farmer and without social advantage, obtained marriage to a man of standing and reputation.

The Colonel married on 21 July 1885 in a splendid wedding ceremony at St Paul's in Knightsbridge. Possibly influenced by his father's attitude, James seems to have hated Florence Gibbs from the outset. He described the new bride as 'A stupid, plain, pigheaded and self-willed woman, with no tact of any description, did not make good impression at first but probably more the fault of her training than of her disposition . . .' The year 1886 began with an all-too-brief bout of happiness. The battle lines had not yet been drawn and it might have been any ordinary happy family which James described on 9 January: 'The Colonel, Florence and kids went for a drive in the sleigh.' But, before long, Florence was the target of the family's collective vindictiveness. Not less than a week later, after a day spent getting young Olmar packed to begin school, James wrote: 'Mrs Hamilton I find begins to get inquisitive about my affairs . . . In addition, she doesn't treat the children and the Colonel as well as she ought. She will regret it . . .'

Florence was isolated at Fairholm, far away from London and from anyone who might sympathise with her, and she was completely dependent on her husband's circle and the approbation of her hostile stepchildren. Each day recorded another misery. '20 January: Mrs Hamilton becoming more subdued. 21 January: Telegram at dinner from Mrs Gibbs asking if Florence was ill. The latter must be up to some mischief or other.' It is possible that James might have made her feel doubly unwelcome by emphasising the fact that Fairholm was *his* house, and not hers or even her husband's.

Florence's relationship with her stepdaughter, Cissy, who desperately needed the warmth of a mother substitute, also began badly. James recorded: '28 January: Cissy and Mrs Hamilton had a row at night . . . carrying on with a high hand.' Slowly but relentlessly, the children began to gang up against their new stepmother. They played tricks on her and belittled her.

The atmosphere at Fairholm was poisoned. Despite the birth of a child, the marriage deteriorated while James was in London in 1886. On visits back to Fairholm, James fanned the flames of disaffection. Aided by his father, he and Cissy ensured that Florence's life was made as insufferable as it could be. It was clear before the year was out that the marriage was over.

A campaign to get Florence to leave was initiated by the whole family. After a fight between Florence and her husband, she locked him out of her bedroom. The children brooded about this slight to their father, and then, in counter-attack, went out at two in the morning and fired off a gun under her window. The Colonel, by then also a part of the plot, came running down right on cue with another gun while bellowing loudly, 'Thieves!' Florence was understandably frightened out of her wits. There is little of Florence's testimony until the time of the formal separation in the early 1890s. Then, she claimed to have been cruelly treated, pushed down the stairs, and to have received no support at all from her husband, even when she had discovered numerous caricatures of herself and her family in the guise of pigs, plastered all over the walls and furniture, or when she found out that her nickname was 'PD' or 'Pig-Dog'. Florence was tough and outspoken, but it was clear that she could not hold out forever. The ten thousand pounds per year was exacting a painful price.

James must have escaped back to London's freedom and independence with some relief. All his problems at this time were symbolically enacted at Fairholm. It was no longer for him the enchanted island, the refuge which it had been when he escaped from school to its beauty and peace and its hallowed memories of his kindly mother.

Although James was in need of family support and understanding from someone other than his father he never made a close friend of any of his numerous uncles or aunts. But he was certainly not lonely, and his years in London saw him evolve into a Victorian swell who entered Sandhurst after many stops and starts. James saw a great deal of the Leylands (the family of the Colonel's second wife) and, with a lifestyle more relaxed than his own kin in Scotland, they provided him with experience of a different way of life. James pronounced them 'rough diamonds, but kind, and you can do what you like there [at 49 Princes Gate], such as smoking and drinking whisky in the drawing room'.

Part of the indoctrination process of aspiring military officers like

'Brought up with Military Ideas'

*Olmar, James, Cissy and Father at Fairholm (1887). Lying in front is Val.*

Stevenson-Hamilton included strong notions of Empire. To them Empire was an ideal: it was the holy grail of service, untainted by any modern notions of oppression, exploitation, or the domination of native peoples. The Union Jack was a sacred banner under which the rebellious were subdued, the ignorant educated, the heathen converted and other European powers which challenged the might of Empire, chastened. The 'white man's burden' was a vision unfettered by the complications of later doubts and cynicism. In February 1884 Stevenson-Hamilton exulted, 'Baker and Keofit [are] in the Sudan, Hooray! Commissions for the lot of us! Cavalry! Hooray!!' After the fall of Khartoum, the situation on the Nile made front page headlines almost every day, and James was thrilled about the 'tremendous battle in Egypt'.

It was during these turbulent few years in London that James also discovered women. The only females with whom he had really been acquainted prior to his London escapades were his sister, Cissy, his grandmother, and other family members. It was difficult for young men like Stevenson-Hamilton to meet eligible women of a suitable kind, and those whom he did meet would certainly have been heavily chaperoned. It was well known that London provided an opportunity for 'easy money' in exchange for female 'virtue'. Apart from those who worked the streets, however, there was a kind of prostitute who relied on the patronage of a relatively small number of clients. Such women, well dressed, beautiful and often, paradoxically, models of good breeding, were frequently well informed and excellent conversationalists, and stood more in the tradition of the great courtesans of earlier centuries. Their fees were correspondingly high. In any event, James began to visit 'tarts' (as he and his friends called them) in a professional way.

He seems first to have discovered them in Scotland, in Lanark, and later to have learned that some of his male relatives had done the same. By November 1886, in London, 'Gladys' was his regular 'friend' and she appears to have been fond of him too, for he writes: 'There were two other fellows there when I came, but she trundled them downstairs, where they sat for two or three hours, kicking their heels, swearing and otherwise amusing themselves as best they could . . .'

On 16 August 1886 James was relieved to hear that he had passed for Sandhurst and was ordered to join on 1 September. His problems, however, were not at an end. He had indeed passed but not very well. He needed to obtain higher marks in order to get into a regiment which would not be too expensive, for by now it was clear that Florence's money would not be available to help him. On reflection the Colonel was not at all pleased and asked James to tender his resignation from his cavalry cadetship. 'Thought deeply and hard about the best thing to do. The Colonel is against it. It seems hard after the exams to give it all up.' He wrote to his army tutor for advice, and Coutts was objective enough to let the young man know that he probably did not have the ability to get into the infantry, but that, if he re-wrote the examination, he might improve his marks and so be able to gain entry to a better regiment.

So James went back to London and began to prepare himself for the next round of examinations. In the event, he did a little better and, when the marks were published in *The Scotsman* on 14 January 1887, he had obtained 6 273 points, an improvement of 210 points (68th position in the Sandhurst list). These were low scores and still did not give James any leeway to pick or choose with regard to regiments, but he had faith in his father's ability to 'bring his influence to bear' once the Sandhurst training was completed.

When he entered Sandhurst in March 1887, apart from his very short stature (he was only 5 foot 4 inches tall), he was the very epitome of the dashing young trainee cavalry officer. The year's course comprised two terms.[8] At Sandhurst the subjects were tactics, fortification, topography (map reading), military law and military administration. Candidates were also required to take part in drill, gymnastics and riding. There were huge grounds around Sandhurst (as there still are today) where students could dig trenches, construct breastworks, build and blow up bridges and pontoons, and study the strategy of battle in a practical way. James had ridden since he was a boy at Fairholm, but now he was learning the art of total control over his mounts, and he was also mastering the finer points of caring for horses under war conditions. He made good friends, drank whisky in the mess, and, in fact enjoyed himself more than he had ever hoped he would.

While he was at Sandhurst, James put Fairholm out of his mind. The other children had both gone off to school and although there were agricultural tenants on the land there was no one living in the house. On a brief visit in July 1887 he found Fairholm 'deserted and damp'. The Colonel was living at Braidwood because Florence refused, not surprisingly, to live at Fairholm. She often escaped to her parents in London, and, as a couple, Florence and James were more apart than they were together. However, there must have been times when they reached some kind of accommodation because two other children, Adela and Laura, were born of the marriage.

James was now nearly twenty. He continued to be a snob, and laughed at the 'airs and graces of people pretending to be ladies' and commented on having to share a carriage with a 'beastly Cockney'. He still looked physically immature, and when he wrote his journal on 2 October 1887, he noted: 'I am twenty today but few people would think I was so old. Quite pensive about it.'

At the beginning of 1888 James passed out of Sandhurst, doing moderately well in the examinations.[9] He then had to make the choice of a lifetime: what regiment to join? Each regiment had its own traditions and peculiarities. Some offered better experience and better chances for quick promotion than others. James's father was keen on the 6th (Inniskilling) Dragoons, which had a good reputation and was not expensive by the standards of the time. In addition, the Colonel had connections which favoured the Inniskillings and he spoke to friends on the matter. It was a regiment favoured by the Scots, and from the outset it was recorded that 'The Inniskilliners [sic] do not care for the English, but they like the Scots, most of their parents being Scotch.'[10] In the event, the Inniskilling commission bore fruit, and on 8 March James received his appointment as Second Lieutenant with effect from 13 March. Just three days later he was told to get ready to leave for Pietermaritzburg in the colony of Natal in South Africa where the regiment was stationed at that time.

He returned to Scotland for a month's holiday before setting off to South Africa. On 17 May, he recorded that 'The Colonel was a bit sad and so was I but judged it best to be philosophic. We are not a demonstrative family. Specially sorry to leave the Colonel now he will have no one to confide in, though I cannot have been much consolation.'

Stevenson-Hamilton's anxiety over separation from his father was soon superseded by the excitement of departure. The first novelty was the sight of Lisbon – an attractive city peopled by ugly citizens, was his conclusion. Madeira he considered delightful, so English, in fact, that it 'ought to be annexed'. His opinion of this pretty island may have been coloured by the fact that James had begun a shipboard romance with Hilda Browne. She was the first South African he had met, and she was returning to rejoin her family in the Orange Free State where her father was a country doctor. To their delight, James and Hilda found that they had a number of common acquaintances among the Sandhurst cadets and so initiating conversation was easy. Soon James was recording exuberantly in his journal that he 'sat with her all afternoon and also after dinner. This is a jolly life.'

All too soon the flirtation, the 'gin flings', cards and games which passed the time in the most pleasant manner, came to an end. The *Moore* docked in Cape Town on 7 June 1888. James found the much acclaimed Table Mountain 'disappointing' and the town itself 'beastly'. The *Moore* sailed on two days later, docking first at Port Elizabeth and then at East London, where the inevitable sad parting from Hilda came. Their later correspondence did not last long, for Hilda and her family moved continually around South Africa, but Stevenson-Hamilton always thought about her fondly when he neared East London on his many later voyages around the Cape coast.

Just a day after Hilda's departure, the *Moore* docked at Durban. Though feeling 'down on my luck still', James began to look forward to joining his regiment, which then formed the garrison in Pietermaritzburg and was stationed at Fort Napier. He soon found himself thoroughly at home in the army and he made the closest and most lasting friendships of his life with many of his fellow officers. These two years spent in Natal were crucially formative for James, creating in him a love of Africa and an appetite for adventure.

## 'Brought up with Military Ideas'

At the time of Stevenson-Hamilton's arrival Pietermaritzburg had a population of about nine thousand whites. Lying about one hundred kilometres inland from Durban, the town was less tropical in climate than Durban, and its situation in a hollow surrounded by hills meant that it was stuffy in summer and cold in winter. It was well developed both economically and socially – the presence of the garrison was one of the main factors which influenced Pietermaritzburg's growth. Many officers were high-spirited eligible young bachelors who took the lead in arranging sporting activities and encouraging theatrical events, balls and fêtes. Their resplendent uniforms brought colour and pomp to the streets of Pietermaritzburg, for James commented that 'In Maritzburg we wore [the] same uniform as in England, except that we had white tropical helmets with a gilt spike on top and a short blue patrol jacket with lapels instead of the cavalry frock coat.'

The duty of the garrison was to defend the colony and soldiers were deployed wherever they were needed in the region – Natal or Zululand – in order to quell 'troubles'. The difficulties faced by the British administration in the 1880s centred on relations with the Zulu who, after the Anglo-Zulu War of 1879, were confined to a smaller kingdom north of the Thukela River. After the Zulu army had been defeated at Ulundi in July 1879, the kingdom was partitioned into 13 portions, each under the control of a chief. Seldom has divide and rule been so effective a strategy for total subjugation of a people, for the region became caught in a fatal web of intrigues and factional loyalties and alliances. Dinuzulu, the heir to the throne of Shaka and Cetshwayo, led a faction which negotiated assistance against their rivals from an unlikely source: the Boer community to the north. The price the Boers extracted was almost the whole of Dinuzulu's western territory, which was called the 'New Republic' with its capital at Vryheid (freedom). Britain tried belatedly to re-negotiate this extensive Boer land-grab, not on behalf of the Zulu, but rather because it was clear that British hegemony in the region was being seriously challenged. The solution, essentially, was the partition of Zululand between Boer and Britain, an arrangement that could not satisfy Zulu demands.

In 1888 the crisis came to a head. With Zulu allies provided by Mnyamana, the elderly former chief minister of Cetshwayo, a British force totalling about five hundred men set out to arrest Dinuzulu in June. There, in the Ceza bush, they found nearly two thousand of Dinuzulu's supporters waiting for them and there was a short engagement before the smaller force withdrew to Nkonjeni for reinforcements. Eventually the Zulu royalists were defeated, but the kingdom continued to seethe beneath an exterior of calm. The British government resolved to increase the strength of garrison regi-

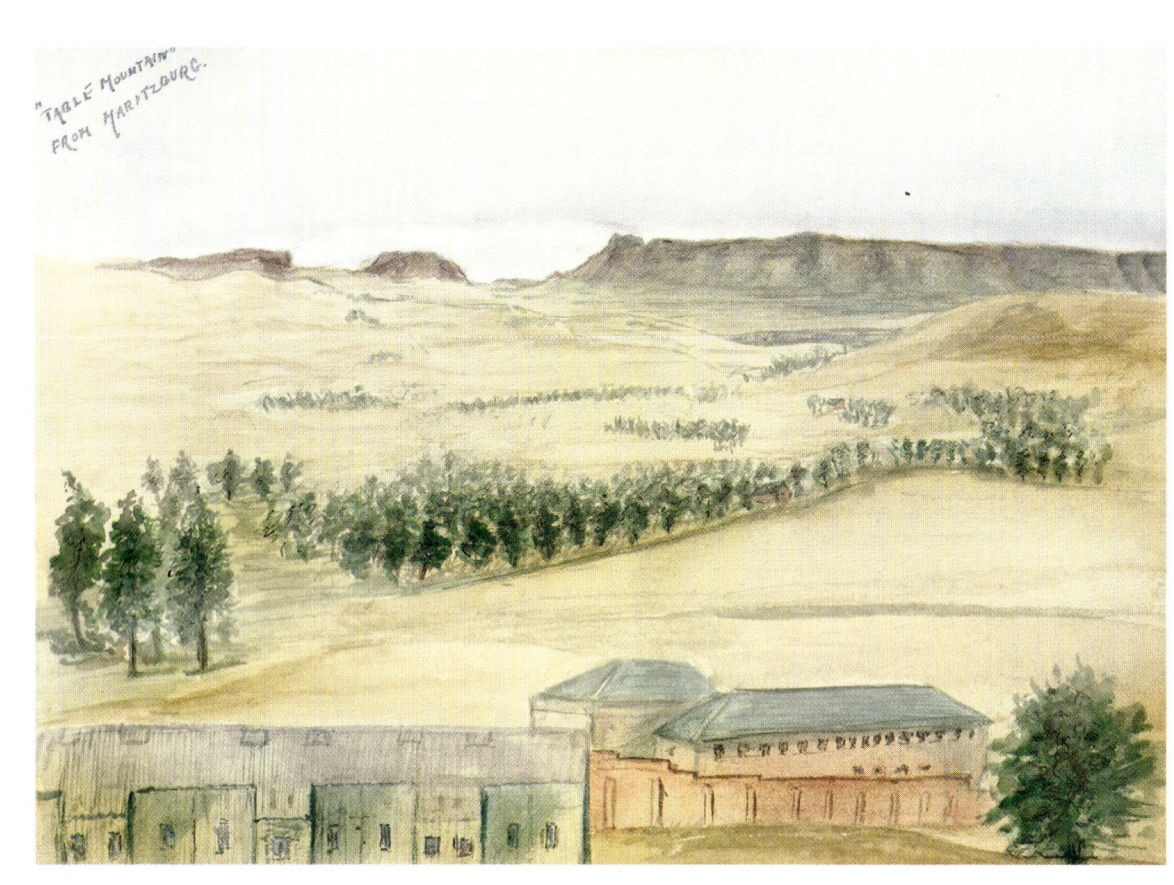

*Table Mountain from Pietermaritzburg.*

ments to the point where they might quell any future uprisings or disaffection, and James Stevenson-Hamilton was one of those who had been sent out to supplement the numbers.[11]

James visited Zululand twice in 1888. He was there from 26 July to 14 August and then again a fortnight later from the end of August to 20 September. He saw no more military action thereafter. It may have been these brief sorties into Zululand, an area of incomparable beauty steeped in ancient lore, which first kindled in James a love of both the African landscape and the outdoor life. The 'Zulus are magnificent', he declared. He encountered his first African antelope and shot at it, but missed. The following day he came to a realisation that would shape his future, writing in his diary, 'I like this life.'

Both the landscape and the African people interested him. It was exciting to cross the great White Umfolozi River in the dark and arrive on the Ulundi plain, the site of the battle which had ended the Anglo-Zulu War. With James at that time there were also various African contingents under British officers, including a group of Basotho and Zulu police. When they reached Nkonjeni, Stevenson-Hamilton began to feel that he was at last really doing what he had been trained to do, 'This is my first real day of joining the regiment,' he declared. But Stevenson-Hamilton's group did not see any military action and the impetuous youth in him was extremely disappointed. 'I suppose', he noted gloomily in his journal, 'we'll be withdrawn and there won't be another row for a long time.' He desperately wanted some exemplary stories to send home; stories which might resonate satisfactorily in the minds of his illustrious military uncles and, of course, which might impress his own distinguished father. But, for the time being, the fighting was over, and, after a few days in alternating dust storms and heavy rain, nurturing his new 'imperial' (the kind of pointed beard which was fashionable at the time) Stevenson-Hamilton returned with his detachment to Pietermaritzburg.

Regimental life was fun and interesting. James and his fellow officers were mostly very young, and some had been his companions at the London crammer, or at Sandhurst. Only the two commanding officers, Lieutenant-Colonel Froom and Lieutenant-Colonel Martin, were in their late forties. Froom had shared a study with James's father at Rugby and he may well have been instrumental in obtaining James's acceptance into the Inniskillings.

Victorians loved nicknames and soon everyone had a nickname of his own, based on word play associated with surnames or on personal characteristics. Captain Allenby, later the celebrated Field Marshal, was 'Applepie', or 'Pie' so named because of his love of order; Captain Forbes was 'Four Bs', Lieutenant Mosley was 'Moses'. Other names were less flattering: Sanders was 'Fatty', Cox was 'Cockass'. James made a list of his brother officers and their physical characteristics. The list shows most to have been relatively tall, ranging from just over six foot to 'Jorrocks' Jackson, at five foot six inches, down to Stevenson-Hamilton, the shortest of them all. His stature might have led to James being dubbed 'Sos', perhaps meaning 'little sausage'. He never explained how he got the name, but it was the one by which he was known to his old friends from the regiment all his days.

Colonial garrison duty was certainly different from the set piece manoeuvres at Sandhurst. Young officers filled their days attending to their horses, putting them through their paces, carrying out drill, seeing to adjutant duties, patrols and parades, and to the maintenance of their equipment. The nights always began with the ritualised, full-dress, formal mess dinners which were so important a part of British regimental life. Zulu dancing was sometimes arranged and this could include an 'Intombi' race of naked unmarried girls. In the evenings there was often a campfire.

Apart from his success as an amateur jockey Stevenson-Hamilton did

*Stevenson-Hamilton (wearing straw boater) with companions from the garrison (1889).*

not distinguish himself in Natal. On the contrary, he admitted in his journal that he was not a good horseman and had to do a lot of hard work to approximate to the high standard of riding which was *de rigueur* in the British cavalry. In his early days, as the most junior officer he was allocated some of the least pleasant duties, for example, on one occasion being instructed to clean the wine cellar after a Sergeant had committed suicide there. James noted laconically in his journal that the regimental dog had already licked up the man's blood and so there was really nothing left for him to do.[12]

Although his journal indicates that James found his two years in Pietermaritzburg pleasurable, there is also an underlying restlessness. He had written to his father in November 1888 that there would always be 'some little war breaking out in this country every year or so', but this was not the case. In the absence of offensive military action, James had no chance to make a name for himself in the field, and so there could be no reason for him to rise on the ladder of recognition and promotion. There was little for junior officers in such a situation to do other than to entertain themselves. Life settled into social routine. They played polo a great deal, became deeply involved in horse racing, and at night they gambled and played cards. They also played pranks, such as collapsing tents on the occupants inside. There was a great deal of heavy drinking, particularly after dinner when time hung heavily on the hands of these energetic young men. The officers amused themselves at the theatre almost every night. There were entertaining plays and pretty Pietermaritzburg ladies in the audience.

Thoughts of home did not greatly intrude into James's life in Pietermaritzburg but there were exceptions. Without doubt the most important day in this regard was his twenty-first birthday on 2 October 1888. He wrote:

> This is the day I inherit. I come of age today and come into Fairholm and Kirkton. This is the day I have looked forward to as long as I can remember as one that would be a red-letter day. There will probably be something going on at home as it is nearly seventy years since granduncle, the last male heir to come of age, attained his majority.

Sadly, the day did not measure up to the new Laird's high expectations. It was, he wrote, a 'damned poor day': his riding was extremely unsound, he had a run-in with a colleague, he was badgered with questions by the Colonel, and, to cap it all, his servant asked to leave his service and go into the canteen where the pay was better. James felt thoroughly disillusioned, enough so to write in a fit of depression that the realisation of lairdship 'was a fraud; various little wretched annoyances united to upset me and make the day a poor one'. Things did not improve in December when a letter from his father outlined his financial situation as formal owner of the family estates. There would not be a penny more than an income of £700 a year after taxes had been paid. While military life abroad was not very expensive, life as an officer in a cavalry regiment could certainly not be sustained without a reasonable income. Uniforms, saddlery and horses cost between £600 and £1 000 per annum depending on the regiment, and high annual expenses were also incurred for dining and entertaining as well as sporting and social occasions.[13] James's lack of income was thus a worry to him. On Old Year's Eve 1888 his thoughts were on home:

> As I write I have a picture of last year in mind; Jack Roberton and I had shot a deer in the snow at Fairholm; bells began to ring 'Dunlop's Donkey' and then the New Year's blasts began. What a difference twelve months make. Here I am of age at last, the dear old place mine, with my commission and having seen service in the field in Zululand. And yet I don't feel as thankful as I ought to. Providence has been very kind to me and how have I requited it?

The highlight of 1889 for James was his visit to Johannesburg, the talk of all the world as its unimaginable riches in gold were beginning to be exploited. The future of the town seemed insecure and, just before Stevenson-Hamilton's visit, *The Star* newspaper had posed the question of whether in three years' time Johannesburg would be a bustling city or whether it would have gone the way of other mining towns elsewhere in the world and 'sunk back into a condition of arrested development'. Stevenson-Hamilton's vivid record of his trip to Johannesburg is a historical gem, for he provides details of the buildings ('the houses look as if they dropped from the sky, and just settled where they happened to fall without any design'); the unbelievable dust ('every passing vehicle raises a stifling cloud that hangs indefinitely in the air, and by evening the town . . . seems veiled in a dense yellowish cloud'); the characters of the town; the theatres ('crammed every night; concerts on Sundays, dances and entertainments of all kinds going on'); and sporting events (horse-racing and boxing) he attended; as well as the general atmosphere of bustling energy and excitement ('When one reflects that two years ago this huge place didn't exist and now . . . is growing every hour, one realises the force that gold has to collect a population in a short time.'). He went down a mine,

> being lowered a hundred feet in the bight of a rope, and crawling through long tunnels eighteen inches high. I saw five or six lbs. of quartz crushed, and then panned in a basin, leaving a little heap of gold dust at the bottom . . . It is absurd people down country and overseas belittling the Johannesburg mines: the Rand has an immense future before it. All the mines are hard at work, and the crushings along the main reef improve every month.[14]

Regiments were often not permanently stationed in colonial garrisons and it was in May 1890 that the 6th (Inniskilling) Dragoons first heard that they would be leaving Natal later in the year, to be relieved by the 11th Hussars. James was disappointed to be returning to England because he had planned to visit Nyasaland (present-day Malawi) on a hunting trip, and he was looking forward to it, having (as he wrote) 'wanted to do something like this all my life'. His mood was soured by disappointment and he wrote in his journal 'I hate soldiering.' By the beginning of October, the regiment was ready and prepared for departure. James felt that there was nothing particularly to look forward to in England. Natal and Zululand had been quite different from anything he had previously experienced, and nothing even in the Scottish wilderness approximated the magnificence of scale and the haunting beauty – and excitement – of the African landscape. Stevenson-Hamilton thought that he might try 'to wangle an ADC [aide-de-camp] billet in India through uncle Nat', but his plans were no more definite than that. By mid-November he was back home, billeted in Preston Barracks, Brighton, and he had also re-engaged his 'old room' in London.

Almost immediately he wished he was back in Africa. He missed the racing, the riding and the sun. 'One feels a nobody here,' he reflected. 'The fellows talk of nothing but dress and hunting and the much superior game of racing is taboo.' On 21 November he called on his father in London, and found him 'looking older and very depressed and fussy. There has been some row in the family and they are all assembled in town. What an unfortunate family we are.' He returned to Brighton in very low spirits and found that he just could not settle down.

# 3

# 'No Goal or Object'[1]

## Regimental Life in Britain
## (1890–1898)

WHEN JAMES STEVENSON-HAMILTON returned to Britain he was still a very young and inexperienced Second-Lieutenant who appreciated that he needed more training and experience in the field in order to make a name for himself in his profession. While the army was still a respectable way in which a gentleman could gain fame and make a living, during the 1890s the military had been hit hard by economic cutbacks and the fluctuating fortunes of the governments which succeeded each other. Moreover, because the Empire was in a period of relative peace, Stevenson-Hamilton's career did nothing but mark time. The realisation grew during these years that in his preference for individual action and responsibility he was not the ideal cavalry officer of the 1890s, but he lacked both the confidence and the opportunity to change his direction.

Questions of money, or the shortage of it, also plagued him. Even though James had attained his majority and Fairholm and other properties were now his own, it was a period of agricultural recession. Tenants' rents and crop prices fell, and James's income as a landowner was limited. Even the increasing prosperity of coal-mining around Fairholm brought him no compensation. In fact, its major impact was to spoil the countryside he loved so much.

Although his journal reveals a frivolous lifestyle, James had a strong sense of duty and responsibility. Perhaps, what he called his 'dissipated' existence was also a relief from his worries and obligations. He seems to have veered between two extremes: a diverting and entertaining public life, and a private life of anxiety and unease with himself. He felt keenly his duty to his father and knew how much it would hurt him if he abandoned the army.

James spent most of these years occupied with his military duties, although periods of leave were long and frequent for officers in times of peace. For three years his regiment was quartered at the old and dilapidated Preston Barracks in Brighton, on the Lewes Road.[2] Brighton and its environs was a congenial area, especially for a horseman. The weather was often pleasant and opportunities for hunting on the South Downs abounded. Many of the newly rich had built country houses in this area and attractive young cavalry officers were always welcome guests. Moreover, the regular train service brought Brighton conveniently close to London for evenings of theatre, dalliance, club visits and dinners. Like other regiments on home service, the 6th (Inniskilling) Dragoons moved around Britain stationed in different cavalry barracks. At the beginning of 1894, they were in Shorncliffe for five months so that Preston Barracks could be renovated. Thereafter, they spent the summer training at Aldershot, followed by some time in Manchester (until June 1895), Piershill Barracks in Edinburgh (until November 1897), and then moved to Ireland (Dundalk and the Curragh) until the outbreak of the South African War.

Brighton was a premier seaside resort, the first in Britain of those fashionable places to which people could escape for a period of relaxation and leisure. Throughout the year the town had a holiday air. Given the diversions for which Brighton was famous, it is hardly surprising that Stevenson-Hamilton devoted so little attention to military pursuits. In the absence of a significant war, he and his fellow officers spent a great deal of their time hunting, visiting, making friends, getting up to pranks, and attending theatres, dinners, balls, and parties of all kinds. In many respects, it seemed a wonderful lifestyle, but the kind of life which James and his fellow officers enjoyed was a relic of a bygone age.

The army system was more and more out of alignment with the needs of a rapidly changing British civilian society, a fact that became painfully evident at the time of the South African War. Despite an ongoing process of reform, modernisation of the military proceeded in fits and starts, causing resentment from the forces themselves. Both the army and the navy were ponderous, tradition-bound, slow-moving, resistant to sensible innovation, and increasingly ill-suited to coping with the kind of threats which faced the Empire as the century drew to its close.

In his biography of Allenby, Wavell describes how the chief military preoccupation of the time was the perfection of 'precise and stereotyped parade movements under the adjutant and drill-sergeant'. Consequently, the peace-time training of individual regiments such as James's remained concentrated on mathematically precise riding, closely co-ordinated mounted drills, and on the care of horses.[3] The important highlights were the regular bi-annual and annual inspections. The army was a place 'where the ambitious subaltern sought distinction in the hunting-field, on the polo-ground, on the racecourse, and even in the ballroom rather than in any manoeuvre area...'[4] Society itself was slowly becoming more professionalised at this time, but the Victorian army remained stubbornly reactionary.[5] The horrors of mass destruction and carnage which characterised the First and Second World Wars were then still quite unknown. As Winston Churchill expressed it, the chance of death was very small, 'only a sporting element in a splendid game'.[6]

In the army at that time there were technical developments in artillery, and as a result the effectiveness of the sword wielded by a mounted cavalryman became more and more compromised. In fact, the day of the massed cavalry charge as a tactic in battle was over, and a prolonged debate was held about the future of the cavalry and, in particular, about whether or not mounted infantry would supersede it. Paradoxically, the 1890s did not see the end of the cavalry, rather a great deal of attention was devoted to the question of how it could be transformed and made more efficient. Regular training courses were provided and officers were encouraged to pass examinations and acquire additional skills.[7]

Almost immediately James returned to Brighton he became depressed. He missed what Africa had offered. It was, however, pleasant to remain close to the friends he had made in Pietermaritzburg. Their number was augmented by a few new faces, and James soon befriended other young officers of his regiment, especially 'Chang' Morse and 'The Pup' Paterson. To begin with James's career got off to a good start. In January 1891 he heard that he had got his long-coveted promotion to Lieutenant (he was 23 years old). But the elevated status brought little change to his way of life or to his responsibilities. He soon discovered that he did not relish the army routines of peace-time southern England. While James was an excellent horseman, for example, winning the regimental point-to-point in 1893, he was not brilliant in the accomplishments required of a cavalryman. In fact, he often performed quite badly on parade, even when he was making a special effort to shine. The bulk of the training while at Preston Barracks was focussed on trying to achieve perfection in parade ground drills, and perhaps South Africa had already taught James that attention to unnecessary detail was not the way to win a modern war.

In February 1891, immediately after his promotion, he was ordered to attend classes in pioneering. Instead of being delighted and seeing in this an avenue in which might distinguish himself, he resented the fact that it took him away from country pursuits, and he wrote 'I wish I could get out of it' in his diary.

Stevenson-Hamilton's experience was an individual one. While he hated the formal side of his cavalry duties, preferring the equestrian and sporting side of country life, Aldershot under Sir Evelyn Wood was remembered very differently by others: 'They were good days those in the early nineties in Aldershot.... There was a glamour ... a romance of dash and colour.... It was soldiers, soldiers everywhere.'[8] The thrill of war was certainly attractive to Stevenson-Hamilton and he pored over the military paintings of well-known *Illustrated London News* artist, Richard Caton Woodville, which were shown at the Royal Academy in May 1895. It was what James regarded as mindless, unnecessary attention to detail that he disliked so much.

Perhaps if James had been given some special responsibility or if he could have been made to understand the point of what he was required to do, or even if he had been more assertive and responsible, life for him in the 1890s might have been very different. When a new squadron system was introduced in March 1892, he wrote: 'Awful day, the amount of slanging and cursing in the regiment quite unnecessary; the system is awful, so is to be cursed by one's own Colonel. I'd rather be in the infantry with less to do.'

Soon he began to contemplate the unthinkable: perhaps he might leave the army. But he really had no options and he appreciated that it was 'no good chucking the service unless you have a large income. A soldier is entertained by other fellows, it is the other way around with civilians.' In November 1893 he admitted, 'I might have done well in the literary or journalistic profession, or become a third-rate artist or understudy for the villain in a fourth-rate theatre – I have a leaning towards them.' On another occasion he pondered in his introspective way:

> I wonder if I hadn't taken this army for which I have no taste or zeal, what would my career have been? In the army, there is no reward for effort, so you get slack, no talents are developed and you think only of amusement. And after twenty years? The shelf. The army is the worst profession. The few plums are chiefly luck. My son – if I have one – I shan't influence.

In April 1894 he re-read his 1889 journal and then wrote: 'I feel worse. Five years older and haven't advanced a single bit. Since I've been in England my life wasted. No talents exercised, not excelled, have no goal or object and consequently discontented. Just an ass in everything.' His birthday was always an occasion for writing sentimentally in his journal. In 1895, when he was 28, he admitted to feeling 'much older than my age.... It is a damn nuisance. Time passes round us ... [My mother's] presence sheds a gentle soft light ... as I write it, it all comes back. I'm a soul longing to express itself and not knowing how.'

## 'No Goal or Object'

He felt that he really needed scope to make a contribution and he was not happy in being a pawn in the game of military life. As his negative attitude became more and more apparent in the performance of his daily duties, it is hardly surprising that he was soon 'jawed out' by a number of officers including his new regimental chief, Lieutenant-Colonel Alexander Charles McKean. In October 1893 James knew that he was 'in trouble with the Colonel and I wish I could get away'. He summed up 1893 as a particularly unhappy year, perhaps the worst of 'any since adolescence'. Without doubt the most important occasion in the cavalry year was the annual review by the Inspector-General of Her Majesty's Cavalry, who, at that time, was General Sir George Luck. As Churchill reminisced, 'It was a fine thing in the '90s to see General Luck . . . manoeuvre a cavalry division of thirty or forty squadrons as if it were one single unit. . . . When the line was finally formed and the regiment or brigade was committed to the charge, one could hardly help shouting in joyous wrath.'[9] It was Stevenson-Hamilton's ill fortune to fall foul of General Luck, and he was extremely distressed because a poor inspection was the kiss of death for an aspiring cavalry officer. He wrote on 9 August, 'Luck reported badly on me in the inspection. Below the average in knowledge of drill. Made a fool of myself [and] so can't expect anything else.'

Increasingly James knew that his future in the regiment would not be bright, and that he should try to find something else to do as a career. He began to think that becoming an aide-de-camp to some prominent military person might be a solution and, with his father's assistance, he applied to join Lord Lamington's staff in Queensland, Australia. It never occurred to him that he might be unsuccessful – but he was. 'This last week I've had the biggest blow to my own esteem ever. So upset. To write off the blow to my esteem I've written off for a billet as a correspondent in Ashanti in the hope of a bullet or fever putting an end to so worthless and harmful a life.' Although he does not record what his father thought of this new line of action, the Colonel nevertheless loyally busied himself with canvassing connections for his errant son. It proved to be extremely difficult to find 'billets' since there was a lot of competition and James had already been snubbed with one humiliating refusal.

Nothing seemed to brighten the horizon, not even the prospect of war. There was hope at the beginning of 1896, when the Jameson Raid took place: 'Jameson has invaded the Transvaal, I guess he'll take old Kruger prisoner.' But the news of a few days later was disappointing to Stevenson-Hamilton, 'How could they have been beaten by a lot of dirty Dutchmen?' he asked. But, as far as military intervention was concerned, this came to nothing. Indeed, the Raid was a humiliation for Britain in international circles since the collusion (later proven) of top politicians was widely suspected at the time.

In spite of all efforts, no openings materialised and James was obliged to remain unhappily in his regiment. In fact, he had decided to stay where he was and get his captaincy before making a change. He tried to apply himself to his studies and began a signal course on how to use lamps, a more demanding exercise than signalling with flags. After two months, he noted, 'I'm very bad at signalling and don't expect a certificate.' He failed the examinations ignominiously, but took them again and this time scraped through.

James Stevenson-Hamilton's diaries reveal a little about his opinions on the politics of the decade. The working classes were flexing their political muscles, and many perceived this as a sinister and disturbing portent of what the twentieth century would bring. Around the time of the 1892 election, when strikes were on the increase, James's comment was, 'Government turned out on Thursday in a no-confidence vote. Parnellites behaviour disgraceful. New government can do lots of damage in one year.' It was Mid-Lanarkshire which nurtured the career of James Keir Hardie, a founder of the Scottish Labour Party in 1888 and the first person from a mine labourer's background to enter the Houses of Commons in 1892. With Fairholm surrounded by coal mines and Larkhall, one of the hotbeds of unionist activity, just a few kilometres away, James could hardly ignore what was happening. Indeed, he feared and hated the socialists and members of the trade union movement.

Lanarkshire's political difficulties were compounded by economic woes. Fairholm was hard hit and when James was informed of the detailed financial situation by his father in December 1890, he was aghast: 'Not a penny per annum seems to have been saved on the estate in the last fifteen years and I find I have absolutely no capital.' It might be supposed that Fairholm was in a better financial position than other country estates elsewhere in the British Isles for collieries seemed to be everywhere. But subterranean mining was so extensive that earth subsidences occurred in many parts and even the Duke of Hamilton's Palace began to collapse into sinkholes. Greed was the driving force behind the coal mining industry and the result was that the district around Fairholm soon became scarred and appallingly polluted. In addition, the overproduction of coal became a problem and prices slumped. Scottish industry was backward and undiversified and thus internationally uncompetitive.[10] Since the population was growing and immigration from Ireland continued, there was massive unemployment and social and economic dereliction in the whole area. Workers began to seek employment elsewhere and, in the 1890s, Glasgow stopped growing. The economy of Scotland, once so prosperous and booming, was sliding into poverty and stagnation and proving fertile ground for socialist philosophies.

The Stevenson-Hamiltons were caught up in these changing circumstances but had little choice in their reaction. They could not sell their ancient property and, anyway, the income derived from land was very limited. Now that he was the owner of Fairholm, James found his father not only unable to help him, but rather quick to count the pennies. James was surprised in November 1891 at how 'very businesslike' the Colonel was: 'he even charges me for telegrams he sends to me about things. Very, very Scotch, getting more and more that way, will probably get that way myself. I'm sure he's feeling the difference from his spending power of yore.' The irony was that he was regarded in the regiment as a man of money, for all cavalry officers with property were still assumed to have it. James took refuge in his ancient lineage, and took offence when some 'middle class London society' criticised hunting. 'They know nothing of the proper thing to do, or about the life of English gentlemen with its shooting and hunting,' he boasted.

James and his father were extremely fond of each other and they had much in common. They spent many a convivial evening drinking the Colonel's special claret, and they often went riding and fishing. James was very proud in April 1896 when his father was made a royal aide-de-camp. This was something to which he might also aspire. But, in spite of the close relationship between father and son, there was no real intimacy. It was the kind of Victorian filial relationship about which so much has been written. James, in fact, was much closer to his deceased stepmother's brother, Fitzcrawford Leyland, to whom he admitted that he had 'opened his heart to more than anyone. The Colonel will never give one the chance.'

The stepmother dilemma had worsened in the years that James had been away. The Colonel and Florence were seldom together: she spent much of her time in London while he lived mostly in Scotland. James did nothing to ease the situation. When one opportunity presented itself in June 1891, he behaved in a very immature way when he 'passed beloved stepmother and her parents in the Park. I swaggered past and did not recognize them. Why should I? The woman is not a lady, nor interesting, clever, pretty, accomplished or amiable. Why the Colonel stays I don't know.' In September 1891 he recorded the following entry in his diary: 'Stepmother at Braidwood, I suspect to make it hot for Cissy – but most people cut her dead. She threatened to prosecute Olmar for trespassing on Braidwood. She is dreadful – a character and face which even the Gorgon would have shuddered before.'

The animosity between Cissy and her stepmother gave another dimension to the problem. James Stevenson-Hamilton, passionately hating his stepmother, naturally took his sister's side, blaming 'Pig-Dog's low pitch of manner' and the fact that she was 'not a lady. She also, I hear, trains her spawn to call their father "the Scotch pig". Talking of such people makes me quite ill.' Since the passionate hatred which had evolved between stepmother and stepchildren caused them to be locked in a fight to the death, no one was sure of the right course of action, but James complained that it was 'Dreadful to deal with that class of people except as menials, but the position has been forced on us so maybe we should make the best of it.' After seven years of marriage, the Colonel and Florence separated formally and Stevenson-Hamilton was insistent that his father, the stepmother and their children relinquish his name – they were mere Stevensons, they were *not* Hamiltons: 'I don't want to have the old name dragged into the dirt . . .' Within a month the matter was settled and the son recorded that it was 'satisfactory to know that those dreadful people no longer bear one's name'.

It would be pleasant to be able to record that James's relationship with Cissy, his sister, was smoother and that she was loving and devoted. James certainly doted on her when he returned from Natal and was delighted to find how beautiful she had become. He did not think that being 'shut up in the depressing company of the old Colonel' was a good idea, and he tried to enhance her lonely Scottish existence by giving her 'the Fairholm drawing room to do what she likes with'. But Cissy remained unhappy and her brother agonised over what to do for her. Even a move to London did not change Cissy's life. It took about a year for James to get thoroughly annoyed: 'She's a bit of a fool I'm afraid.' Soon he realised that she was always bored, found fault with everyone, and was completely without any emotional resources. She never read and hated music. He complained about her irresponsibility, particularly in the vexed question of her relationship with her father. James could appreciate that there were two sides to the story. His father certainly needed the support of his older children during his times of great emotional distress. But he could also see that the Colonel, 'at the zenith of his affluence and enjoyment, left the children for months on end; he never took them about. Not wittingly, he was young and made the best of it, but he should have been more responsible himself. He is reaping the rewards now with Cissy. She treats him off-hand.'

Olmar was somewhat less of a problem, for at least James did not feel himself responsible for his younger brother. In March 1891 Olmar sat for the preliminary entrance examination to Sandhurst, but was apparently unsuccessful because of poor eyesight. In 1893 he decided to follow in his grandparents' footsteps and leave Britain in search of a better life in Australia: 'really the best thing he could do' James observed, feeling that he was 'now fairly started in life'. By the following year Olmar was full of complaints, about which James was fairly philosophical. Dissatisfaction seemed to be a family trait: 'Like the rest of us, he always has a grievance.' After two years, when Olmar had still not settled down, James was concerned, 'I suppose Australia is difficult but [we are] ne'er do well men in our family, [we are] restless, [with an] inability to settle down – I have it, fatally I know.'

Whenever he was in London, Stevenson-Hamilton saw the Leylands, his deceased stepmother's wealthy London family. But he was more critical of them at this time than he had been when he was a teenager relishing the informality of their lifestyle. In August 1891 he noticed one evening that 'Mr Leyland was drunk and very boorish. The Leylands have very snobbish airs, [and are] ostentatiously rich. Without their money they'd be no one. Have contempt of poverty. Brutes! But I shall drop them in future.' When Frederick Leyland died, his two illegitimate children were taken care of in his will, but there was 'Nothing for the Colonel. He had a glimmer of hope that there would be.' Leyland's was not the only family death in 1892. Uncle Andrew Stevenson's funeral took place in October. The nephew recorded that the magnificent 'Jem Mace' had died of 'creeping paralysis . . . Eventually violent, his wife had to get the police. They took him to a *pauper* lunatic asylum, the utmost squalor and misery . . .'

In December 1894 James first noticed Gwladys, the daughter of Uncle Rob Stevenson and his wife Aunt Claire (née Aitkin). He wrote, 'Uncle Rob looks younger than ever. I don't care for Aunt Claire. Gwladys . . . is about six foot in height and promises to be nice-looking.' Four years later, James recorded: 'Wanted to take Gwladys (promises to be very pretty) to the Palace but Uncle Rob wouldn't hear of it. All old-fashioned prejudices regarding girls despite his own reputation.' James got around the problem by taking Cissy and Gwladys to the Savoy but did nothing to ensure his popularity with his aunt or uncle, noting, 'Took Gwladys home about 1, much to her parents' rage.'

Apart from his enjoyment of sports of all kinds, James used hunting, polo and racing to put family matters out of his mind. The South Downs area was a fashionable locality for the newly rich to build country houses. Their economic power declining, traditional landowners commissioned fewer than one-fifth of the new houses which were built between 1875 and 1915, but wealthy bankers, financiers and industrialists kept the country house ideal alive by undertaking a frantic and opulent building spree in the south. To set up as 'landed gentry' was easier than it had ever been in the past.[11]

Stevenson-Hamilton befriended a number of these families, all of whom were happy to receive attractive and well-connected cavalry officers. James was a great friend of Charles Godman whose father, Frederick du Cane Godman, owned South Lodge (as well as property in Scotland), a massive home which has now been restored as a luxury hotel. Godman entertained his son's army friends with tales about the Crimean War and showed them his wonderful collections of carpets, textiles and pottery.[12] James's particular friend in the new country house set was Helen Lindsay-Smith of Ashfold whose husband was a banker who spent most of his time in London. James was extremely fond of Helen. In fact, she was the kind of woman he might have married had such a person come his way. Helen was happily married, had a young and growing family, and proved a stable and loyal friend to James. She also embodied the serene old-fashioned family values which meant a great deal to James in his troubled twenties. Her warm hospitality and her loving devotion to her children gave James an inkling of what an ideal family life might be like.[13] Being with Helen was uplifting for James, and he said that she and her children made him 'feel patriarchal and grandfatherly . . . So homelike and peaceful, a vision of Fairholm years and years ago. [Then I] stood at our mother's knee . . .'

At balls Helen and James danced together and he came more and more to appreciate that she was a 'wonderful woman, a real pal', although he complained also that 'I do wish Lindsay-Smith would use his wife better. She is my greatest woman friend but I never see her because she is generally in that peculiar condition known as "interesting".' But there were not many like Helen Lindsay-Smith, and certainly none he cared to marry. In February 1895, he met 'Margaret Collyer – very best horsewoman in England, paints Academy-standard pictures, sings charmingly. I never could marry a woman so much my superior.' Clearly Helen did not intimidate him in the same way.

Stevenson-Hamilton regarded it as part of his duty to find a suitable wife who could join him in rescuing Fairholm and turning it into something like the Lindsay-Smith's happy household at Ashfold. But he had learnt from his father's experience that money was not all that was needed. While it was certainly necessary, love was equally important. In March 1892, he admired someone for her '"bel air"; very few women have it, I prefer it to a pretty face. I can usually tell a lady quickly – I have the advantage of my own birth and breeding.' He admitted his snobbery as head of the family of Hamilton openly to his diary, stating firmly, 'If I marry it will be with the interests of the family in my heart, to raise us to something better. . . . I shall either marry one . . . stinking of money, or else I shall take a lady.'

While prospective wives were hard to find, sexual encounters were

*Listening through augur holes.*

easy for good-looking cavalry officers. One of James's colleagues had a very public initiation into the 'mysteries' in May 1892, when 'we bored augur holes in the door, which was useful'. James drew a sketch of a group of young men all straining their eyes and ears through the peepholes. An award certificate followed.

Actresses were easy targets it seems, for they had a reputation, connected perhaps to their provocative onstage dress and the characters they played, for being sexually available.[14] James's journal recalls taking leading ladies to supper after the theatre, and on one occasion he recalls that he had a bouquet for L. (possibly Lillie Burnand, the actress he fancied) 'but she wouldn't come to supper. I daresay this will take a little time, more than it is worth possibly.' In fact, he had obviously miscalculated and the next day he lamented that the 'Nice sitting-room and bedroom at the Clarendon – all wasted. Back to the theatre, missed her, because I was half-an-hour late.'

Another favourite actress was Eve. Surmising from clues in the journal (there are missing pages), it seems that James might have seduced her and then made a hasty offer of marriage which he feared she might hold him to. There are phrases such as, 'I must get out clear without burning my fingers.... Several things would not have happened but for its [his room's] protection and hospitality' (7 January 1894); 'Am still heartbroken. When was I so smitten before?' (9 January 1894); 'Have nothing to do so morbid reflection and self-dissection. Scotchmen have more of this deeper temperament than Englishmen.... Dreadful that this should smite me now that I felt I'd sown sufficient wild oats' (10 January 1894); 'Letter from Eve most discouraging.... Lowe refuses to do anything. I'm helpless here, I feel a brute' (19 January 1894). It is clear from these scattered references that he was as much running away from his own feelings as he was running away from her. He was soon at Ostend and made his way to Aix la Chapelle. He needed, he said, 'time to think and reflect'. He asked his father to come over for a few days since he was sorely in need of unsentimental adult male advice but none was forthcoming from the Colonel: 'He has a thicker head than I thought, for he seems to have the wrong end of the stick and won't come under any circumstances; I don't suppose I would either if I had a son under the same dull conditions – as I never shall I fancy.'

His friends were all getting married, but in each case James was critical of their choice. In January 1898, 'Herbie' married Miss Rodger – but her fault was that she was a Roman Catholic. When another officer married he complained that the wife's family were 'not a remarkably smart class of people'. Part of the problem, he said, was that 'you never meet women in regimental life. Only in their proper place, after dinner shall we say?' and, when one did, there was always a difficulty.

By the end of 1897, with prospects distinctly unfavourable in every sphere of his life, James Stevenson-Hamilton made a firm decision to return to Africa. His friend, John Watkins Yardley, 'The Curate', had been thinking along similar lines and had been corresponding with Major A. St Hill Gibbons who was organising a trip to Barotseland, now eastern Zambia. In September, Gibbons had asked Yardley to make up his mind because plans had to be made and certificates in surveying and other exploration skills obtained from the Royal Geographical Society, adding, however, that these

## 'No Goal or Object'

'are ABC'.[15] In the event, Yardley was unable to leave England because of his mother's illness. Gibbons was solicitous but reminded him that there was no trouble with communications between England and Barotseland, particularly as the railway to Bulawayo was in 'full swing'. However, he added, 'If you come across a man or two who are made of the right sort of stuff and who are willing to come, I think I can promise them the best sport the world can give . . .'[16]

Yardley immediately thought of Stevenson-Hamilton and soon James was negotiating with Gibbons. Yardley sent James a letter which contained a judicious mix of encouragement and warning. In November he wrote: 'I don't know who are going with Gibbons, but if you find they are nice and you like to pay for your trip [you may] enjoy some big game shooting and be able to get back in a year's time.' But Yardley warned James that, apart from the risk of contracting malaria, it would not be a profitable trip from the military or financial points of view, or even gain him a reputation as an explorer. Gibbons was a self-publicist and 'would look to that for himself'. Yardley explained that Gibbons had not got government approval or support and that it 're-solves itself into a personal trip to explore the Marotse country'. But Yardley also encouraged James by saying that he had liked Gibbons when he met him, and that he 'struck me as intelligent'.[17]

Stevenson-Hamilton was tempted. He contacted Gibbons early in January and was pleased to receive by return of mail a short outline of the proposed expedition. Exploring the Zambezi Valley and Barotseland and returning to Britain through the Great Lakes of East Africa and the Nile River sounded extremely attractive to a man chafing against boredom and keen for adventure. He tried to get other opinions on Gibbons's character. His friend, F.D. Pirie, also warned him about Gibbons, and said that he did not like him at all, adding: 'I do not place an enormous amount of reliance on Gibbons's word. If interests clashed it would be a case of looking after No. 1. This is only my opinion, I have no facts to go on.' He also warned James about ensuring that the legal contract be altered before they left because 'it is very one-sided at present. I would think that Gibbons with dictatorial powers would be very nearly unbearable. You mention Selous, but he and Gibbons are in an entirely different class.'[18] James needed others to join the expedition and tried to get his friend Marshall to join the party, but Marshall declined citing his grave reservations about Gibbons as the primary reason.

Although so many considered opinions from good men could not be wrong, Stevenson-Hamilton was not to be deterred. Africa beckoned. James confided to Marshall, 'Strictly between you and me, I don't take Gibbons very seriously and I think it just as likely or not that the expedition in its main objects will break down, but I look at it this way – we can only get leave to go out in this way, and once out there we have our gun and are on the spot...'

Within a few days James met Gibbons, decided to take the chance and to find others to join them. Early in March he began to take classes in how to use a theodolite and other surveying techniques at the Royal Geographical Society. He seemed a suitable candidate and Gibbons asked whether he wanted to be put up as a Fellow. All was settled and, at the end of March, James wrote, 'I'm prepared to pay £500 for change of scene and if I lose it, it won't break me and at the worst I will just miss a season's hunting and I shall escape jolly Sir George Luck and get a year's leave into the bargain.'

Eager to leave Britain, he said farewell to his regiment at The Barracks in Dundalk, drank an 1865 claret with his father, and said his goodbyes to the Lindsay-Smiths. Then, at the last moment, he hesitated. On 28 May he wrote:

> Off at last. A fool perhaps for leaving the only kind of life I care for? So many friends, I didn't know I had them. No one can understand why I'm going. a) Running to seed in England. Having too good a time and deteriorating morally and physically. b) State of the regiment with a weak colonel. Had it not been for the Colonel's [his father's] 'stick to your profession', I would have left years ago. Would have been finished if I had run up against George Luck again.

Stevenson-Hamilton needed a complete change, and he was about to have one.

# 4

# 'This Life Just Suits Me'[1]

## Barotseland
## (1898–1899)

WHEN IT SET OUT from England for Africa, the Gibbons expedition had a substantial agenda. As he described his goals to the Royal Geographical Society, Gibbons said that, firstly, he wanted to determine the 'geographical limits and tribal distribution of Barotseland'; secondly, he needed to make a proper map of the region (Stevenson-Hamilton's task was to assist with this); thirdly, a careful study of the resources and commercial possibilities of the area was to be undertaken, and, finally, the navigability of the Zambezi and its tributaries was to be ascertained.[2] Once these objects had been accomplished, the party would, hunting wildlife all the while, head eastward towards the Great Lakes of Africa and return to England via the Sudan and Egypt. Such was the grand design.

But Gibbons also had a private agenda which he told Stevenson-Hamilton about when they were corresponding about the trip. This involved land acquisition, and Gibbons wanted to peg out a very large area in Barotseland which Cecil Rhodes's British South Africa Company had conceded to a syndicate, as well as a personal grant for Gibbons himself. There was also the question of selecting a site for an enormous 'game park' in anticipation of a time when such a reserve might become feasible. In addition, Gibbons wanted to erect a monument to the memory of the great David Livingstone.[3]

The Gibbons Expedition was a personal entrepreneurial venture, not constituted under the formal auspices of any colonising or exploring body. It was funded almost entirely by the group itself. Sir John Ardagh, Director of Military Intelligence, gave a small official grant-in-aid, and the Royal Geographical Society supplied the survey instruments free of charge and gave James a three-month training course in their use.[4]

Gibbons seems to have considered himself a latter-day secular Livingstone, following in the master's footsteps and sharing his obsessions. In 1858 Livingstone's great goal had been to navigate the Zambezi inland from its

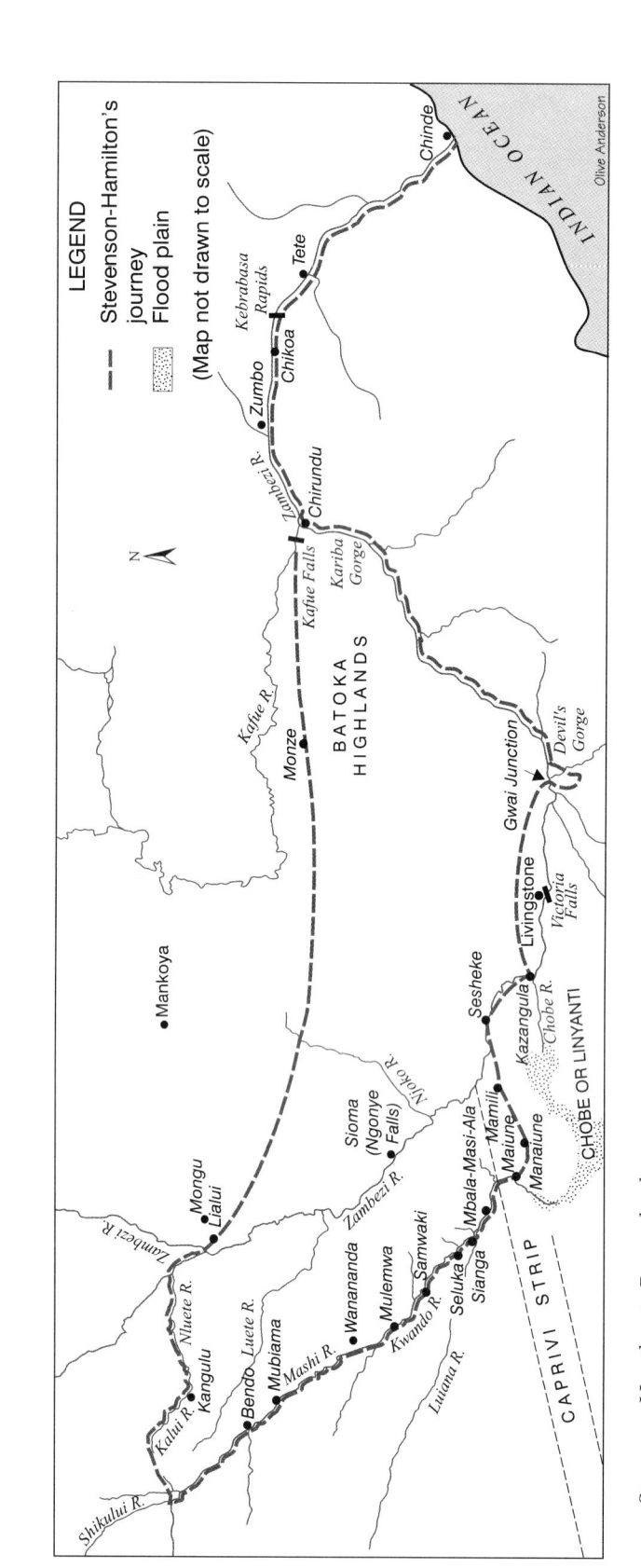

*Stevenson-Hamilton in Barotseland.*

## 'This Life Just Suits Me'

mouth, hoping to reach the Victoria Falls. His party was well equipped and its staff were competent, but the dreadful Kebrabasa (Cabora Bassa) Rapids in the west shattered once and for all Livingstone's grand dreams of promoting 'Christianity, Commerce and Civilisation' along the Zambezi highway. It was a personal disappointment from which Livingstone never recovered.

Gibbons set out in the hope of proving that he could better Livingstone's record. It was an enterprise of daring and boldness, and it is little wonder that James was lured by the offer of joining the expedition. Like Livingstone, Gibbons focussed on the Batoka highlands with their apparent promise of suitability for European settlement, writing 'many of the uplands [of Africa] are among the healthiest tracts of the habitable globe'.[5] It was absolutely necessary that writers and travellers like Gibbons, who were encouraging British settlement, should portray the African people and the climate of Africa in the most favourable possible light so that prospective immigrants might be attracted. And local Africans therefore had to be shown to be anxious to collaborate in modernisation, enthusiastic to cease from their 'savage' ways, and keen to become a dependable labour supply. Concerns about the climate also had to be laid to rest, and Gibbons accordingly wrote, 'A long and varied experience has persuaded me that the climate of Africa is far from being as black as it is painted.'[6]

Although the adventure of exploration was certainly attractive, the opportunity to hunt the extraordinary wildlife of Africa was undoubtedly the major reason why James Stevenson-Hamilton was so enthusiastic to revisit Africa. He had experience of hunting in England, but African hunting was quite different from the stylised routines at home.[7] There were no game laws in Africa comparable to those of Europe. Even where there were constraints, they were neither taken seriously nor enforced. For example, when Stevenson-Hamilton was hunting in Barotseland he knew that eland were protected, 'forbidden fruit according to Coryndon's [the British resident] edict, but I think the first white man in a new country may be accorded some licence'.[8] Moreover, the need to shoot antelope for food, both for the traveller himself and for his numerous bearers and servants, meant that killing many animals was necessary for survival in remote places.

There was, however, another kind of freedom in Africa, and this was the exhilaration of the timeless and untamed beauty of the African landscape. This kind of 'savage loneliness', personal solitude, and the possibility of an escape from an ordered landscape and society, could no longer be found in Britain. In spite of swollen rivers, torrential rains, impassable rapids, trackless wildernesses, hostile local people, unreliable bearers, starvation, injuries, serious bouts of malarial fever, snakes, swarming insects, crocodiles and other physical hardships, Stevenson-Hamilton loved Africa and African exploration without the slightest reservation or regret. When meeting James after a couple of months of travelling apart, Gibbons observed that he '. . . looked the very picture of health'.[9] Stevenson-Hamilton himself was more effusive: 'Much disgusted with contents of some of the books of travel in this part of Africa which I was reading, in regard to the fuss the authors make about what they are pleased to call hardships.'[10]

Moreover, James was deeply affected by the inimitable beauty of Africa – a primeval landscape, unspoilt by evidence of human habitation or industrialisation and urban sprawl. One night in Barotseland, in May 1899, entirely on his own and away from his African servants, he wrote:

> A lovely clear moonlight night, very cold. Before going to bed, I climbed a big ant-hill close to camp and had a grand view of the veldt by moonlight. There it lay for miles, shimmering in the silvery light, miles and miles of open plains alternating with forest glades and all in such dead silence you could have heard a pin fall . . . I suppose in the direction I looked, one might go for a hundred miles and never see a human habitation. The veldt by night is a sight that one must see to understand the immensity and the loneliness of it, the grandeur of the intense silence and the beauty of untouched nature.[11]

Britain contained nothing which aroused the soul of Stevenson-Hamilton in quite the same way. However, Africa offered more to James than escapism and natural beauty. For long periods, he was on his own and reliant on his own resources and wit in a strange environment. Although he depended on his African guides and helpers, he was responsible for their welfare and for the consequences of his own decisions. Not only did he survive the experience, he discovered how much he enjoyed his own company, and how little he missed the pleasures of 'civilisation' and sophisticated companionship.

One of Gibbons's primary concerns was to forge a tightly knit team in the hope of preventing the kind of animosities on which a number of other expeditions, such as Livingstone's, had floundered. Gibbons believed that his choice of military men who were accustomed to obeying orders of a superior, would make his expedition run more smoothly.

At the time of the expedition, Major Alfred Gibbons was nearing fifty years of age, a good-looking and slightly balding man with considerable experience of Africa. Originally with the 3rd East Yorkshire Regiment, Gibbons had traded the military life for African exploration, and, by the time that

## 'This Life Just Suits Me'

James met him, he had already made three prolonged visits to southern Africa. The first two were to Bechuanaland (modern Botswana), where he had joined the Bechuanaland Border Police. Then, in 1893 and 1894, he had tried to explore the upper Zambezi but had not been able to raise the necessary funding. In 1895 he undertook this expedition (in the path of David Livingstone), and he later wrote it up in his book *Exploration and Hunting in Central Africa* (1898) and in a paper which he read before the Royal Colonial Institute on 10 May 1898.[12]

Despite the warnings Stevenson-Hamilton had received when he was thinking about joining Gibbons, the two men got on well together and it did not take long before they had 'become great pals' and for James to regard Gibbons as 'quite one of the best of fellows'.[13] While considering some of his schemes, particularly the plan to navigate the Kafue River by steamer, impractical – 'I hae my doots', as James expressed it – he nonetheless admired Gibbons's decision-making capabilities and, above all, his remarkable 'energy and steam'.[14] This latter trait did not always suit James's somewhat more phlegmatic personality. In March 1899 he wrote: 'Gibbons is a five furlongs horse; he goes at a great pace and halts pretty often. I like plodding steadily on. I suppose I don't do as much in the day, but my legs are shorter and after all, every man has his own pace.'[15]

Africa brought out James's best qualities and it undoubtedly did him good to see for himself how well he could cope in comparison with someone as experienced and accomplished as Gibbons. Apart from the leader, the other person whom James got to know better than any of the others was Captain F.C. Quicke, whom he had introduced to the expedition. Quicke was a year older than Stevenson-Hamilton and also a cavalryman, being with the 1st King's Dragoon Guards. He was something of an athlete, a champion heavy-weight boxer, and an accomplished hunter who held the pig-sticking record in India and Somaliland.

Quicke was easily given over to depression. He did not take illness calmly and became easily agitated. He also was a compulsive organiser, preferring to attend to the minutiae of details himself when he might have just sat back and relaxed. James wrote on one occasion, 'Quicke as usual all excitement and fuss; wanted to start off in about 10 minutes and drag me with him: he *will* not take things calmly but gets into a fuss over everything . . .'[16] But Quicke's pessimism did not dampen James's own high spirits and James often tried to cheer him up, otherwise, as he observed, 'Old Quicke, left alone, would probably shoot himself in an excess of melancholy.'[17] Despite this, James envied Quicke's keen sportsmanship, for he was a more proficient hunter than James, often finding his quarry when James did not and, in the end, he wrote disappointedly that Quicke had 'much more sport than I have'.[18]

Other members of the team included Lieutenant A. Boyd-Alexander of the Rifle Brigade, a young man of 25, who did not feature largely in the narratives of either Gibbons or Stevenson-Hamilton because he was not with them very much of the time.[19] Boyd-Alexander was a dedicated ornithologist and was happy to pay Gibbons for the privilege of giving him the chance to get to Africa to study and collect birds. Boyd-Alexander did not participate in the exploring programme and spent his time along the middle Zambezi totally engrossed in his hobby. It may, however, be that Boyd-Alexander made a deeper impression on James than he realised, for he taught James the importance of closely observing birdlife.

The other three team members played only a small part in Stevenson-Hamilton's Barotseland experience. There was the medical man, Dr Smith, who was over the age of sixty and quite unsuitable for the Zambezi venture. An engineer was required and this was C.L. Weller, the youngest of the group, aged only 21. At the time, Weller had already served his engineering apprenticeship and had begun his studies at Trinity Hall, Cambridge. Like Quicke and Stevenson-Hamilton, he seems to have joined Gibbons for the adventurous experience. The one member of the group who did not join up in Britain was Theodore Muller, a Swiss, who met Gibbons near Tete. Having had 'considerable experience in the management of natives', Muller was also useful because he knew a number of local languages. Unfortunately he died of dysentery in December 1898, the only one of the party to meet such a sad fate.

Gibbons's preparation for the expedition could hardly have been better. The plan was to proceed to Barotseland from the east along the Zambezi River. Knowing that there were impassable rapids along its course, Gibbons had secured the use of a light-weight aluminium launch which could literally be unscrewed and carried in manageable pieces over the unnavigable stretches of the river. If Gibbons had been right, and if he had proved that the Zambezi was navigable, his name would today rank alongside those of Rhodes and Livingstone as one of the great pioneers of Africa. This extraordinary possibility might explain Gibbons's almost manic determination to succeed and carry on when some of his staff, like Quicke, said that the situation was hopeless. Gibbons also saw to it that they had food for more than a year, as well as clothing, shoes, medicines, trade goods, observation and surveying instruments. At one time, more than four hundred porters were needed to carry their goods.[20] Although highly organised, they also had to improvise at times. At one point, Stevenson-Hamilton shot a vulture and he 'got some quills from his wings, with one of which I now write, and I fear my writing doesn't do much credit to the vulture'.[21]

Barotseland was an extremely remote part of Africa at the time of Stevenson-Hamilton's visit. It is cradled by the western arc of the Zambezi River which rises in the north-west corner of Zambia and then flows a short distance through what is modern Angola before re-entering Zambian territory. From here, the river flows southwards, veering somewhat to the east. At Sioma, about half-way to the river's southernmost point, a hard basalt dyke intrudes, creating the great Ngonye Falls. After the waterfall, the land levels out and this, together with the fact that in the rainy season the Zambezi's large volume of water is augmented by many tributaries (especially the Kwando and the Chobe), causes the river to spread itself out into an enormous flood plain, some 150 kilometres long and 30 kilometres wide. This flood plain constituted the territories of the Barotse people.[22] For many centuries, when the waters rose each year between March and June, this inland sea became alive with dugouts and other fishing craft, while livestock and people took refuge on outcrops of higher ground. Once the waters subsided in winter, cattle returned to graze on the freshly emerging and highly palatable grass, and crops flourished in the accumulated fertile alluvial silt.

In the nineteenth century, the Barotse people, weakened by factionalism, fell prey to powerful invaders from southern Africa – a community of Tswana under Sebituane, whose language and customs came to predominate in the region.[23] However, Sebituane's heir, his son Sekeletu, was weak and the Barotse soon took their revenge, meting out to their foreign overlords the treatment they had received some four decades earlier, rising in rebellion and killing every one of their conquerors – women and children included – in one dreadful, gory night. Thereafter, chief Lewanika ruled Barotseland for almost forty years. His people prospered from the tribute extracted from subject groups and his war canoes dominated the Zambezi. The Barotse of that time have been described as 'political realists with a clear grasp of the complex balance of power which then existed in Central Africa'.[24]

The 1880s had been a decade of great colonisation in Africa, but the imperial powers were reluctant to spend money on colonising ventures. This reluctance opened the way for a frenzy of concession-seeking by private entrepreneurs. In June 1889 Lewanika had signed just such a concession document, granting prospecting and mining rights to his old friend, Harry Ware, in return for an annual payment. Ware sold this concession almost immediately to Cecil Rhodes, the Kimberley mining magnate, Cape politician and greatest British imperialist of the time.[25] Gibbons, acting as an agent for Rhodes and the British South Africa Company on his two journeys into Barotseland, explored Africa as a prospective settler, keeping an eye open for areas that might be attractive and healthy for European expansion. Unlike Gibbons, Stevenson-Hamilton was not promoting settler schemes and was therefore able to savour each day as it came, rather than relate it to any future investment or political gain. This is not to say that he did not appreciate the political ramifications of the expedition or that he was ignorant of the Anglo-Portuguese rivalry in central Africa. In July 1899, while at the most westerly point of his travels, he dined with a Portuguese trader and on Senõr Antonio J. Veëiro's map, James noted, 'I see that the country west of the Zambezi, which is debatable land, is marked "Province of Angola" on the Portuguese map. It's quite likely they are right, but no doubt we shall get it in [the] end.'

Barotseland was pivotal to Rhodes's grand vision of an Africa dominated by Britain because it was sandwiched between two Portuguese territories which cut Britain off from the sea on either side of central Africa. Moreover, a third European power had become involved with the granting to Germany of the Caprivi Strip in 1890. Considerable manoeuvring for influence was therefore inevitable. It was, however, the western boundary of Barotseland which was more important to the imperial powers than Caprivi, because there had been no detailed study of the area and arrangements with the Portuguese saw the boundary run between British and Portuguese spheres of interest in the centre of the upper Zambezi. This bisected Barotseland, Lewanika's polity, and Rhodes was furious. At the time of the Gibbons expedition, arbitration on this boundary was being discussed and the idea was to obtain as much information as possible to lay before the International Arbitration Court.

Gibbons and his party set out from Chinde, a Portuguese town just north of the complex delta which forms the mouth of the Zambezi. There was, however, a British concession whereby various trading companies operated stern-wheeled steamers and traded with Nyasaland and various Portuguese settlements on the lower Zambezi. Gibbons chartered one of these steamers, the *Centipede*, from Sharrers Traffic Company, to take his group as far as Tete, some five hundred kilometres upstream. Unfortunately, this was a year of extremely low water in the Zambezi and the expedition got off to a bad start by taking some three weeks to reach Tete. A day's journey beyond Tete, the party left the *Centipede*, unloaded their goods, and together with their African carriers marched to Chikoa, some eighty kilometres upstream.

At that point the wonderful aluminium steamer which had been brought out with the party was to come into its own and its various parts were carefully pieced together. Men and goods were loaded aboard. But it did not take long for all to realise that the engines were too small for the heavily laden craft to make headway against the strong current of the Zambezi. It was then decided to divide the expedition into two groups. Indeed, the steamer itself was divided, with Gibbons, Quicke, Weller, Smith, Stevenson-Hamilton and 14 'Zambezi natives' using their half as a steamer, while the other half was 'made into a barge with sail and oars' and this contained Boyd-Alexander and Muller. The whole party planned to reunite at the Kafue River junction early in 1899.

Stevenson-Hamilton's group made good progress every day:

> We had a very strenuous time owing to rapids and rocks, and sank the steamer on several occasions. However, it was only necessary to take her to pieces once, at the Kariba rapids, and after surmounting some dozen others with the aid of a tow rope, eventually we were definitely stopped and sank for the last time in 'Devil's Gorge' near the Gwai [River] junction and some seventy miles before the Victoria Falls.

A contemporary British newspaper was proud to announce that the steamer *Constance* (which is what they named it) was the first vessel (with white people in it) to navigate the middle Zambezi River and had gone further than any other craft. When the *Constance* could go no further, Gibbons, Quicke and Stevenson-Hamilton managed to climb out of the gorge with great difficulty and, after a two-day march, found a small village and obtained assistance.

It was a desolate part of the Zambezi in which the group found itself. There were few local villages and no food or carriers were forthcoming. Consequently, Gibbons set off with about a dozen 'personal boys' to make his way to Lewanika at his capital Lialui to get porters – about sixty were needed – to carry all the equipment and trading goods. While he did so, Stevenson-Hamilton and Quicke were left alone for nearly two months with two servants to attend them. They found it hard to obtain enough to eat, 'meal was almost unobtainable owing to crop failure, and there was no big game because the rinderpest [a virulent animal disease which became an epizootic throughout Africa in 1896] had virtually eliminated all wildlife'. This must have been almost unbearably frustrating to young men who had come all the way from England to hunt the fabled giant fauna of Africa.

During February 1899, thanks to Gibbons's forced march and his efforts with Lewanika, the carriers eventually arrived, and at last Stevenson-Hamilton and Quicke were able to leave the little campsite and

*Lialui.*

head for Kazangula. Soon the rain began and it did not abate: 'We were never dry, day or night.' Not surprisingly, the African bearers did not like to work under these conditions and became surly and workshy.

At Sesheke, Quicke left by canoe to Lewanika's capital and then went on to map the area to the west and north. Gibbons and Stevenson-Hamilton went together southwards along the Chobe and parted at the village of Mamili, where they were 'hospitably entertained'. From Mamili Gibbons continued to travel southwards towards the Okavango swamps, while Stevenson-Hamilton went generally northwards, following the course of the Kwando River until near its source. The whole place had become a seasonal swamp. The terrain was extremely gruelling and exhausting. Bearers threatened to desert at every turn, and the area was inhabited and surrounded by unfriendly people who were not vassals of Lewanika and who did not therefore owe him any allegiance or obligation to help out travellers under his protection. This was the most difficult part of the expedition for Stevenson-Hamilton.

At Lialui that August 1899, Stevenson-Hamilton recovered and caught up with Gibbons and Quicke. They also learnt from a letter brought by runner that Muller had died and that Weller, Smith and Boyd-Alexander had all returned to Britain in January. The unscheduled departure of half of the team meant that Gibbons had to alter his plans. The idea of travelling to the Great Lakes by steamer was finally abandoned and Gibbons decided that he alone would head for Khartoum. Quicke was dispatched to survey the northwest region of Barotseland and head for Britain via the Angolan coast. For his part, James was to survey the river system north-east of Lialui, in particular the course of the lower Kafue River. When he reached the Zambezi at the Kafue confluence, James was then required to return along the Zambezi, with the responsibility of arranging for the disposal of the expedition's goods which had been left in the care of the Portuguese at Zumbo.

All three men travelled enormous distances, criss-crossing Barotseland, checking river names, noting the condition of the country and its inhabitants. Stevenson-Hamilton later recalled, 'I did my part of the journey without much incident... During the greater part of the journey out I suffered severely from fever and had to be carried in a *machile* from Chikoa to Tete.'[26] Sighting the Kafue Falls was the highlight of visiting Barotseland for James. From some distance upstream he realised that he was approaching a waterfall, but the going was extremely difficult and at one stage (he was also slightly delirious from fever) he thought perhaps they might be an 'hallucination'. But they were indeed very real and he was most impressed:

> ... they are very respectable – about 70 feet high (60 feet and then another of 10) and a regular mill-race below for 100 yards. Tremendous cliffs rise on each side and a mountain rises 1 200 feet from river just to north. No white man has, so far as I know, seen them before; in fact I never met anyone who knew of their existence.... Having feasted my eyes enough, and tried to think I am sufficiently rewarded ... I climbed back.[27]

Given the modern preoccupation with racial prejudice and intergroup conflict, and also with Stevenson-Hamilton's later career as a game warden in segregationist South Africa in mind, his attitude, as well as that of Gibbons, towards the African people is of considerable relevance. Gibbons certainly wished to depict Lewanika and his 'tribesmen' as accommodating, helpful, and intent on advancing the colonial effort. Lewanika and Gibbons had met before, and it is clear that they had liked one another. The chief went to considerable trouble to supply the expedition with carriers, bearers and guides, and to help under difficult circumstances. Certainly it was in Lewanika's interests to finalise the western boundary so that his followers on either side of the upper Zambezi were not divided between Britain and Portugal, and the success of Gibbons's expedition was therefore important for his internal and foreign policies.

Social Darwinism as a philosophy dominated imperialist thinking at the time. There was – so it taught – a ladder of civilisation, with apes at the bottom, black Africans on the first rung, Indians a little higher, and Europeans at the top. Certainly Africans might rise as they abandoned their traditional lifestyles, but no one doubted at that time that they had a very long way to go. They definitely required discipline and tutoring. 'They are just like children', wrote Stevenson-Hamilton, 'and must be told what to do or else they play the devil with everything.'[28] Statements such as Gibbons's, 'Born and bred to oppression, the African is equally ready to give and receive harsh treatment',[29] were common in the traveller literature of the nineteenth century. Gibbons and Stevenson-Hamilton had no hesitation in threatening their African attendants with firearms if they did not do as they were told, and James decided, as he came to the end of his travels in September 1899, that 'It is sad, but true, that one has to rule these people through fear and not through love.'[30] But Stevenson-Hamilton's attitudes towards his African companions were not absolutely clear-cut: 'These niggers don't resent being snubbed a bit, but rather like you better for it, but I loathe snubbing anyone, even a nigger. It goes against the grain somehow, more fool me!'[31]

In 1953 Stevenson-Hamilton's *Barotseland Journal*, donated to the Central African Archives and edited by J.P.R. Wallis, was published – the only significant part of James's vast diary output to have been brought under the public gaze during his lifetime. At the time of its publication, the elderly man (he was then 86) was unhappy because he had wanted an edited version to be used rather than his raw daily entries. He felt that his diary remarks from that time contained racist statements, indications of annoyance, and a lack of the appreciation which he later developed for African ways, which were neither appropriate nor useful for the 1950s. He wrote when the *Barotseland Journal* was published, 'In the journal I have let myself go about people and places rather strongly at times, but it was not intended for any but my own eyes, and just reflects my feelings at the moment.' He was also astounded that what he had written might be of general interest to a wider public, for 'however interesting it may be to oneself to read of one's own past experiences, it can hardly be expected that others will be interested'.[32]

But the importance of his contribution lies precisely in its spontaneity and honesty and the fact that it constitutes a daily matter-of-fact record which has not been edited, weeded or sanitised. One reason why James's diary lay unused for so long was that the contract with Gibbons specifically included the provision that other expedition members could not publish their experiences before Gibbons's own work saw the light of day. Gibbons's two-volume book, *Africa from South to North through Marotseland*, published in 1904, is very different from James's version of events. It is highly mannered, full of effusive Victorian language, opinion and propaganda, and it is discouragingly long. James's more abrupt and unaffected daily observations have a different kind of charm.

## 'This Life Just Suits Me'

FALLS OF THE KAFUKWE
Nov 1899.

The Kafue Falls.

The duality or dichotomy evident in the attitudes of European travellers is tantalising and many authors have tried to make sense of it. Africa was Eden, but spoilt because it was in the hands of Africans. In addition, it is certainly an unusual proposition for one to be entirely and most obviously at the mercy of a group of people, while remaining their leader and believing that they are therefore dependent on one's judgement and goodwill. The leader – the white man – knew what he had come for, where he wanted to go, and what he wanted to do. But he had no clue as to how to get there, how he would feed himself, or what difficulties or conventions he might encounter. It is remarkable how the innate sense of European superiority survived intact in such unfamiliar, even hostile, surroundings. From the European point of view of the time it seemed self-evident that work and westernisation would improve and benefit Africans, that wars would cease, and that missionaries and 'civilisation' generally would suppress 'the most awful atrocities prevalent throughout the country'. 'Tribal' warfare was regarded as a particularly atrocious aspect of black life, and Europeans were inevitably unable to appreciate the nuances of the politics of the continent. Those who would have been horrified at intervention in the domestic affairs of another European country, could comment without irony, as Stevenson-Hamilton did of the Ndebele: 'And yet ignorant people at home cried out at our "brutality" in conquering these fiends of hell.'[33]

Stevenson-Hamilton, like Gibbons, was very impressed by Lewanika when he met him in August 1899. This admirable chief, a statesman and shrewd observer of the vanities, prejudices and preferences of the numerous Europeans who courted his favour, lived in a 'very large clean house, nicely furnished, carpets, easy chairs, maps, curtains etc.' He wrote approvingly that Lewanika looked like the 'prosperous head of a city firm. His features are perfectly European and his eyes have a good-humoured twinkle when he talks, which he does in a low and nicely modulated tone . . . He impressed me, by manner and everything else, as a perfectly finished gentleman.'[34] The following month Lewanika asked Stevenson-Hamilton to lunch. This was a special occasion and James noted every detail, from the square table, clean cloth and table napkins with ivory rings, to the roast beef, 'excellent gravy', brown bread and jam followed by preserved peaches and sour milk. The waiters were as excellent as the table settings and the food, since they were unobtrusive and polite: 'You have no rush about of servants round the tables, a custom that might be followed with advantage in some cases in Europe.' While James took the opportunity to observe African habits closely, Lewanika, for his part, questioned James equally closely about European ways:

> After lunch had to go through the usual pumping ordeal. 'What pay does a policeman get? What do you get paid for making maps? (a very difficult one to answer!). How much does a soldier get paid? . . .' I vainly tried to turn the conversation. The worst of it is, one know he asks every white man precisely similar questions and never forgets the answers of each, which he compares with previous ones and comes to the unavoidable conclusion 'Well, some of them must lie.'[35]

There are many references in James's journal to the fact that he wished he could communicate better with the Africans who were his constant company. 'If only I could talk to them enough to suggest things. . . . As it is, I can only make myself understood in the very simplest things.'[36] Throughout the journey, Stevenson-Hamilton surveyed their position every day, taking readings from the stars whenever the night was clear. Naturally his assistants saw him performing these tasks, and one night the conversation turned towards astronomy:

> They [the Barotse] think the sun travels across the heavens from E. to W. during day and during the night travels back again from W. to E. but hidden by the firmament which, of course, they imagine to be a canopy of some kind. The moon acts in the same way. The stars are 'shweele' (dead) during the day. I wish I had known enough to go on talking on these most interesting topics.[37]

While trying himself to learn some Barotse words, James also attempted to teach some English:

> Mwala is getting quite *au fait* in English, picking up a lot of words. He is fairly intelligent and comes and sits near my table or at night after dinner by my fire and asks for some word to be repeated over and over again until he has grasped it. I get hold of a few words too, though I have the advantage of being able to put them on paper, but his memory otherwise would serve him better than my civilized one.[38]

Barotseland was the adventure of a lifetime. Stevenson-Hamilton became adept at living outdoors, becoming an expert field cook who was able to improvise when the correct necessities were not at hand. 'Made rather a good brown loaf: I made a white one of flour yesterday by baking under an inverted kaffir pot on a gridiron – much the best way, I find,' he wrote confidently. Then there was the grilled wildebeest steak and fried pumpkin and potato chips for dinner. This manner of doing things is all my own notion. I think Gibbons roasts all the juice out of his meat. At least since I started grilling meat and basting it with lard, I have never had to echo his complaints about the dryness of African meat. The potatoes cut in slices and fried are also a great improvement.[39]

But not all his home-making adventures were as happy. Inclined to be forgetful when leaving in a hurry, he once forgot his gridiron at a campsite and, rather than lose it, he retraced a whole day's march to retrieve it, because he knew that 'you cannot make up these deficiencies in Africa'.[40]

It was, however, his encounters with wildlife while in central Africa that thrilled James Stevenson-Hamilton to such an extent that they helped to shape his ultimate life's work as a conservationist. It is not that his diaries reflect modern environmental thinking since such ideas were completely unknown at the time. What is apparent is that his enjoyment of hunting wildlife, his strong desire for information and knowledge, together with his appreciation of the landscape, certainly led him step by step in a more contemporary evaluation of nature conservation. Like other sportsmen of his time, he was very keen to obtain a specimen of every possible wild animal and, of course, his major trophies. He was not to have the experience of abundant wildlife, for the rinderpest had by 1898 also begun to take its toll in west-central Africa. But every day brought something new, and the lack of a stifling routine was exactly (he now found) what James enjoyed most in life. He noted approvingly in his diary: 'Always in Africa, and especially in this expedition, you never know what is going to happen.'[41]

Stevenson-Hamilton enjoyed his best hunting after he had separated from Gibbons and was alone with his bearers in the Chobe area and on the high ground along the Kwando River. He also hunted whenever he came across an interesting species of wildlife – the Victorian naturalist's impulse to make a 'complete' collection. He was fascinated by wildebeest, which he thought looked from a distance like American bison. When they just stood and stared they even reminded him of the Cadzow cattle around Fairholm. But James was shooting mainly for good game trophies. After having shot one wildebeest, he found that it was a young cow and that its horns were inadequate, and so he was sorry that he had not shot another while he had the chance.[42] He was delighted to kill a roan antelope after an exciting chase through a thicket, 'We ran forward and I was pleased to see the buck lying just where she had stood, quite dead. The bullet had gone right through the neck and cut the jugular vein. It proved to be a large roan antelope cow

(I am death on cows!), standing about 14.2, and a very good head for a cow.'[43]

James also encountered species which were new to him. In May 1899, he shot what he thought was a young lechwe, only to discover that it was actually a sitatunga. He was thrilled to bag a tsessebe, 'handsome antelope of a rich brown colour with coats as fine and glossy as our English race-horses . . .'[44] Like many Victorian hunters, Stevenson-Hamilton recorded his hunting exploits in detail in his journals. These were thrilling to him, and the excitement of the moment comes through clearly in his writing. On those rare occasions when he thought of home, he wrote, 'Another Ascot week. I wonder if I shall attend the next one? What a difference in the life! It is queer though, I enjoy this life more than anything I have experienced.'[45]

He was depressed when there was no big game. 'Shall I *ever* get to them, I wonder, on this trip!',[46] he complained after seeing only guinea fowl for days on end. There was a chance of bagging a giraffe, and occasionally there was a zebra in the distance. By July 1899 he was leaving the game area. But 'I am, however, pretty well content,' he wrote,

> Except giraffe I have got something of every kind of game existing in [the] region I have passed through, though I would like a bull roan antelope and eland to complete collection, and, I think, another zebra. I may get a waterbuck on the Zambezi. I don't expect any shooting after that; the pleasantest part of the trip is over . . .[47]

He did, in fact, get his waterbuck on the Zambezi that September, as well as a warthog and an oribi. On 6 November 1899, he was on the same ground as he had been a year before. A few days later he set off down the Zambezi in new canoes and his progress with a far higher water level was much quicker in comparison with the upward journey. At Zumbo he arranged for the sale of the expedition's stores, boarded the *Constance*, which had been left there by Weller almost a year earlier, and set off down the river. Once back in 'civilisation' at Tete he heard about the outbreak of the South African War. Rumours of the disastrous reverses which the British forces had already suffered made James anxious to support the imperial cause now that the Barotseland expedition had ended. Rather than return to Britain and rejoin his regiment after his spell of African leave, Stevenson-Hamilton decided to make the most of his proximity to the war zone and he headed directly to South Africa.

# 5

# 'My Regiment was in South Africa'[1]
## The South African War
## (1899–1902)

BY THE TIME James Stevenson-Hamilton reached Durban early in January 1900, military operations in South Africa had already been in progress for almost three months and some of the major engagements were over. The Boer forces of the Transvaal and Orange Free State invaded the Cape Colony and Natal and quickly invested the major towns of Kimberley, Mafeking, and Ladysmith. These sieges, combined with disastrous and unexpected British defeats in early December at Stormberg, Magersfontein and Colenso ('Black Week') astonished the British public. Contrary to the initial jingoistic belief in a swift British victory, it had become increasingly clear that ignominious retreat and even more military disasters were real and humiliating possibilities.

Once back in South Africa James longed to get into the action. The war for which he had prepared and longed for had arrived at last, together with the chance of distinction and promotion. After conquering a fresh bout of malaria with large quantities of dry champagne and quinine, he reported for military duty. He learnt that his own regiment was already in the Cape Colony, based just south of the Orange River near Colesberg as part of the mobile cavalry under Major-General John French. After his period of freedom in Africa, James was struck by the unpleasant implications of a sudden return to the rigid routines of cavalry life. Vexing memories of the pettiness of his superior officers and formal rules and regulations of regimental duties began to weigh heavily on his mind. As he made his way to Colesberg, his initial enthusiasm was replaced by gloomy recollections and morose uncertainty. Initially his aim had been to avoid a formal regimental connection and to link up with a group of irregulars. Now, it seemed, he had closed off his options by not having joined such a corps before reporting to the Durban military authorities who, naturally, placed him back with the 6th (Inniskilling) Dragoons.

In spite of all forebodings, he went to Port Elizabeth to make travel and other arrangements. These were considerably protracted – 'how hard

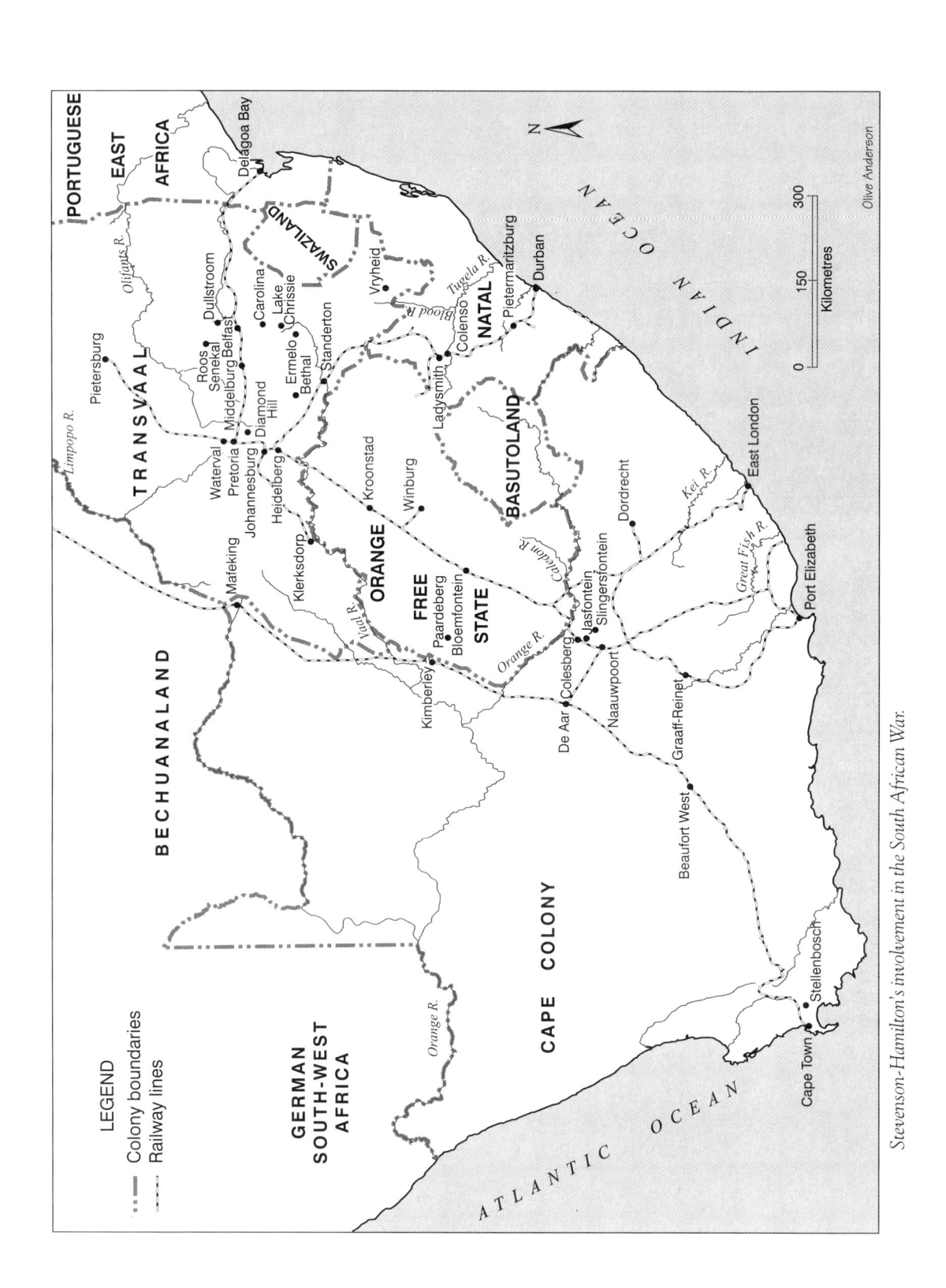

*Stevenson-Hamilton's involvement in the South African War.*

they make it for one to go and risk being killed,' he mused. But eventually he was on the Bloemfontein train and on 21 January disembarked at Rensburg siding, the regional headquarters of the British army some distance south of Colesberg. Once he had rejoined his regiment and seen the situation at first hand, Stevenson-Hamilton's doubts about his decision began to dissipate. His old friend from Natal and England, Major Edmund Allenby, was there, as were many other familiar comrades, who lost no time in telling James of the serious military predicament in which the British forces found themselves.

Lord Roberts's strategy was to consolidate all his forces in a single northwards march first to Bloemfontein and then on to Pretoria. Once those capitals of the two Boer republics had fallen, it was assumed that the enemy remaining in the field would surrender and that war would be over. In order to accomplish this task successfully, Roberts amassed a force of more than a hundred thousand men, and the logistics of moving this army forward while trying to retain an element of surprise, required a good deal of planning and foresight. Roberts's grand strategy permitted only two exceptions to the concentration of men for his advance up the railway line to Pretoria. Firstly, General Sir Redvers Buller (whom Roberts had replaced as Commander-in-Chief in South Africa) was left in command of the British column in Natal and, secondly, under pressure from Cecil Rhodes who had been trapped like an angry wasp in the besieged diamond-mining town of Kimberley, a considerable force was being detoured to the west to effect the relief of that town.

The situation in which James now found himself was influenced by the need to end the siege of Kimberley. When war broke out, the Boers had crossed the Orange River, taken Colesberg, and then pressed southwards. Active skirmishing with the British forces in the district had retarded their progress into the colony thereafter. The semi-desert landscape in the area of Colesberg is bleak, the veld broken only by the typically flat-topped *koppies* (small hills) of the Karoo. It was not easy terrain in which to engage or pin down a highly mobile enemy. However, in order to consolidate his grand march and relieve Kimberley, Roberts had to weaken his position around Colesberg, all the while keeping the Boer commandos occupied. The diminished number of British troops in the area were under the command of Major-General R.A.P. Clements and when Stevenson-Hamilton arrived the Major-General's task was to harry the Boers and prevent them from making further incursions into the Cape Colony – while the rest of the cavalry raced across the Karoo to relieve Kimberley.

When Stevenson-Hamilton rejoined his regiment, there were three active squadrons under the command of Lieutenant-Colonel H.C. Page-

Henderson: 'A' squadron was led by Captain A.R. Mosley, 'B' by Major Thursby Dauncey and 'C' by Allenby.[2] From December onwards unplanned and *ad hoc* skirmishes were the order of the day all along the railway line. The Boer commandos were independent of any centralised command, and they were highly mobile, self-reliant and had a reputation for daring and improvisation. The British were not slow to learn this new kind of warfare, and the dangerous realities of the military situation had already forced Clements to adopt tactics and a style of line organisation which was only slightly more formal than that of the Boers themselves. The railway from Cape Town was the means of supply for all aspects of the British war effort. To defend it, Clements divided his forces into two main groups, one on either side of the railway line.

It was in these surroundings that James had his first taste of battle, and he loved every minute of it. Independence of action – which is what James had hankered for – was encouraged because the situation demanded it. Stevenson-Hamilton's group included some of Rimington's Guides (a scouting unit) led by James's regimental friend, Mike Rimington. In this kind of engagement James was given his first taste of military egalitarianism and classless interaction. As one of the Guides expressed it in a letter home:

> Do you know Colonials? . . . England has not got the type. The Western States of America have it . . . When you come among Colonials, forget your birth and breeding, your ancestral acres and big income, and all those things which carry such weight in England. No forelocks are pulled for them here; they count for nothing. Are you wide-awake, sharp, and shrewd, plucky; can you lead? Then go up higher. Are you less of these things? Then go down lower. But always among these men it is a position simply of what you are in yourself.[3]

Until the capture of Bloemfontein in March 1900, James was leading precisely the sort of life he liked most and this style of warfare suited him perfectly. He felt exactly as did the officer whose memoir is quoted above. He was content to be in an atmosphere where ability and achievement were recognised, in which discipline was minimal, and in which *success* counted above all – rather than slavish adherence to formal regulations and petty codes. James lived in the open veld, sleeping at night on the ground, surrounded in every direction by open countryside, and meeting unusual and interesting people. These experiences were made more exciting by the ever-present dangers of warfare, for there were also the challenges of learning about the Boers and their instinctive grasp of tactics. In the war zone in which James found himself, mobility and scouting were all-important and life-saving decisions had to be made on the spot and at a gallop.

By a happy turn of fate, James's expertise in veld-craft – gained in Barotseland – and his temperamental preference for independent thinking and action were now at last paying dividends in his military career. By 3 February his competence was recognised when a telegram invited him to meet Major-General French, who immediately sent him to take charge of an isolated post on a farm called Jasfontein. There, about a dozen of Rimington's Guides and fifty Tasmanians under Captain Cyril St C. Cameron were placed under his command.[4] Without delay he began to organise the fortification of the farm, while at the same time placating a farmer named Kotze who claimed that his farm had been raided by one of the patrols. On the same day, he stopped two Cape carts from making their way down a country track and was surprised to find 'two fair rebels probably carrying information'. He was embarrassed and did not know what to do. 'It is a nuisance running into women in these times,' he said. He allowed them to outspan at Kotze's house and even to entertain his men by playing the piano. However, when 'lots of kissing and giggling' began, James sternly ordered the women out and set them on their way home. This was certainly not the kind of war which one read about in military textbooks or learned about at Sandhurst.

Stevenson-Hamilton's first experience under heavy fire was during the attacks on Slingersfontein on 9 February, and he found it both exhilarating and very exciting. He described the 'bullets whizzing everywhere'. Later in the engagement, while hiding on the slopes of a *koppie*, he spotted a company of mounted Boers retiring along a ridge. He instantly grasped that if he and his men could occupy a further line of *koppies* which he could see some distance in front of the retiring Boers they might snipe at them as they retired, and so he and about twenty others galloped across the intervening plain – only to be cut off by another party of Boers whom they had not seen. James and his men immediately took shelter. Heavy fire was exchanged and a bullet scraped the top of his sun helmet. As the exchange developed, James found himself in the company of three Tasmanians, all cut off, as he was, from the main body of his troops. They lay absolutely still, holding their breath, and waited to be surrounded. When the firing seem to die down to some extent in their immediate vicinity, they jumped on to their horses and galloped away so fast that they later could not even tell whether or not they had been fired upon.[5]

Because his own self-confidence, powers of observation and judgement had increased tremendously during his Barotseland expedition, James began to see more and more clearly that the regimental commander, Page-

Henderson, was 'really making a mess'. On 25 February he declared that his superior officer was incapable of giving coherent orders 'except to retreat'. On that particular day James was especially angry because a retreat which he had been ordered to undertake was, he believed, not at that moment in the best British interests. Accordingly, on the following morning he met the Boers under a flag of truce and found out that he had indeed been right – the Boers had already evacuated their position, as James had suspected all along – and Page-Henderson should have ordered the British forces to remain where they were and exploit the new situation. This encounter between Stevenson-Hamilton and the Boers was cordial. He was impressed by their manner, gave each of them a cigar, and noted that the Commandant wore small earrings. He was pleased that, throughout their discussions, he kept his white flag fluttering aloft because, although the Boers could see him from ten kilometres away, his own men nearly opened fire on him. To make matters worse, an Inniskilling Private later came up to Stevenson-Hamilton and did not recognise him. The hapless junior was 'jawed out', and James declared himself 'sick at the comparison of the quiet, efficient and easy-going manner of the enemy with the wild, excitable demeanour and the damn bad manners of our men'. Allenby would have agreed: 'I must say, I rather like Brother Boer,' he confessed to his wife.[6]

After the defeat of General Piet Cronje and his large Boer force at Paardeberg at the end of February 1900 and the relief of Kimberley thereafter, the tide turned in favour of the British. Until he arrived in Bloemfontein a month later, James virtually had a free hand in the Orange Free State. Each night he and his men stayed at deserted or 'friendly' farmhouses, gathering the Free Staters together in order to read to them Roberts's proclamation which ordered them to hand in their weapons. Letters from home arrived for the first time, and James received two pieces of good news. Firstly, his brother Olmar, a tea planter in India, was coming out to join the war with Lumsden's Horse, a volunteer regiment raised in India.[7] Secondly, his troublesome sister, Cissy, was off to Queensland, Australia, with Lord and Lady Lamington (Cissy's old friend, May Hozier). 'The best thing she could do,' he declared.

The pleasures of responsibility and freedom of action could not last forever and Stevenson-Hamilton's troubles began when he reached Bloemfontein on 4 April 1900. At first, he could not find Clements's army, but he then learnt that it had been broken up and he himself had been relegated to an infantry brigade. Although he was still for the moment formally attached to Rimington's Guides, the Tasmanians had left having been incorporated, to James's dismay, into a combined Australian force. Even more of a pity, however, was the lack of supplies, the poor condition of the horses, and the palpable animosity between the civilian and military administration. In Bloemfontein 'the army was a great inert mass', and James's worst nightmare was to be part of such a entity. What could he do to prevent himself from being sucked into it? He tried to obtain an intelligence position but he heard nothing about his application for some time. Ever impatient when in contact with army bureaucracy, he felt that things were not going his way. Page-Henderson wanted him to return to the regiment because he (Page-Henderson) was leaving to command the Cavalry Depot situated in Bloemfontein.

Not only was the regiment being depleted, but there had been a complaint against Stevenson-Hamilton from a farmer named Visser who had accused James of stealing a large quantity of butter. 'This is untrue,' raged James, who explained to Page-Henderson that, when he went to this farm, Visser had been absent without a pass. Because James had reported Visser for this, Visser was now getting his revenge. But Page-Henderson had taken his decision and told James that 'after scally-wagging about the country over the last few months' he would henceforth have to toe the line. Allenby, now in command of the regiment, also wanted Stevenson-Hamilton back. When Lord Roberts decided that no more cavalry officers could be seconded to other divisions, James tried to escape by pulling all the strings he was capable of, but by 25 April he had to admit defeat. Roberts's decision was the 'last nail in my coffin'. He was very dejected and wrote: 'No chance now of special opportunities for distinction. Makes one peevish and in danger of losing interest for the moment.'

He was in a fulminating mood when he returned to Springfield camp where the three squadrons were together once more with the Cavalry Brigade. There James first came into close contact with Thursby Dauncey whom he would come to loathe by the end of the war. Dauncey, new to the regiment, was in overall command of squadrons B and C, and James was placed in C.[8]

Roberts planned a quick advance to Pretoria but he was delayed in Bloemfontein for almost two months. Only by 3 May was the General ready to leave and three days later James wrote, 'Great advance on the Vaal. No order, confusion. Baggage coming up late.' A cavalry is dependent on horses and the only mounts available were out of condition and unfit for the arduous and unaccustomed uses to which they were being put. Because it was winter, there was little natural fodder, although James and his companions often overcame this difficulty by expropriating forage from the farms through which they passed: 'taking a leaf out of the irregulars' book and oblivious to orders', he admitted.⁹ The poor state of the horses' condition increasingly retarded the cavalry's advance. Indeed, it was the South African War that exposed deficiencies in horse management, and even the most experienced cavalrymen were unable to perform fundamental manoeuvres efficiently because of the weakened state of their horses. Spiers argues – and Stevenson-Hamilton's comments would support this – that the traditional British cavalry training of the time placed excessive emphasis on *stable* management while the knowledge, care and treatment of horses in the often punishing conditions of field service were neglected.¹⁰

The slow advance to Pretoria continued uneventfully and the cavalry passed unchallenged through many small and dreary towns on the way. No one at this time had any idea of the overall and long-term strategy of the Boer High Command. What had become evident after the Paardeberg defeat was that they had abandoned their practice of setting up defensive laagers, and had regrouped themselves into small, mounted, guerilla bands. The Inniskillings often caught tantalising glimpses of these elusive commandos disappearing to the north. Perhaps they were merely saving their resources for an attack at the right moment? No one knew for sure. As James and his squadron neared Johannesburg, excitement mounted. There were now two vital questions on everyone's minds: would the Boers, before they retreated, destroy the rich gold mines of the Witwatersrand, and to what extent would they try to defend Pretoria, their capital city? Johannesburg fell without resistance and James took the opportunity once more to examine the town that he had visited in 1889. He was not greatly impressed: 'Town not grown much since 1889, but shops and buildings better generally.'

After a day at leisure the march to Pretoria began. 'A long day through the most terrifying hills [the Magaliesberg] in the latter part,' James wrote. While the main force eventually got to Pretoria unopposed, the cavalry, including Stevenson-Hamilton, took a wide route around the capital in order to rescue British prisoners from the farm Waterval, an event accompanied by much 'shouting and delight'.

For James, the happiness of at last arriving in Pretoria was undermined by the fact that he was becoming increasingly angry with Dauncey for – as he believed – unnecessarily endangering the lives of his men. On 6 June, Dauncey sent Lieutenant G. Meek and Sergeant Broadwood (who could speak Dutch) to a group of Boers who were 'standing on a hill to ask them if they wanted to surrender'. James was aghast when he realised what had happened, and not at all surprised to hear that Meek had been fatally wounded and that Broadwood had been taken prisoner. Not only had he lost a friend in Meek, but James was becoming more and more concerned about being led, literally to the slaughter, by someone who, in his opinion, was seriously and dangerously deficient in military skills and judgement. He tried once more to get out of his regiment. On 20 June, he heard that a new military police organisation was to be formed and he applied for a post, but did not get it.

As the British approached Pretoria, the elderly president of the Republic, Paul Kruger, abandoned his capital and left in his special train for Delagoa Bay. After the fall of Pretoria, many Boers felt that there was no point in carrying on and many commandos began returning to their homes. But those who were left behind rallied. On 11 and 12 June they engaged the British at the Battle of Diamond Hill, just east of Pretoria. Stevenson-Hamilton and his squadron held on to a small hill for the whole day and recorded very few casualties. Although the outcome of Diamond Hill was inconclusive, the Boers, after inflicting extremely heavy casualties, retreated from their positions and a period of stalemate ensued.

Despite a few bouts of stimulating military action, what Stevenson-Hamilton most dreaded had come to pass: he had become a mere cog in the vast military machine of the British army. He knew no more about what was happening than the average Tommy, and complained to his journal, 'We hear only the wildest rumours and only get the overall picture from out-of-date English papers.' From the conventional military point of view, the war should have been over and the Boers should have been treating for conditions of surrender. In the crisp Pretoria winter, the Union Jack fluttered over public buildings. Many on the British side already supposed the war to be ended, and correspondents and others were already packing their bags and leaving for home. Memoirs and books summarising the events of the war even began to appear. Only a few astute commentators started to appreciate that the capture of Pretoria had not ended the war.[11] In fact, far from being over, the war had not even reached its half-way mark. The Boers calculated that they could go on fighting indefinitely if they relied on their farms for supplies and so they began a period of guerilla warfare.

For almost two years thereafter, Stevenson-Hamilton's travels in the military allowed him to observe much of the subcontinent. He came to know the distinctive features of animal and plant life, as well as the unique geographical setting in which each species flourished. He suffered in all weathers, but loved the hardship. He developed his powers of observation and further developed his remarkable capacity for that self-reliance and self-discipline which he had first learned in Barotseland.

But he was thoroughly discontented with the cavalry. Although Stevenson-Hamilton articulated the problem rather vaguely in his journal,

Dauncey's poor leadership was in many ways symptomatic of the wider dilemmas facing the cavalry which was severely criticised even while the war was in progress. Sometimes James defended his position: 'The papers at home are talking about the cavalry subaltern as a sad exception to good qualities of British officer. Some of those smug people should come out here and see for themselves.' But, despite his loyalty, he could see that the cavalry was simply no longer appropriate for modern warfare. While he was in the Colesberg area, Stevenson-Hamilton had learnt how crucial reconnaissance was, and he would have agreed with both Erskine Childers and Lord Roberts himself that, generally speaking, the cavalry lacked proper reconnaissance techniques, inspirational leadership, and overall and individual initiative.[12] Naturally there were exceptions in men such as Rimington and Allenby but, unfortunately for Stevenson-Hamilton, his contact with men of their calibre had been intermittent at best.

For Stevenson-Hamilton a long period of frustration began after the fall of Pretoria. From July until September 1900 he was deployed in French's cavalry with Allenby in command of the regiment. James liked and admired Allenby, writing an appreciation of his qualities – 'it was a pure delight to serve under him' – in a later biography of Allenby written by Field-Marshal Wavell.[13] At the time, however, Stevenson-Hamilton's journals do not record this 'pure delight'. Indeed, he had little contact with Allenby.

He did, however, come to appreciate his own strengths and weaknesses and learned to analyse and observe human nature and assess the capabilities of others. He realised consciously at this time his hatred of being second in anything at all. As the years went by, he mentioned this more and more in his diaries, and described how it was unacceptable for him to be 'Number 2'. He knew that it was best for all concerned if he ran his 'own show'. Such self-reliance not only pleased and satisfied him; it optimised his abilities and strength of character. During the South African War he always achieved most and was happiest when he was in control – even if the force he commanded was very small. Although a loner by preference, he certainly did not possess the kind of prickly personality (as some do) which made co-operation with others impossible. On the contrary, he welcomed responsibility and saw it as a means of controlling his own fate.

Part of his disillusionment with his war experience may also have been related to his desire to excel – for his family's sake as much as for his own. By the time of the South African War, James urgently needed to distinguish himself. His training had been completed 12 long years before and while Natal in 1888 had initially seemed very promising, it had turned out to be a military damp squib. Thereafter James's professional prospects had seemed bleak. He now realised that opportunities for fame and distinction in war were not lurking around every corner. The South African War offered him unparalleled opportunities for military distinction as the Egyptian campaigns of the 1880s had given his uncles. But James, to his dismay and despite being mentioned twice in dispatches and being made a Brevet-Major (an increase in rank although without corresponding pay), was unable to make the most of it. The army was led in its lower levels by men like Dauncey, and in its higher ranks, by 'terrible old fossils' like Major-General Fitzroy Hart who, despite being the Commander of the 1st Infantry Brigade at Aldershot, had 'failed to grasp the new tactical thinking'.[14] General Buller, Commander-in-Chief of the whole army in Natal, suffered from a dangerous drinking problem and was so inept that even the Boers sometimes laughed at him. James concluded that the 'deserving are neglected and those who have loafed are lavishly rewarded. England is not a good country to serve, or rather the English government isn't.'

By patrolling the perimeters of the Delagoa Bay railway line, the cavalry hoped to cut the Boers off totally from the outside world and force them to negotiate an official surrender. As is well known, this did not happen. That late winter and spring were very cold and stormy. Horses and men died and a shortage of supplies added to the intense physical discomfort. It was difficult to maintain discipline. After Middelburg had been occupied on 27 July, James was incensed by British looting. He complained that the 'men fall out on patrol and can't be found, while actually they are rushing like tigers through some wretched house pulling things to bits'.[15] By September, the war seemed to be going well for Britain. The Transvaal was annexed and soon ex-President Kruger crossed the border and fled into Mozambique, from where he left for Europe. Surely the war was over?

But what now seemed inevitable to the relentlessly logical minds of British politicians and strategists alike once again failed to materialise. Once again dreams of a swift and clean end to a cruel and wasteful war turned out to be another tantalising mirage. Even at this point, with their beloved president now a fugitive from his own country, the Boers gave no hint that they were prepared to surrender. In January 1901, James was writing that 'the show drags on and I don't know what we're all fighting about now that Kruger has cleared, as it was supposed to be him and his government we were out to upset'.

In 1901 it became obvious that a war of attrition had begun. The commandos did not lay down their arms. They simply went their separate ways, haphazardly harassing British troops wherever opportunities presented themselves. All the British could do was to retaliate as best they might. The chances for significant military strikes lessened with each passing month and it soon became clear that unconventional tactics of some kind would have to be employed in order to defeat the enemy. It was at this point that Kitchener made the decision to apply his 'scorched earth' policy. Many at the time considered the burning and destruction of Boer farms and placing women, children – and Africans – in concentration camps as justified and inevitable, but others condemned these initiatives as barbaric and excessive. Kitchener also eschewed traditional army organisation, preferring instead columns which conducted 'drives' into certain areas so as to create havoc for the Boers. Stevenson-Hamilton was part of a cavalry reorganisation which inaugurated 'flying columns' to conduct these drives. Eventually vast squares of the stark, burnt-out and impoverished countryside were enclosed by blockhouses and barbed wire and the Boers were encircled and driven back against these barriers like hunted animals. Prisoner-of-war camps overseas in Ceylon and elsewhere burgeoned. Even in such desperate circumstances the Boers did not give up. They were fighting for their very survival, and Kitchener's inhumane strategy only served to harden their resolve.

When summarising his life many years later in what he called a 'Tabloid sketch of my life', James described this period as follows:

> The division then returned to Pretoria via Carolina, Ermelo, Bethal and Heidelberg. Our horses and transport oxen were exhausted and we were badly harried by strong forces of Boers. Our most serious engagement was at Tefreden Hill near Lake Chrissie where three weak squadrons of the regiment – about 75 men in all – were attacked by about 800 mounted boers. The Brigade consisting of Carbineers and Greys had halted some miles back and if Allenby had not managed to get up two guns and the Greys hurriedly, we might have had a disaster. As it was, we lost Lieutenant A.W. Swanston killed; Captain J.W. Yardley, Lieutenants J. Harris and E.S. Paterson wounded; Lieutenants Terrot and Gibbs prisoners (later released); some twenty other ranks [were also] casualties.[16]

Stevenson-Hamilton blamed Dauncey for this debacle. It was not the first time that James rankled at the thought of his superior's military incompetence. He obviously regarded himself as the better soldier and noted with pride that 'a few days later near Ermelo I was rearguard with my squadron and had a very trying day, being afterwards sent for and specially thanked by Allenby for the work of my squadron in which only one man was killed (we were about 25 strong)'.[17]

Although 'Stevenson-Hamilton's squadron did good work'[18] and in spite of the courage of the ordinary British soldier in the field, the Boers remained unbowed. There was little constructive or cheerful in James's life. However, he was in Pretoria with his brother Olmar for a few days where there was polo and a band playing merrily in Burger's Park. But at that same time, James received disquieting news about his sister Cissy. She had fallen out with the Lamingtons in Australia and almost immediately had become engaged to a Mr Hay of Adelaide, a widower with two children. As far as James could tell, Hay had no money and no prospects. All he offered Cissy were responsibilities.

The great 'drives' became ever more frequent as 1901 progressed. First Stevenson-Hamilton was sent to the farms to the north and north-west of Johannesburg. Boer women and children were rounded up and supplies and livestock were commandeered. James does not seem to have been personally involved in this distasteful task ('I hate to see farms burnt,' he wrote), and it appears as though the cavalry were used in a supportive and defensive role so as to prevent Boer commando retaliation. Then Queen Victoria died: 'She should have outlived the war,' James lamented. He had known no other British monarch and her death occurred at a time when her country was engaged in a war against innocent women and children. It seemed like a bad omen for the new century.

Things were even worse as far as the regiment was concerned. Allenby had left after having been given his own column: 'A pity, he was very good. A fine soldier to be under, never lets one down, very strict, fair. Leaves responsibility to squadron leader.' Rimington, too had his own column. The most horrible fate befell James: Dauncey was installed as temporary commanding officer and James was therefore under his direct command. He managed to escape for a short period when he was sent to escort prisoners to Standerton. He had orders thereafter to march to northern Natal to accompany stores which had been procured for the forces in the Transvaal. This was exactly the kind of enterprise he loved. 'It was rather exciting', he remembered later, 'as I had a very small force and there were a lot of Boers about who had broken back through our line, but we got through after many alarms but no fighting.' Even the miserable weather – it rained constantly for the entire six weeks and there was fog on all the high ground of Natal – did not dampen his spirits.[19] This sortie was immediately followed by a wonderful month of leave in Natal.

It was an anticlimax to return to the Transvaal and the dreariness of the interminable war after a taste of civilian life. One consolation for James was that he was posted to operate in an area new to him – the area north

*'C' Squadron, Heilbron (1902).*

of Belfast and the Delagoa Bay railway line, and the countryside around Dullstroom and Roos Senekal.[20] In spite of the expertise of the distinguished-looking General Sir Bindon Blood, a new arrival with a lifetime of military experience in India, the drives in this district were not a success, and General Ben Viljoen remained at large, always managing to keep one step ahead of the British. Once again James found himself sleeping in the freezing highveld in a South African winter, patrolling up and down ravines and river valleys, only occasionally finding a military target to destroy – such as a well hidden mill. 'Still we wander on . . . On this trek no one gets any orders, nor knows where anyone else is, or why. Bindy Blood takes no interest. He lives at Middelburg and is a pretty useless person.'

For once there was good news for James when he arrived back in Pretoria after some months in the field. Rimington asked James to come to the Orange Free State 'with 150 men, my own officers and swords'. But any elation he might have experienced soon soured. According to James, Dauncey was furious because, in his view, Rimington was poaching the best men from the regiment. Dauncey's version of events is not known and the regimental history does not mention any animosity between the officers.[21] But for James, without a doubt, this was the worst period of the war. Dauncey not only remained in command, he now bore an active grudge against James. Matters between the two came to a head at the beginning of August near Heilbron. According to James, he (James) had held a court martial and Dauncey had tried to have a counter-trial in order to quash James's sentence.

The new year of 1902 dawned and another fracas was precipitated by an adverse report which Stevenson-Hamilton had submitted alleging that Dauncey had given him contradictory orders, first to retire, and then to remain where he was. This had landed James in a serious plight with a group of attacking Boers, and he considered that he was lucky to have had only one of his men killed.[22] It was the kind of situation which Dauncey had created (and which James had noted in his diary) more than once. On this occasion, James, provoked beyond endurance, decided to take action against his superior officer. After hearing about this, 'Dauncey lost his head and galloped about screaming but luckily someone told the Colonel [Rimington] what was going on.' It was touch and go, but the personal battle lines between the two men were drawn, and James reacted to the new stalemate by applying for leave. For a blissful fortnight he relaxed in Johannesburg and even undertook a short trip to Durban. In mid-March, Rimington, who seems to have acted as a protector of the outspoken James, became indisposed for the first time in the war and was hospitalised at Elandsfontein for a month. Stevenson-Hamilton appreciated what this implied for himself: 'Now that the Colonel has gone, Dauncey has a heaven-sent opportunity to get his own back . . . Thank God he is only an Inniskilling by adoption and very recent at that. When a poor creature of this sort is one's superior officer he has mean and spiteful ways of being unpleasant.' Then James himself was sent off to hospital in Heilbron as he was laid low by an attack of fever. He had been feeling ill for a while and, after leaving hospital, he was given ten days' leave to recover.

While sick, he heard 'wild rumours' that peace might be declared at last, and it did, in fact, seem that the end of the war was imminent. But Stevenson-Hamilton's personal war continued. On 9 May he wrote in his journal that Dauncey was drunk. After being insulting and abusive to Stevenson-Hamilton, Dauncey put him under arrest: 'I don't know what for. He felt like it, and being drunk, did so.' This was James's only explanation. The next day he noted: 'Being under arrest, I have no work to do.' Both officers were called up before Rimington, now recovered from his illness. James recorded the following entry: 'Dauncey compiled a long and lying report on what happened. He had to apologise for calling me names and I was told off for answering back to a superior officer. Dauncey was going on leave and I told Ansell plainly that he could tell the Colonel that I would not serve under Dauncey as commanding officer.'

As soon as Dauncey returned from leave on 28 May, James made plans to avoid him. As peace was now at last being negotiated, James wrote: 'Now the dirty dog is coming back so I have applied for leave. I shall take some temporary job or other to tide me over until he gets kicked out of the regiment as he is certain to be sooner or later. Nothing on earth will induce me to serve with him or under him.'[23]

This was not an emotional, spur-of-the-moment, journal entry. James had made a decision to stay in South Africa, although he did not know what he would do once the war was over. His resignation from the 6th (Inniskilling) Dragoons, although temporary, seemed at the time the worst possible way for him to end the war which he had hoped would bring him glory and fame. He had arrived in South Africa full of enthusiasm and optimism and now his intuitive forebodings about rejoining his regiment were justified. Instead of finding the distinction he had hoped for, thanks only to Dauncey (the awful 'spoke in the wheel' as James called him) he had been plummeted into endless petty politics and personal animosity. Moreover, he had learnt at first hand that his efforts had not even been directed into an 'honourable' war, in the sense that European soldiers might have been able to respect. Certainly, there had been strategic reasons for British policies of farm-burning and African and Boer concentration camps, but this was not the kind of war of which someone like Stevenson-Hamilton could be truly proud.

But James had spent his adulthood as a military man and, apart from a short period exploring Barotseland, he had known no other way of life. Returning to live at Fairholm might have been attractive, but he sought adventure on the one hand, and on the other, his private income was insufficient to live on in Britain. While he was in Johannesburg shortly after the Treaty of Vereeniging had been signed (at Melrose House in Pretoria), James was entertained by his friends and, while a rare snowfall blanketed the mining town, he was introduced to Sir Godfrey Lagden. At that time Lagden was certain to be selected for high office in the Transvaal Colony as Commissioner for Native Affairs. On 11 June 1902 Stevenson-Hamilton happened to mention to Lagden (as he had to others) that he was looking for a civilian position. By 22 June Lagden had one to offer. Part of his portfolio was to oversee the colony's game reserves and he asked whether James would be interested in becoming Game Warden of the Sabi Game Reserve in the eastern Transvaal lowveld. Although there had been many applications for the post (James had not applied) none had impressed Lagden. James did. At first James was uncertain whether to accept or not, hoping that something more substantial (perhaps with the British South Africa Company in Bechuanaland or Rhodesia) would come his way. But there was no better offer forthcoming, and so James accepted the position in July 1902. As Lagden said, it was an 'interesting and sporting job',[24] especially for a man 'brimful of pluck and resource'.[25] A totally new chapter of Stevenson-Hamilton's life was about to begin.

# 6

# 'My Own Creation'[1]
## Sabi Game Reserve
## (1902–1914)

ALTHOUGH THE GAME WARDENSHIP was an offer which appealed to James Stevenson-Hamilton's temperament, he was disappointed that it had low official status – 'rather a subordinate position' in fact. However, he accepted the job, at a salary of £500 a year and an additional allowance of £180. Although he realised a couple of days later that, if he 'had had the sense to ask for it', Lagden would have agreed to £600, the deal was closed.[2] Shortly thereafter he set out for his new domain – the Sabi Game Reserve in the eastern Transvaal lowveld. In his published memoirs, *South African Eden*, he described the first day he saw the area which was to become his 'own creation'. In the first place it was the landscape which appealed to him: 'the wonderful panorama of mountain and forest', leading to the 'land of mystery beyond', the soft colours of 'green, yellow, and russet brown . . . with increasing distance merging into a carpet of blue-grey'. Then it was the wildlife, the birds in particular, 'chattering among the trees' and the vague sounds which rose from the distant forest. 'It is', he concluded, 'the voice of Africa, and with it comes to me a sense of boundless peace and contentment.' Throughout his life, these were the sensations and emotions which drew James so closely to the lowveld, and brought him back to it every time he sought a change, or tried to escape.

The start of his new career was not particularly auspicious:

> I was on the point of entering a country of which I knew practically nothing, with instructions to convert it as soon as possible from its time-honoured status of a hunter's paradise into an inviolable game sanctuary. My mandate had been vague, general, and . . . I had no visible authority behind me. No special regulations for the game reserve had been drafted and even the new game laws were not yet in being . . . Viewed as a game reserve the country was disappointing. Even allowing for the time of year and the consequent lack of much

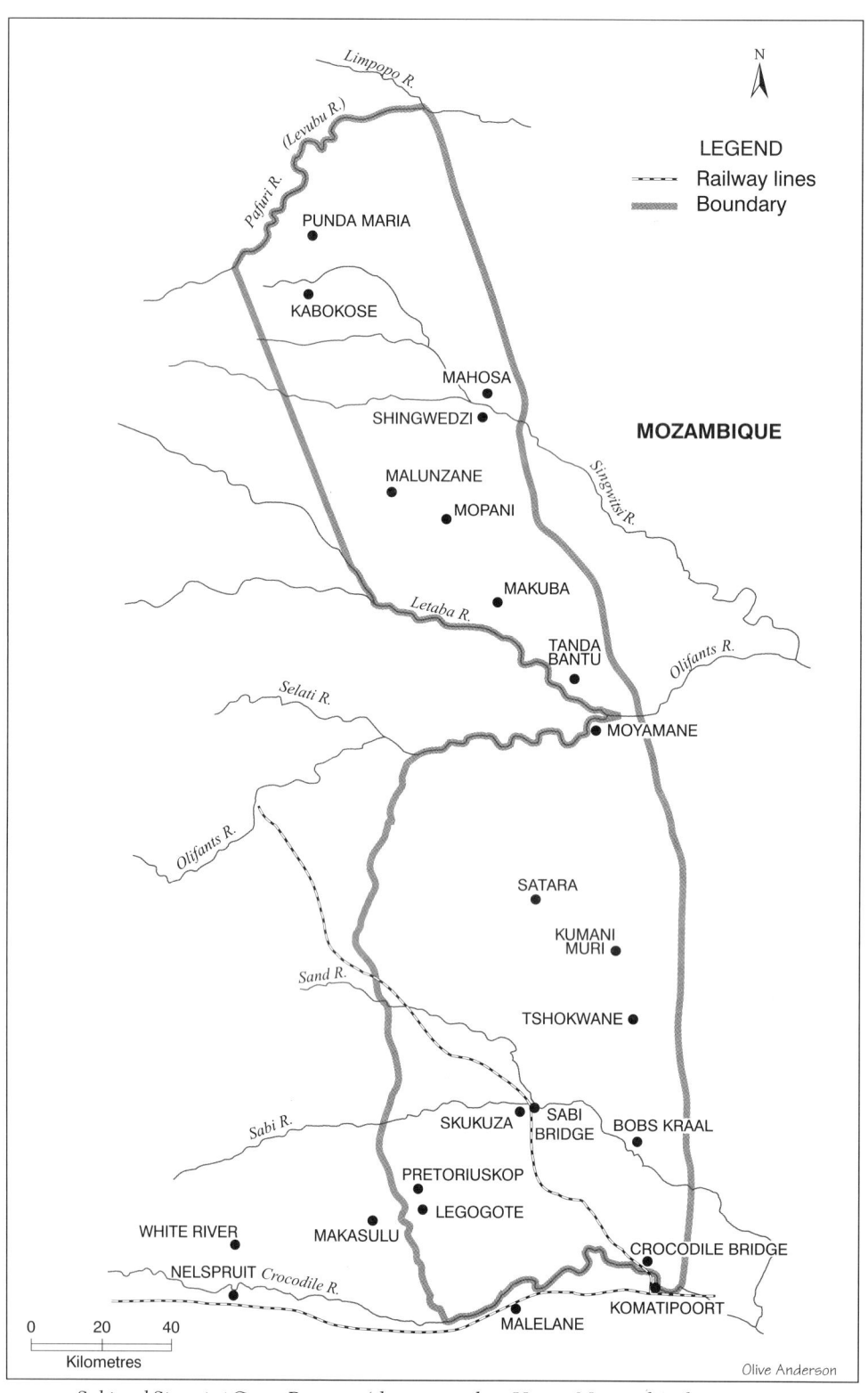

*Sabi and Singwitsi Game Reserves (showing modern Kruger National Park camps).*

water in the veld, one would have expected to see at least some indication of larger wildlife. Yet there was not even an old spoor to indicate that anything of the kind ever had existed there.

Despite his apprehension, Stevenson-Hamilton could not have begun his career in wildlife and park management at a more significant time. Africa, a continent long famed for the uniqueness of its abundant wildlife, had been ravaged by profligate hunting. Many species were threatened and it was evident that active steps would have to be taken if any were to be saved. The end of the South African War brought new factors into the conservation equation of the Transvaal. Since becoming a colony in the British Empire, the Transvaal had become enmeshed in the policy considerations which applied to British imperial possessions throughout the world. The new British civil service which was imposed on the Transvaal was familiar with the notion of game reserves since a number had been established in various colonies and some had been mooted for the Cape Colony as well.[3]

There were four game reserves in the Transvaal which were acquired by the British administration when the war ended. The oldest was the small Pongola Game Reserve which could be found in the south-eastern corner of the country (proclaimed in 1895). The second, the Sabi Game Reserve, situated in the eastern Transvaal tropical lowveld, comprised the region between the Sabi and Crocodile Rivers. Both these reserves were located in extremely hot and tropical districts which were generally too unhealthy for widespread settlement by Europeans. The Pongola Game Reserve had been established in order to protect access by the Transvaal Republic to the Indian Ocean through Zulu and Swazi territory at a time when Britain's policy was to encircle the Transvaal and prevent her from laying claim to any strategic coastal port.[4] By contrast, the impetus for the establishment of the Sabi Game Reserve in 1898 had come from local officials and the sporting fraternity in the gold-mining districts around Barberton, headed principally by Richard Loveday. The third reserve (established in 1896) consisted of a small area on the outskirts of Pretoria and the fourth, on the Springbok Flats near Warmbaths, was proclaimed in April 1898. At the outbreak of the South African War, only the Pongola Game Reserve had a warden. The townlands of Pretoria did not require one and negotiations for wardens of the Sabi Game Reserve and the Springbok Flats were in progress when hostilities erupted.

James Stevenson-Hamilton's reserve, the Sabi, was the first to come to the attention of the new civil service. There is even some evidence that the British were unaware that the area was a Republican game reserve. This is based on the fact that Abel Chapman, a former hunter and keen game protectionist, submitted a detailed proposal to the authorities in December 1900 for the establishment of what he called a 'National Game Reserve'. Whether Chapman knew that the southern end of his proposed game reserve had already been proclaimed is a moot point, but local people knew about it. Even before war had ended, the Mining Commissioner at Barberton, Tom Casement, had taken the game reserve under his wing, reporting poaching and even appointing a game warden. The first was Captain H.F. Francis, but he was killed in a military engagement just a month after being installed, and Casement replaced him with W.M. Walker, a former gold prospector from Moodie's diggings, who joined the Imperial Light Horse at the outbreak of the war. Walker seemed to be a good candidate because he was 'well acquainted with the low country and [spoke] Dutch and Kaffir fluently'. Walker was appointed on 24 October 1901 but proved a dismal failure in the position. He never lived in the reserve and, in fact, only visited it once by rail. His superiors soon realised that they were wasting their money, and he was dismissed at the end of January 1902.[5] Such were the two incumbents of the warden's post before Stevenson-Hamilton.

Although James was unfamiliar with the eastern Transvaal and did not speak Dutch or any black language, he possessed many other qualities which suited him to the task. He was administratively efficient and lived according to a self-imposed military discipline. His sojourns in Africa meant that he had built up a good deal of immunity to disease and privation. He was also intelligent, articulate, observant, unmarried and had displayed qualities of leadership during the war.

Life in the new game reserve could hardly have been more different from regimental routine. James found himself entirely alone. The environment was strange and he virtually had to create his own job. In this situation his innately methodical approach to life stood him in good stead: he undertook a long trek to every corner of the reserve in order to familiarise himself with what it contained. By early September 1902 he was ready to present his report to Lagden. Lagden's purpose in re-establishing the game reserves in the Transvaal was to set aside areas for sport hunting. It was hoped that some revenue might be earned from high fees which sportsmen would be willing to pay for the privilege of hunting big game. With this in mind, Stevenson-Hamilton's first concern was that the reserve was very small. The tiny area between the Sabi and the Crocodile Rivers contained no game at all and it was clear that, even if it were to be stocked, the area would be too small to constitute a significant wildlife reserve. Stevenson-Hamilton suggested to Lagden that 'it would be to the greatest advantage were the piece of country

*View of Sabi Game Reserve looking east from Legogote.*

north of the Sabi River, and bounded on the north by the Olifants River, and west by the Selati Railway added to the Game Reserve'.[6] Right from the outset James worked towards making his reserve a world-class environmental project. He declared that with the northern addition it was

> much the finest game district in the Transvaal . . . Although the big game is but a shadow of what it was a few years ago, I still have no hesitation in saying that more exists here than in all the rest of the Transvaal put together, and that after a few years of careful 'nursing' we shall have a Reserve which cannot be beaten, if not in the world, at all events in South Africa.

Lagden was converted to Stevenson-Hamilton's idea and the warden began to put his plans into practice. By April 1903 his arrangements for proclamation were well under way, and he was already working to obtain agreement about two distinct extensions. Firstly, the western and southern boundaries of the reserve needed to be altered. Apart from two privately owned farms, only state land was involved, all of which was reportedly 'unsuitable for farming operations'. The second extension was to be the northerly one, the boundaries of which almost followed the watershed on the western side and the Olifants River on the north.

However, there was an enormous obstacle in the way of this crucial northern extension. More than half of the land required was in the hands of private owners, principally land companies such as the Transvaal Land and Exploration Company, Oceana, and Henderson Consolidated Lands. Undaunted, Stevenson-Hamilton went to Johannesburg and Pretoria and persuaded these companies to allow him to incorporate their farms into his game reserve and to give him powers to administer and police them for a period of five years.[7] Before these crucial meetings took place, James believed that it would be difficult to bring the companies around to his point of view. Happily the negotiations proved far easier than he had dared to hope. Stevenson-Hamilton made an excellent impression, with the landowners delighted that 'such a thorough sportsman as Major Stevenson-Hamilton is in charge'.[8]

Another incidental success for Stevenson-Hamilton was the establishment, at almost the same time, of the Singwitsi Game Reserve. Stevenson-Hamilton had no hand in its proclamation, which was suggested in December 1902 by a resident of the Soutpansberg district, L.H. Ledeboer, who was later to become one of Stevenson-Hamilton's game rangers. Once again, Lagden was quick to agree to the scheme, and in May 1903 what came to be called the Singwitsi Game Reserve was proclaimed.[9] It included the area lying between the Letaba River on the south and the Pafuri (or Levubu) River on the north, and was bounded on the west by a line running between these two rivers, and on the east by the border of Mozambique. Stevenson-Hamilton explored the new game reserve during September and October 1903 and expressed delight with it.[10]

Although Stevenson-Hamilton by now controlled an enormous area, more was to be added. The Sabi and Singwitsi reserves were almost continuous on the Transvaal's eastern boundary with Mozambique. The next part was far removed from them. When Stevenson-Hamilton was told, late in 1902, about the existence of the Pongola Game Reserve on the borders of the Transvaal, Swaziland and Zululand, he thought that it might be worth investigating and he mentioned the prospect to Lagden. The reserve was no glittering prize. It consisted of only six farms and, although there had once been a gamekeeper in charge, the position was no longer filled. In addition, it contained very little wildlife.

Ever enthusiastic, Lagden again moved quickly and on 21 April 1903 the Executive Council approved the re-establishment of the Pongola Game Reserve.[11] Major A.A. Fraser was given the post of warden in a position that was subordinate to Stevenson-Hamilton, whose title now became 'Warden of the Government Game Reserves'. Stevenson-Hamilton visited his new deputy at the end of 1903. He was impressed by the scenic beauty of the reserve but was disappointed to have to confirm that there was very little game in it. After making a thorough investigation, Stevenson-Hamilton concluded that the Pongola was really too small to be a proper game reserve. The narrow ravine which formed its nucleus made it unsuitable for attracting game from Zululand in the east while, on the westward side, the reserve contained only animals which were temporarily present during their migrations from the Lebombo Mountains towards more permanent waterholes in Swaziland. Stevenson-Hamilton told Lagden that the reserve would have to be enlarged if it were to be viable and that, if that were not possible, the entire reserve, or possibly a portion of it, might be utilised as a 'game nursery' or 'deer park', so that wild animals could be bred and tamed for supply to zoological gardens throughout the world.[12]

The government was less enthusiastic about enlarging the Pongola Reserve than it had been about the Sabi, and Stevenson-Hamilton soon decided to abandon it. In February 1904 he transferred Fraser to the warden's post in the newly established Singwitsi Game Reserve. He felt that the Singwitsi Game Reserve was far more important to game protection than the Pongola since it was much larger in area, consisted of widely differing vegetational types, and contained a great variety of wild animals. Stevenson-Hamilton was anxious about leaving the Pongola Reserve without white supervision (only two black rangers had been left in the area), but nothing could be done at the time. Although sympathetic, the Department of Native Affairs refused to increase the game reserve budget, and various civil servants in the area were too occupied with other issues to take much of an interest. In the years after 1906, the Pongola Game Reserve suffered from benign neglect until it was formally deproclaimed in the early 1920s.

Since his territory had now expanded to cover two extremely large game reserves, Stevenson-Hamilton employed additional staff. After giving the matter considerable thought, he organised the administration of his reserve by dividing the area into sections and placing a white game ranger, assisted by a number of black 'police', in each. The rangers' tasks were to arrest poachers, patrol their section of the reserve and report generally on game matters. Stevenson-Hamilton believed that the position of ranger carried some responsibility, but he seems to have had a low opinion of the men who worked for him. He declared that every Lowvelder was a 'wrong "un"' and that 'all the flotsam and jetsam apply to me; I suppose they think it will be an easy life with not much to do except drink and so will suit them'. While he wanted to give them real responsibility, he felt that they could not be trusted with it. Also, because communications were poor, Stevenson-

Hamilton did not have very much personal contact with his rangers. There were no roads in the reserve other than a couple of wagon tracks.

In time, Harry Wolhuter, a farmer and storekeeper who was one of the first rangers and the man in charge of the western section from his home, Mtimba, near Legogote, was to become Stevenson-Hamilton's close friend. In his memoirs, *South African Eden*, Stevenson-Hamilton recalled their first meeting, describing the lanky young Wolhuter as 'tall and spare, with a heavy black moustache, a man of quiet determined manner and few words, he looked exactly what he was: a typical farmer, bushman, and hunter of the best type'. Other appointments were less successful and a number of early game rangers, Rupert Atmore and Edward 'Gaza' Gray, lasted a very short time. However, there was better luck with Thomas Duke and Dick de Laporte – both known to Stevenson-Hamilton having been members of Rimington's Guides – who displayed considerable aptitude for their jobs. When Stevenson-Hamilton was away, De Laporte often acted as warden. Stevenson-Hamilton's biggest problem was Major Fraser in the Singwitsi. In many respects Fraser was a loveable character. Stevenson-Hamilton considered him 'a sportsman in the higher sense of the word, and a born gamekeeper – essentially of the Highland variety. No gillie it must be said, even of the most hardened type, could have excelled him in the absorption of unlimited quantities of Scotch whisky without the slightest visible effect.' Fraser controlled the Singwitsi Reserve with ten African police and was hard pressed to stop the widespread poaching which took place. The area was also – as Stevenson-Hamilton described it – 'the haunt of a number of what may euphemistically be termed "frontiersmen" . . . [who] . . . made a hand-to-mouth living by illicit labour-recruiting, poaching elephant in Portuguese country, and no doubt selling firearms and ammunition to natives'.

The small budget for salaries and expenses within which Stevenson-Hamilton had to operate made it all but impossible to attract white employees of the highest calibre. In June 1902 the allocation for the Sabi Game Reserve was increased from £2 150 to £4 000 per annum.[13] In 1903 Stevenson-Hamilton estimated his expenses to be in the region of £5 000, of which £900 comprised his own salary and allowances, £1 740 the salaries and allowances of four white rangers, and £1 404 the salaries for black police.[14] No increase in the budget was granted after the enlargement of the reserve, even after Stevenson-Hamilton had asked for £8 000 and had pointed out that the greatly increased area would need to be properly administered. A few schemes were explored to enable the game reserves to generate at least a portion of the revenue they needed but unfortunately none of these was successful.

*View up Sabi River from the warden's quarters.*

Stevenson-Hamilton personally enjoyed a great deal of freedom and discretion in the administration of his authority. He publicised his game reserve widely so that people would become aware of its existence. Anyone entering the reserve needed a permit, and so the warden was aware at any given time of which officials might be inside the game reserve boundaries. He tried to allow as few as possible to enter, and he himself was appointed Resident Justice of the Peace as well as Native Commissioner. Even the police were unwelcome and, at the beginning of 1903, Stevenson-Hamilton arranged that the South African Constabulary leave the reserve and he and his rangers be given full police powers. As Justice of the Peace, Stevenson-Hamilton needed a public prosecutor and clerk of the court. The authorities sent him G.R. Healy, a young Irishman. Because he also lived at Sabi Bridge, Healy was Stevenson-Hamilton's closest white neighbour. He helped the warden with chores around the camp and they regularly enjoyed a game of tennis. Healy, however, had company other than Stevenson-Hamilton, for he had a stream of live-in female companions. The warden envied the fact that these women kept the house tidy and cared for Healy devotedly, to the extent that James confided to his journal, 'I only wish Mrs Grundy would allow me a housekeeper too, but I fear not.'

It is doubtful whether Stevenson-Hamilton realised at this early stage that game protectionism would be his long-term career and his great life work, but he was nevertheless punctilious in the exercise of his duties. At the very beginning he wrote that 'when I am interested in a job, I like to see it through properly'. Stevenson-Hamilton's personality was unusual in that while he revelled in an active outdoor life, he did not resent office work and enjoyed writing reports and keeping administrative procedures running smoothly. His regular reports to Lagden were always on time, correspondence was always dealt with quickly, and matters were never left to ride.

Stevenson-Hamilton's titles and powers in the reserves could well have become meaningless, but a test case provided him with the opportunity to demonstrate his authority. In August 1903 he lodged a charge against two senior officers of the South African Constabulary for shooting a giraffe and a zebra in the game reserve.[15] The case created a stir, and in due course involved the Game Protection Association, the Chief Staff Officer of the South African Constabulary, the Lieutenant-Governor, and even the High Commissioner's Office.[16] Because Stevenson-Hamilton had been convinced that the case would be 'a travesty of justice' and 'enough to make one chuck one's job', he was relieved when the two men were convicted, although he considered that the fine they received in lieu of a prison sentence was a light one.

Stevenson-Hamilton experienced many difficulties in exercising his duties as he defined them. It was important to him that he was allowed independence of action: 'I hope the Department will back me up and let me run things in my own way; in which case I think the show will be a success, but interference from outside will be fatal.' Lagden himself did not live up to Stevenson-Hamilton's expectations. After having initially held a high opinion of him, Stevenson-Hamilton, even by November 1902, considered Lagden to be 'an old woman [who] won't push things ahead'. Stevenson-Hamilton also wrote that Lagden, who had begun life 'in the London Post Office ... conveys to me the idea that he thinks he can treat me, who am quite independent of my present employment, and only work for the love of the thing, as if I were a junior clerk'. In fact, by 1904, Stevenson-Hamilton had concluded that officialdom in the Transvaal was composed of 'a lot of blackguards' and 'low class dogs posing as Englishmen'.

Stevenson-Hamilton suffered because the existence of the game reserves impinged upon the interests of numerous government portfolios. The game reserves occasionally bore the brunt of jealousies that sometimes flared up between various departments, particularly Lands, Native Affairs and the Colonial Secretary. Not only was the government, in Stevenson-Hamilton's opinion, slow to take needed action, but Lagden did not consistently support Stevenson-Hamilton's proposals, especially when anything controversial was proposed. Influencing Stevenson-Hamilton's difficulties was the fact that Lagden's own political career in the Transvaal appears at times to have been precarious. An indication of this may be seen in the way in which game reserves were removed from the jurisdiction of the Department of Native Affairs in July 1905 – without Lagden's knowledge or consent – and then allocated to the Colonial Secretary.[17]

In later years, James confided to a close friend that opposition spurred him to effective action.[18] He was certainly not a popular figure in the eastern Transvaal for many years, probably because he was so efficient in executing his duties. Although he mentioned that 'everyone in the Lowveld seems to run down everybody else', he himself often invited the antagonism he encountered. Indeed, in some respects he seems to have enjoyed this unpopularity, confessing that he felt more determined to remain in his post 'now that I know the rascals want to get rid of me'.

Threats to the game-protectionist empire which Stevenson-Hamilton was constructing in the eastern Transvaal came from many quarters, although it seems that he may have over-stated the opposition he encountered – for he usually managed to run the reserve exactly as he wished. Because he regarded all visitors to the game reserve as potential poachers, he was able, for example, to persuade the government to preclude both prospecting and mining within the reserves. In July 1903 Stevenson-Hamilton was able to prevent the railways administration from mining coal along the course of the Crocodile River. As the decade progressed there were increasing efforts to develop the agricultural potential of the Transvaal and the fact that the game reserves 'locked up' valuable state land merely for the pleasure of future sport hunters became a focus of attack. While disease and climate continued to act as deterrents to white settlement in the lowveld the continued existence of the game reserves was assured, but as early as January 1904 it was being said that the area was becoming healthier and more valuable every year.[19]

Not only did the game reserves encounter opposition from those whose task it was to promote the economic development of the colony, but they were even attacked by sportsmen – the very group whose interests the game reserves were designed to serve.

It is ironic that an increase in the number of wild animals within the game reserve led to difficulties. Because the herds of antelope had increased, so had the number of lions. Some people thought that there were too many lions and that they were leaving the reserve and destroying domestic stock. Stevenson-Hamilton argued on the contrary that the observed increase of game in the reserve 'tends to keep the carnivora within the district and not drive them out'.[20] Lagden supported Stevenson-Hamilton in this instance and wrote, 'As regards the Lions, it seems a very unsporting thing to countenance their utter destruction and I am not in favour of that.'[21] The Lydenburg branch of the Game Protection Association lobbied to have part of the game reserve opened up to hunters but the central committee of the Association as well as Stevenson-Hamilton argued that this idea was not only premature, but that the Lydenburg group was making 'a farce of game preservation'.[22] It must be remembered, however, that it was not envisaged at the time that the game reserves would be denied to sportsmen in perpetuity, merely that the time was not yet ripe.

Other local residents also resented the game reserve. When he first arrived in the lowveld, Stevenson-Hamilton wrote that 'Scallywags largely inhabit this portion of God's earth. [It is the] natural home of the lost legion.' The person who headed up the local Selati railway line, he called 'a frothy little 4-lettered cad. Have to put up with them here.' He encountered a large group of whites living on the south-western border of the reserve who hunted game regularly. They were known as the 'Wit Rivier Boers', ('the other Boers call them "the wild people" and say that they are worse than the natives', he wrote).[23] The warden felt that the game laws were 'waste paper' to the Boers but, although they had a 'low opinion of all Englishmen', he sometimes had a grudging admiration for them, despite his feeling that they were a 'curious blend of simplicity and cunning'. 'Veld Boers are not a rough peasant like the English think', he mused, 'but the most intolerant and exclusive of aristocrats in the world.'

Stevenson-Hamilton also had to establish working relationships with the Africans in the region. In 1902 Stevenson-Hamilton wrote scathingly about whites who exploited Africans:

> Great fuss in Johannesburg papers about the native question; it is said they are being treated all wrong; fulminating heavily about 'Colonies having their way'. Actually the scarcity of native labour is at the bottom of the talk. The natives made so much during the war that they won't work and also they are now busy planting. The Johannesburg gold bugs want compulsory labour introduced although of course they don't put it quite like that. In everything connected with the native every single white man wants to have a finger in the exploitation pie![24]

Stevenson-Hamilton did not align himself with these 'gold bugs' and was critical of the methods used and profits extracted by people who arranged migrant mine labour. In his relationships with Africans, Stevenson-

Hamilton was essentially a practical game ranger. The history of game reserves as areas to which either no one, or else only the privileged, had access, meant that resident Africans had no place within their boundaries. Thus, when Stevenson-Hamilton arrived in the Sabi he forced the Africans to leave. The warden initially attempted to execute the removal with some consideration for the needs of the people involved, suggesting for example that they should be relocated at a time suitable for the cultivation of crops. He anticipated no resistance to these forced removals, declaring that the residents 'were perfectly ready to move whenever or wherever they were told'.[25] However, some months later, he was accused of setting fire to huts in order to compel people to move, although his superiors in the Native Affairs Department insisted that it was only huts which had already been evacuated that were being burnt.[26] By August 1903 some two to three thousand people had been removed from the Sabi Game Reserve,[27] while as late as 1906 a group of Africans living on the perimeter complained that 'the government wants to drive them away from the low veld so as to include these parts in the game reserve'.[28]

Within a decade, however, Stevenson-Hamilton had changed his attitude towards African residents, provided that their numbers were not too large. By 1912 he was arguing that the ideal game sanctuary 'should contain as few native inhabitants as possible. (Complete absence of the latter is rather a disadvantage than otherwise.)'[29] Two reasons can be advanced for this change of heart: Stevenson-Hamilton came to appreciate that Africans could provide labour and, as tenants on crown land, they paid rent and were thus a source of revenue.

When it was established in 1903, the Singwitsi Game Reserve was also the home of many Africans. Stevenson-Hamilton did not advocate expelling them, contending that 'the damage they do in a year will not equal that done by a few Boers in a week'.[30] A further expedience may have been that Stevenson-Hamilton relied on locals to inform him or the rangers about poaching violations. Obtaining information on poachers was an important part of the rangers' duties, and there were unusual ways of getting it. For example, in January 1909, Wolhuter was given a seven-year-old child in recompense for a debt which the child's mother could not discharge. Stevenson-Hamilton was amazed at the situation, which the Wolhuters took in their stride. The warden noted, 'the youngster at all meals, on the floor, eats with a spoon. Follows Wolhuter everywhere. Does odd jobs. Wolhuter says good thing having him as he tells him all he hears amongst the kaffirs.'[31]

The warden employed a number of Africans as 'police' to assist the white rangers and patrol designated areas of the reserve, commenting on any intrusion of poachers and other untoward occurrences or observations. As scouts and guides, Stevenson-Hamilton could not do without the 'native police'. They accompanied him wherever he went in the veld, teaching him veldlore, the best routes to follow, and where the best waterholes were. Publicly and privately he was proud of their achievements, and wrote about them as follows in his memoirs:

> Native police were provided with suitable and becoming uniforms and there quickly grew up a strong feeling of *esprit de corps* . . . The majority of our reserve native police were loyal, trustworthy, courageous, and hardy; all possessed some knowledge of bushlore, were well acquainted with the country, and were largely immune from fever. They knew that they were paid to see that the game was not poached, and whatever their secret thoughts may have been as to the sanity of such a policy, their actions were not in the least affected thereby; the man who killed a buck was a criminal!

There was another employee who was particularly close to James, his cook and personal servant, Ali Sharif, a Swahili from the Comores who had been with the warden since 1903. In 1912, James was devastated when Ali was killed in an accident on the railway line which ran to Sabi Bridge. Ali was indispensable to James as a servant and trusted friend, and for years he had taken care of every detail around the house and in the camp. The day after Ali died a note with the news was brought to the warden and he wrote disconsolately in his journal:

> I have the feeling at present that I cannot carry on here without my faithful old friend. . . . I cannot bear to live in the place of which he was such a familiar figure. Consanguinity and race are nothing; he was the most faithful servant, and I've been lucky to have had the experience at least once in a lifetime.[32]

Within a decade, Stevenson-Hamilton's game reserve was a resounding success. Moreover, despite the odd vituperative remark in his journal, he was entirely happy, perhaps for the first time in his life. His daily record is noticeably free from the agonising self-dissection of earlier years. He stated that the slow workings of government bureaucracy are 'the only drawbacks in an otherwise perfect state of existence'. By 1910 the main aim – to provide 'a nursery for the propagation and preservation of the South African fauna' – had been accomplished. For example, according to Stevenson-Hamilton's observations, in 1902 there had been no black rhinoceros, elephant, eland or ostrich in the area; there were about fifteen hippopotamus, five giraffe, eight buffalo, twelve sable antelope, two roan antelope, five tsessebe, forty blue wildebeest, one hundred waterbuck, thirty-five kudu and numerous impala, reedbuck, steenbok and duiker. By 1909 there were twenty-five elephant, seven or eight rhinoceros, fifty or sixty buffalo, numerous hippopotamus and eland, and large herds of roan antelope, kudu and many other species.

Furthermore, to a great extent this state of affairs had been personally accomplished by Stevenson-Hamilton. By concentrating power in the office of the warden, he had prevented various government departments from turning the vast game reserve into either a 'native reserve', or a prospecting and mining area, or even a locality for white settlers. Because he had built up a justifiable reputation as a man who had great knowledge of game, his opinion had prevailed in government circles, and officials had been persuaded not to allow Transvaal sportsmen to invade the reserve. By disciplining and training his staff he succeeded in his goal of effectively patrolling the vast tracts of land that formed the reserve, and he was also increasingly successful in apprehending miscreants who flouted the game regulations. In addition, by expelling Africans and by controlling the lives of those Africans who remained within the reserves, Stevenson-Hamilton curtailed subsistence hunting in the district.

Although he encountered opposition from many quarters, his most important ally – the legislature of the Transvaal – never deserted him. The Legislative Council supported all his endeavours, one member going as far as to compare the reserve with Yellowstone National Park in the United States and deeming it 'the duty of the Government to take this matter in hand, and make these preserves something in the nature of a national institution'.[33] By 1910 Stevenson-Hamilton had reached substantially the same conclusion, and he also began to express the view that game reserves should remain strictly preservationist in perpetuity and never be opened to hunters.[34]

# 7

# 'Puzzling are the Ways of Wild Animals'[1]
## Sabi Game Reserve
## (1902–1914)

JAMES STEVENSON-HAMILTON made an enormous contribution to environmental protection by setting high standards of management and administration in the Sabi and Singwitsi Reserves. He worked in a very large area under difficult conditions, without roads, modern communications, comfortable housing or other adequate infrastructure, on low pay, and with untrained staff. There is no question that his work as a civil servant, controlling as he did large rural areas devoid of administrative infrastructure, should be evaluated in the same way that one evaluates people such as Sir Alfred Sharpe of Nyasaland, Robert Coryndon of Uganda, and other colonial administrators of the time. His game reserve was, in effect, a large colony which he administered single-handedly.

As well as being a talented practical administrator, James was also a thinker and writer and a master of wildlife observation. This he was able to indulge in the most constructive way throughout his life. His routine included going about the game reserve every day, observing everything carefully, then pondering what he had seen at leisure and turning his hand to writing about it.

In *South African Eden* he describes his life as follows:

> About June I would start on my annual inspection tour of the northern Shingwedsi [sic], Letaba, or round the northern part of the Sabi reserve along the Olifants River. For such a trek the ox wagon, as well as the pack donkeys, and perhaps a couple of horses would be taken, with as much as two months' supplies of food and horse fodder. Arrangements would be made for mails to follow by runner to agreed places. It was a delightfully free and easy method of getting about and offered the widest opportunities of seeing the country. Accompanied by a couple of police boys, one rode on ahead, followed at some little distance by the donkeys running free in front of their attendants, the little bells, hung by straps to their necks, pleasantly tinkling. With the

*The warden's annual tour.*

wagon came more police, and domestic servants leading the dogs, lest these should feel tempted to give chase to some of the many animals visible all around them.

When the distance travelled seemed sufficient, and a pleasant shady spot was reached, with water at hand, one could decide to stay there for the rest of the day and the night, or as long as might appear desirable, and so would dismount, off-saddle, and sit down under an inviting tree to await the caravan . . . from the recesses of the wagon appear camp-table, chair, bottle, glasses, all the things tending to mitigate the asperities of life. The cook boy quickly has a fire under weigh, the kettle boils anon, and tea is ready. If it be intended to spend the night in this place, there is a general scattering to carry out well-accustomed duties. Some gather firewood, others set about with axes and bill-hooks, the making of the essential zeriba, tents are pitched, water fetched, and oneself may take a solitary stroll round to explore the environs, returning at sundown to see the animals tethered, fed, and all snug for the night, before settling down to one's own excellent dinner by the campfire, eaten amid the slowly swelling sounds of the night; the call of the little Scops owl, the throbbing of the crickets, the yelp of the jackal, perhaps the distant rumble of a lion bestirring himself from his daily slumber . . .

After returning from the annual tour, perhaps about the middle of August, I generally established myself at a permanent camp for about three months, surrounded by all the domestic animals, because grazing at Sabi Bridge ceased to exist after July. From 1910 onwards I made a regular practice of going to Tshokwane . . . Having eventually built a commodious camp at this place, I usually stayed on until the rains in November made it possible to take the animals back to Sabi Bridge. The summer months from December to the end of April were devoted to the arrears of office work, to visiting rangers at their different stations, and, so far as weather allowed, to hunting carnivora in the neighbourhood of my station. It was a good and full year; there never was a moment when time hung heavy, and it was all one's own, to do with as one would, without any outside interference. This last was perhaps the greatest charm, apart from the life itself and the nature of the work. It is impossible to imagine anyone having a freer hand than I had during all these years with regard to matters within the reserve; I could make or mar it as I pleased, and alas, nobody was likely either to praise or blame me whatever happened!

Stevenson-Hamilton combined an aesthetic appreciation for the magnificence of African wildlife with strong intellectual interests. He soon realised that the kind of enterprise he was involved in had a philosophical base more sophisticated than a blinkered hunting ethic and he set about learning what he could about game protection. The process of detaching himself from his roots in the army and accepting his new calling came slowly. At the start he had not thought of leaving the cavalry, but had merely applied for a spell of leave. When the time came in 1904 to make a choice between returning to the army or remaining at the game reserve, the decision was a difficult one. James returned to England to consider his position. The scales were almost even, with prospects in both jobs very unsure. Stevenson-Hamilton always

*Tshokwane.*

found taking such decisions extremely unsettling and he was tormented by the fact that he might make the wrong choice. He was worried that he was

> past the age when social delights appeal to me and soldiering in peacetime has no interest. [If I] plunge into the unknown, the Colonel [his father] won't like it, and though he isn't a great judge, I don't like to worry him . . . I can't make up my mind, I want to be in both places at the same time. I want to go back but don't want to give up this, my own creation.

Early in December he returned to his regiment, which was stationed in Dublin as it had been before the South African War. A pleasant development, and one which might have tempted him back, was the fact that Dauncey was no longer with the 6th (Inniskilling) Dragoons. James was delighted. 'Kicked out', he noted with satisfaction. But otherwise, he did not like what he saw. Most of the fellows were out hunting, as though nothing had changed with the century or with their maturity. Then, lunching at the Cavalry Club, he was told about 'the new army system; much discontent. There are no candidates for cavalry though there are over one hundred vacancies. They need to pay better . . . It is hard to know what to do.' What persuaded him perhaps was the realisation that 'everyone seems to have six medals', and that many of his contemporaries were commanding their own regiments. It was apparent that he would have to start again at the bottom of the ladder. By March 1905 he was pleased to announce that 'I am to be gazetted straight out.'

What made the choice so difficult was that while James was relieved to have cut his ties with the army, he had reservations about his long-term future in the South African civil service. He particularly resented being at the beck and call of politicians – an irritation that remained with him throughout his life. Since he was always analytical, a part of his personality enabled him to think critically about events, people and opinions. He himself, while certainly adaptable, never followed a new idea simply because it was fashionable. When younger he had deeply respected Englishmen in general, but he had since learnt from observing many civil servants in the Transvaal administration that there were 'bounders' among them too. He did not have the patience to become caught up in the petty intrigues of civil service politics, with rivalries between state departments and officials protecting their little empires. That was what he had detested about the army.

Unfortunately, in his position he could not remain aloof from politics. There were two significant changes of government which affected Stevenson-Hamilton's career in the years before the First World War. He had joined the civil service in 1902 when the Transvaal was a colony directly under the control of Britain. But after the British election of 1906, Responsible Government came to the Transvaal. Because the English-speaking component was so fragmented, it was inevitable that when elections were held in February 1907, the Afrikaner party, Het Volk, would win the day. However, Responsible Government was not merely another contest between Boer and Briton for control of the Transvaal. In fact, it represented the desire for a new kind of colonial nationalism rather than a return to the 'Krugerism' which Stevenson-Hamilton so disliked. White South Africans were maturing as a 'nation' and the authoritarian coercive tactics of the imperialism to which Milner subscribed were slowly losing ground to a more conciliatory and inclusive approach.

Publicly, Stevenson-Hamilton remained on amicable terms with politicians from all parties (an ability he maintained throughout his life), and from a personal point of view he was not alarmed by the change in colonial status. But he did fear the impact which such a change might have on his game reserves if government support were to diminish as British sportsmen in high positions were gradually replaced by local interests. One senior civil servant, as soon as wind of Responsible Government was in the air, told Stevenson-Hamilton that his 'show [the game reserve] was doomed'. There was indeed agitation to have a public road opened through the game reserve, and Stevenson-Hamilton had to tread carefully. Aware of the popularity of Het Volk, he cultivated a friendship with one of its leaders, Edward Rooth, a prominent Pretoria lawyer, who seemed to support the idea of game preservation. His friendship with the sophisticated Rooth brought home to Stevenson-Hamilton that the cultivated Afrikaner urban fraternity was quite different from the 'wild Boers' at White River. Stevenson-Hamilton did not favour the Het Volk policies, believing that they were based on anti-British 'racial animosities'. It worried him that he had been prepared to give up his life in a contest with such people, and now he was employed by them. However, there were other politicians whose views were closer to his own and he cultivated them too. Richard Loveday was one: he had agitated for many years during the mid-1890s to have the Sabi Game Reserve proclaimed. A vociferous critic of Het Volk government, Loveday was a candidate for the Transvaal Progressive Association and one of his main platforms was support for maintaining the game reserves.

On the day after the election result, the warden visited the government offices to ask what official game reserve policy would be. All that was required was a notice in the *Government Gazette*, and his 'show' could indeed have been doomed. Feeling very vulnerable about his employment and the beautiful game reserves to which he had devoted the love and labour of the past five years, the warden wrote a comprehensive report and assiduously lobbied the new politicians. Many of them, including Rooth and the new Minister of Lands and Native Affairs in the Het Volk government, Johann Rissik, were 'dismal [pessimistic] about the game reserves'. Then Stevenson-Hamilton went to the swearing-in ceremony for the new legislative assembly and discovered, probably to his own surprise, that the 'Boer members are good men, while the British – or so-called British – are not up to much'. In fact, despite the fears of Rooth and some of his fellows, salvation for the game reserves appeared in the form of one particular man – Jan Christiaan Smuts. Although young, Smuts was a veteran of Transvaal politics, and was also an extremely enthusiastic conservationist, naturalist and botanist. After the election he was appointed as Colonial Secretary and was thus ultimately responsible for making any final decisions about the reserves. Stevenson-Hamilton came to know Smuts well and respected him greatly. A few years later, James wrote: '[He is] a charming man, my ideal of a statesman. [He is] wasted in South Africa.' On his own initiative, Smuts founded or supported game reserves and, when Stevenson-Hamilton really needed help in the 1920s, Smuts went out of his way to assist. Throughout the three years of Responsible Government the game reserves remained intact. Indeed, Smuts even added a reserve of his own to the number in the Transvaal. This was the Rustenburg Game Reserve, a large area between the Marico and the Matlabas Rivers in the western Transvaal on the Bechuanaland boundary.[2]

The question that dominated politics in South Africa at this time was the amalgamation of the four colonies into the four provinces of a unified South Africa. While this would be one of the greatest constitutional and political events in the history of the subcontinent, it was not clear to anyone precisely what kind of country would emerge after May 1910. Once again, Stevenson-Hamilton had to adapt to a changed political environment, but he himself had changed by then. In 1902 his loyalties had been purely British. But, in 1910, for him as for so many others, the issue was not quite so clear-cut. As he admitted at the time, 'South Africa is a marvellous place for holding one.' As time went by he found himself more and more concerned with South African issues – while imperial ones meant correspondingly less and less. Others in South Africa felt the same way. Stevenson-Hamilton was influenced by reading Sir Percy Fitzpatrick's *Jock of the Bushveld*. Daringly, for the time, Fitzpatrick called South Africa 'home' and conspicuously identified himself as 'South African'.[3] Identity was not tied up in their cases with politics or race in the first instance, but with the physical landscape which they had come to love. This dichotomy, or duality, never ceased to be a personal problem to James, causing him a good deal of pain and uncertainty, particularly in 1914, at the outbreak of the First World War; in the 1920s when the future of the game reserves seemed so unclear; and again when he finally retired in 1946 and had to choose between remaining in South Africa or returning to Fairholm. On each of these occasions he felt the pull between his adopted home and his ancestral home and country – was he South African or British in his loyalties and identity?

The longer he stayed in the lowveld, the more James became attached to the landscape – just as he was emotionally attached to Fairholm, in Scotland. Although he certainly liked the wildlife, it was, in the end, the sense of place which prevailed and inextricably held him in thrall. Fairholm was important to him because of the family connections which stretched back for centuries. The game reserve was different – although its spell was just as great. James had not inherited the reserves. In many ways he had created them and so they represented a more personal achievement.

When James had been a child, he had explored every 'nook and cranny' of Fairholm. He was to explore the Sabi Game Reserve just as thoroughly and to use his knowledge to influence public opinion in favour of game protection and ecology. The state of the science of natural history and environmental conservation at the start of the twentieth century was quite different from what it is today. There was far more wilderness, less settled agriculture, less modernisation, and correspondingly a greater abundance of wildlife resources of every kind. But as the realisation grew that wildlife was diminishing at an alarming rate, governments as well as civil society became involved in game laws and game reserves.

As the twentieth century was born there was international debate on what steps might be taken by the European community to save Africa's wildlife. A conference was held in London in April 1900, where, for the first time, European powers met to discuss nature protection in Africa. 'The Convention for the Preservation of Wild Animals, Birds, and Fish in Africa' was the document drawn up by the conference and it was signed on 19 May 1900.[4] These imperial developments impacted on the Transvaal, the game reserves, and hunting legislation that Lagden introduced at the time Stevenson-Hamilton became warden of the Transvaal Game Reserves. This dominant British environmental philosophy was greatly influenced by nineteenth-century sport hunters and the publicity which they had given to African wildlife. The imperial hunting literature was generated by sportsmen and naturalists from the upper classes of European society. Because they could afford to ignore the material considerations of hunting for an income in a way that Africans and Afrikaner settlers could not, British attitudes were largely sentimental. Many of these protectionists by the end of the nineteenth century were referred to as the 'penitent butchers' – former hunters who had changed sides. Hunters who seemed proud of the vast numbers of animals that they killed were out of favour, while there was praise for those who were 'the most sparing and the least wasteful'.[5]

This attitude had come about because as imperial interests in Africa had expanded, wildlife came to be considered an imperial asset. It was aesthetically pleasing and thus enhanced the value of the Empire. A scene with wild animals which wandered freely about the countryside was reminiscent of paradise – and what paradise was a true paradise if not under British control?[6] Edward North Buxton, a leading British conservationist of the time and later a friend of Stevenson-Hamilton, described the great game of Africa as 'a precious inheritance of the Empire to be most jealously safeguarded'.[7] The penitent butchers in Britain arranged themselves into the typically British institution of a club: the Society for the Preservation of the Wild Fauna of the Empire. Founded by Buxton in December 1903, this society assumed the role of the volunteer arm of imperial game protection, forming an important pressure group which commanded the attention of the highest authorities in Britain.[8] The Society's ideas were those that Stevenson-

Hamilton knew from his British experience and from his reading, but he was soon to find that the ideals of the penitent butchers did not work in the same way in the settler society of the Transvaal.

In 1902, after a period of dormancy during the South African War, the Transvaal Game Protection Association was resurrected.[9] Although it voiced substantially the same general principles on game protection as did the Society for the Preservation of the Wild Fauna of the Empire, in reality, any conservationist aims were secondary to the Transvaal Association's primary function of serving the interests of the small group of sportsmen and landowners who were its leaders. It was, moreover, an extraordinarily racist organisation. The Transvaal sportsmen could not conceive of the fact that they were in any way, either as hunters or as economic modernists, responsible for destroying wildlife. They blamed the disappearance of wildlife entirely on black Africans, despite considerable evidence to the contrary. The Association spent most of its time targeting Africans and trying to curb subsistence hunting. Its other target as a sporting club was to prevent biltong hunting, which, to a large extent, was still carried out by sections of the Boer population. Stevenson-Hamilton and many in the Transvaal colonial administration were suspicious of the Association's motives from the outset and, on the warden's advice, the government consistently refused to award the Association any funding.[10]

While he took a close interest in the development of legislation to restrict hunting, Stevenson-Hamilton's primary preoccupation was with game reserves. He was extremely conscious of the fact that the Sabi Game Reserve was, apart from the game reserves of Zululand, the last refuge of the large antelope of the subcontinent, and he argued that the 'extermination of these last relics of the once numerous fauna of the country would be more than a pity, both on grounds of pure sentiment and on those of more practical interests'. He believed strongly that the Sabi Game Reserve was excellent for its purpose because of its remote locality and paucity of white or African settlers. At first he, like Lagden, favoured an extremely strict restriction on any hunting whatsoever for a few years, and thought that once the numbers had increased, the game reserves could generate revenue by providing shooting grounds for wealthy sport hunters.

It did not take Stevenson-Hamilton long to change his thinking about using the reserve as a sporting facility for the rich. He came to believe instead that game reserves should adopt as their guiding principle the establishment of undisturbed sanctuaries in which game animals could increase in number and mutually balance their numbers in a natural and ecological way. It is extremely doubtful that he would have had any success with his views had the land of the reserve been regarded as anything but worthless. However, as the decade proceeded, it became clear that the cost of maintaining game reserves in a strictly preservationist manner had to be calculated in terms of the withdrawal of such reserves from direct involvement in the economic development of the country. In the decade following 1910 several important factors combined to threaten the existence of game reserves. These included a growing scarcity of land, the local extinction of the tsetse fly (which made previously inhospitable areas disease-free), and advances in medicine, agriculture and mineral exploitation.

James Stevenson-Hamilton's role in South African game reserve philosophy was a seminal one. Although one of his books was dedicated to 'the guardian spirit of the Low-veld',[11] he was not a mystic or a pantheist, but essentially a practical conservationist. Although he had earlier expressed private reservations about his career in the Sabi Game Reserve, he had by 1910 become convinced that the reserve had an important future. He came in time to think that there were three principal reasons for protecting wild animals: they must 'remain available for the investigations of naturalists, the legitimate aspirations of sportsmen, and the visual gratification of the public of another generation'. He distinguished between a 'sanctuary' which legally enjoyed absolute inviolability in that no shooting whatsoever was permitted within its defined area, and a 'preserve', which was 'an area wherein animals are preserved for the use of a privileged few'.[12]

Stevenson-Hamilton did not advocate the haphazard establishment of game reserves, and he did not support unviable reserves, preferring to concentrate effort where it would be most beneficial. He in fact told Smuts that the Transvaal required areas in which hunting could take place, and that an excess of game reserves would be counter-productive to game protection.[13]

Although Stevenson-Hamilton was extremely interested in animal population dynamics, concentrating particularly on the increase in species numbers, he was a naturalist after the Victorian mould rather than a scientist. In fact, throughout his life he distrusted scientific findings. At first his scepticism manifested itself in the accusation that scientists hunted commercially under the guise of museum collection, but in later years he came to believe that scientists, particularly veterinarians who considered the diseases carried by game to pose a constant danger to domestic stock, presented a real threat to the continuing existence of wildlife.[14]

Because attitudes to animals are always changing, the word 'game' has been used deliberately in this book. While today there is an appreciation of the linkages between all biota, whether plant or animal, at the time when

*Lion skulls at Sabi Bridge (1924).*

James Stevenson-Hamilton first became a protectionist, there was an unbridgeable divide between 'game' and other wildlife. The precious species, and those to which the conservation effort was directed, were large antelope – the 'game' or desired quarry of the sport hunter, the commercial hunter and the subsistence hunter. Any creature which competed with the human hunter for antelope as prey was considered to be 'vermin'. It seems strange to modern conservationists that two of the 'big five'[15] – lion and leopard – were thus actively hunted with extinction as the aim.

Vermin were described in the most loathsome terms at the beginning of the twentieth century, and the terminology itself was deliberately designed to kindle hostility and hatred for innocent species. Crocodile, for example, were despised because they were 'an animated trap, something lower than the meanest of reptiles' which made one's 'flesh creep', while hyaena were referred to as 'a hideous family'.[16] The list of species considered to be verminous was considerable and included lion, leopard, cheetah, wild dog, crocodile, jackal, hyaena, birds of prey, and many reptiles. Certain vermin species were considered to be particularly worthy opponents of man, chief of these being the lion, for centuries regarded sentimentally in mythology and folklore as the 'king of the beasts'. The killing of a lion was supposed to require great bravery and strength, and many hunter-writers included self-serving tales of exciting adventures with 'the great and terrible man-eating cat, the monarch of the African wilderness' among their anecdotes. In the early days Stevenson-Hamilton spent a considerable amount of time as warden in baiting lion, either with dogs or with exposed carcasses in order to cull their numbers.

But within a year or two, Stevenson-Hamilton began to develop his own conservation ethic. While he continued to kill lions, he came to argue that they were necessary to balance nature's food chain, and that it was *humans* who had upset the balance. He began to write on the subject of game reserves and discovered that he had a talent for influencing public opinion. Now, a century later, the Western world has become inundated with pictorial and written material about African wildlife. There are picture books, scientific books, videos and films, all readily available. It is accordingly difficult to imagine a world – James Stevenson-Hamilton's world – in which these creatures did not form part of the experience of the general public.

Ahead of his time, Stevenson-Hamilton felt that it was his duty to proclaim his ideas to a larger public. He wrote critically of Fraser, the ranger he had placed as warden of the Singwitsi Game Reserve:

> It seemed a matter for regret that, possessing as he did many latent abilities, Major Fraser always obstinately refused to be anything more than a gamekeeper. Though he wrote an excellent, well-phrased letter in a good legible hand and, on the few occasions when he happened to be in the mood, showed himself to be proficient with both pencil and brush, he would never make any notes nor transmit what he knew, except by way of casual conversation. Thus much of his wide – and in some ways unique – knowledge of beasts and birds died with him.

This vignette, unfavourable to Fraser, shows by implication what Stevenson-Hamilton believed *his* duty to be.

A competent author and lover of words and writing, Stevenson-Hamilton published numerous articles on game protection for journals such as the *Transvaal Agricultural Journal*, *The Field*, *Blackwood's Magazine* and the *Journal of the Society for the Preservation of the Wild Fauna of the Empire*. In his first published work, 'Game Preservation in the Transvaal' in the 1905 *Journal of the Society for the Preservation of the Wild Fauna of the Empire*, he described the revival of the 'game nursery'. Allaying settler fears, he explained how this had been beneficial because the 'natives' were no longer allowed to hunt, and were therefore concentrating on cultivation or had entered the labour market. He explained to readers his administrative policy of diligently eradicating carnivora so that they would not leave the game reserve and enter nearby farmland. He added information from his annual reports about the increase in game and conditions in the reserve.

By 1907 he was writing to deflect opposition to game reserves, presumably because of his experience at the time of Responsible Government in the Transvaal. He wrote 'Opposition to Game Reserves' for the *Journal of the Society for the Preservation of the Wild Fauna of the Empire*. He argued that reserves were needed because hunting legislation was clearly failing and that the position would worsen with economic development. He felt that suitable semi-wild country should be identified and set aside as reserves. Any reserve should be large, carefully guarded and 'sacrosanct'. He appreciated that the pioneer phase in southern Africa had passed, but argued that game reserves did not retard economic development. They existed only where white settlement was impossible. Nor could opposition be effective on the grounds that lions and other carnivora bred exponentially in reserves. They did not breed uncontrollably, he argued, because there was a 'Balance of Nature', and he described the (now well-known) fact that lion populations only grew once their prey species had increased in number. Without adequate food supplies, as was the case in the Sabi Game Reserve, which still had very few antelope to boast of, the warden frequently came across very thin lions, and cubs which had died in infancy. In answer to the charge that reserves harboured tsetse fly and could thus reintroduce sleeping sickness (which had disappeared with the rinderpest in the Transvaal in 1896), Stevenson-Hamilton said that he felt that the evidence was in fact extremely dubious. There were also other articles he published in the *Journal of the Society for the Preservation of the Wild Fauna of the Empire* in 1909 and in later issues.

Because this journal was not readily available in the rural Transvaal, Stevenson-Hamilton also wrote for the local *Transvaal Agricultural Journal*. In his 1907 'Notes on the Sabi Game Reserve', the warden said that game reserves should really be called 'game sanctuaries'. He reiterated the same arguments about worthless land, carnivora, tsetse fly and African hunting, and emphasised that the 'idea underlying the establishment of the Game Reserves was primarily to effect the rescue from complete destruction of the last of the big game, by providing a surer, more special, and efficient method of protection than was possible in the rest of the country, and under the ordinary game laws'. The article was enlivened with photographs and descriptions and comments about some of the smaller mammals which farmers might encounter. He also directly took to task those sportsmen who averred that Africans were the main destroyers of wildlife. 'This is not true . . . [but] an easy and comfortable way of shirking responsibility.' He pleaded for true sportsmanship and a real respect for game laws. Only such attitudes might prevent the extinction of some species – a grim possibility that had already occurred in the United States. The article also appeared in Dutch.

Stevenson-Hamilton based all these articles on material in his daily journal, in which he recorded his activities and observations and collated them, together with relevant literature, in the course of time. He was a competent typist and the family archives contain the drafts of numerous articles on which he worked as he developed his ideas.

Breaks on holiday leave from the game reserve were welcome, although not very frequent. Regular visits to England were not possible, and so Stevenson-Hamilton took the opportunity, in March 1907, of visiting his friend Robert Coryndon, then still in Barotseland. Stevenson-Hamilton and Coryndon discussed the possibility of a game reserve, which had been one of the unfulfilled objects of the Gibbons expedition. Perhaps the idea of moving on from the Sabi into something larger in central Africa appealed to James. But Coryndon was unenthusiastic, arguing that as the countryside was still full of game, a reserve was unnecessary.

Vacation leave in the winter of 1908, a longer period of three months, was spent with R.C.F. Maugham, the British Consul for Portuguese East Africa, whom Stevenson-Hamilton had come to know well from his frequent visits to Delagoa Bay and their exploration of the Zambezia province of Portuguese East Africa.[17] It was this journey that Stevenson-Hamilton recorded in the *Geographical Journal* as 'Notes on a journey through Portuguese East Africa from Ibo to Lake Nyasa'. He thoroughly enjoyed the experience, which was partly a business trip, for he and Maugham were to map a previously unsurveyed part of the territory at the expense of the British Foreign Office. It was a change from the Sabi Game Reserve and from British Africa. James used his phonograph to record and play voices and music to the local people and they, like the African police force in the Sabi, were intrigued and amazed. Portuguese dinners were rich – 'eight to ten courses of the same goat in different guises and good red wine' – and he always felt dreadful the next day. He then visited Lake Nyasa and, having been made aware of the depredations of the slave trade, he took a boat around the lake for a better look. He was pleased to have 'seen new and highly interesting country which few Englishmen have [seen]'.

Stevenson-Hamilton's other long trip through Africa began at the start of his year's long leave in 1909. He decided to travel through east Africa, the Sudan and Egypt before going to England. His companion on this occasion was Ali, his Comoran servant, an invaluable interpreter. No interpretation, however, was needed for the following advertisement for boat hire in Beira: 'Hon. Sirs who desire of boats, should entrust themselves to the estimable and laudable Dionisio. To entrust your body to Dionisio is as if to entrust your soul to God. Remember – you only die once.'

At Zanzibar, the warden appreciated that 'one breathes the East here', but there was little else that he liked about humans in east Africa. Firstly he was critical of the many 'lady explorers in Africa for self-advertisement' and of the places where one was 'pestered by "Cape to Cairo" vagrants' who demanded hospitality from the local people while they were 'tramping about Africa for a bet or for notoriety'. Secondly, the colonists in Nairobi made an unfavourable impression, a 'selfish lot, only exploiting' and giving nothing in return. He wrote that it was 'dreadful to think of the greed and selfishness of low class whites which will cause extermination [of wildlife] – and they are British!'

While disliking intensely most of the humans he met, he was by contrast enthralled by the landscape, its abundant wildlife and his hunting companions. The former United States president, Theodore Roosevelt was one of the party. Energy 'exudes' from him, wrote Stevenson-Hamilton. Roosevelt, together with his son, Kermit, was staying in the sumptuous home of American millionaire, W.N. Macmillan. Other hunting companions included C.R. Hobley, prominent in the Society for the Preservation of the Wild Fauna of the Empire, the Acting Governor, and members of the game department, with whom he could compare experiences. The open plains with their 'variety of wildlife' amazed him: 'the country is full of game, far beyond anything I have ever seen'.

The hunting trip ended in December 1909 and Stevenson-Hamilton travelled through the Sudan and Egypt on his way to Britain. This was his second visit to Britain since taking up the wardenship of the Sabi and he used his British connections on both occasions to advance his career and to meet the most influential people in his field. In 1904, taking his precious trophies with him, he went directly to Rowland Ward to find a good taxidermist. Soon he was attending all the meetings at the Royal Geographical Society and acquainted himself with Dr R. Chalmers Mitchell of the Zoological Society of London. He lunched with Buxton, the leading protectionist, who encouraged him to write for the *Journal of the Society for the Preservation of the Wild Fauna of the Empire*.

On this 1910 visit to Britain James was unencumbered by regimental business and could thus devote himself to wildlife matters as well as giving attention to his family. His long period of absence had taken its toll on his previously wide circle of friends, and he made the following note in his diary in London in February 1910: 'In town. No one much about – very few people I know.' But the lack of social opportunities meant that while he was in London he was able to concentrate on issues of game protection before proceeding to Scotland. He was already sufficiently distinguished in his field to be taken around Rothschild's impressive museum at Tring by the owner himself. He saw Buxton again and visited Frederick Courteney Selous, the great southern African hunter at his home (and private museum) at Worpledon. Stevenson-Hamilton was fêted by the conservation fraternity and, at the annual dinner of the Society for the Protection of the Wild Fauna of the Empire, he was seated close to the famous Selous, his friend Sir Alfred Pease, and J.H. Patterson (author of *The Man-Eaters of Tsavo*). Among his fellow diners, were the naturalist and author, H.A. Bryden, Waldorf Astor, Sir Alfred Sharpe, Lord Hindlip, Robert Baden-Powell, Theodore Roosevelt, Lord Curzon, Lord Rothschild, Lord Lugard, the Earl of Crewe, and other establishment luminaries.

He also had to reconsider his family position in 1910. He had remained close to his brother, Olmar, who had visited him in the game reserve in November 1902 when his career began, and he was sorry to see him leave and return to India. In 1905 James had received a desperate communication which elicited from him the following comment:

> Olmar appears to be pretty sick of everything and wants badly to go to the Egyptian army. Also a permanent allowance. I don't think latter is a good thing. I would always pull him out of a hole, but if he once became a remittance man, I should say he would simply drift and never make good at all. He is naturally lazy and without ambition.

But Olmar seemed to have settled down, having married cousin Gwladys, whom James had once taken out. James re-established close contact with his father, still living at Kirkton. In 1904 his father had stood in a County Council election and, according to his son, 'was beaten by 100 votes [by] Mr Gold, "one of the people" and drunken at that'.

There was a great deal of talk about politics among his friends and Stevenson-Hamilton listened to political speeches at Hyde Park whenever he was in London. The future of landowners under the growing tide of socialism seemed bleak and his father's electoral defeat was an indicator of what was in store. 'Personally wish I wasn't tied by land,' he confided to his journal. Fairholm, which he loved so passionately, was turning into a burden. In addition, he noted from his military friends that 'racing [is] dying, soldier racing [is] dying, steeplechasing too; no support from public'. The social landscape of England was changing. Even Helen Lindsay-Smith's son, Algy, was (unimaginably) 'a *socialist!!* Full of mannerisms and side – nothing less like a radical socialist. How very unusual life is in England.' Things were certainly changing and he despaired when he saw Fairholm. The new coal pit was an 'eyesore', and the 'new wood has disappeared.... All so changed that I don't know that I would care to live there now.'

But what alternative was there? At the end of 1910 when the time came for him to decide whether or not to return to the Sabi Game Reserve after his long leave, he remained unsure about what to do:

> The Colonel is shaky. Shall I live in England? I like my work in South Africa, the country, the people. Olmar and Gwladys are happy in India. Leyland has a wife and mother-in-law. The principal trouble at home is money matters. Politically things are bad. The income from Fairholm is likely to diminish. If I ran it, it would improve. While the Colonel lives I can't make any changes. I'm becoming bald, my teeth are coming out, I'm getting old.

Realising that the unification of the four southern African provinces into the Union of South Africa was about to take place and might threaten his position in the Transvaal, and feeling seriously debilitated by his chronic malaria which he first contracted in Barotseland in 1898 and which recurred from time to time, Stevenson-Hamilton thought that the time had perhaps come for a change of career. Two possibilities presented themselves. The first was a game reserve position in east Africa, which he felt might be in the nature of a promotion. But he was not offered the job. There was another short-term possibility which also tempted him, especially as it allowed him to postpone his final decision on whether to leave South Africa permanently or not. In 1910 'the Secretary of the London Zoo, Dr Chalmers Mitchell, asked me if I would go to South Africa as the Zoo agent to organise a collection of South African wild animals to be presented to King George V on his accession'. With his travelling expenses paid and an offer of a salary of £1 a day, he recorded in his diary that he was 'rather tempted'. He accepted but then was immediately tormented by doubts: 'A good deal worried about things. Indecision is such a curse and whatever one decides one generally seems to regret.'

*Early game photo (taken by Paul Selby).*

Collecting the fauna for the new King's Collection involved Stevenson-Hamilton in a considerable amount of effort. He had to visit all parts of southern Africa. The work was 'getting people interested and forming committees' and the aim of the scheme was to obtain representative wildlife from the Rhodesias, the protectorates and from every South African province. The animals so acquired were

> got together at a selected spot in each territory. [Then] we had [them] all sent to Pretoria Zoo where two keepers sent especially from London came and collected them. [The animals] arrived safely in London, [and were] given to the King, who handed [them] . . . over to London Zoo. I was congratulated on my work and [was] given the silver medal of the Society.

It was easier to collect game in some areas than in others. Northern Rhodesia, where he was fairly well known through his friendship with Lewanika and Coryndon, was the most co-operative. His task in Southern Rhodesia was also simplified because the Duke and Duchess of Connaught were there at the time, having come out to southern Africa for the opening of parliament in Cape Town ('Duchess not as pleasant as the Duke – cross and formidable'). On the Duke's staff was Hamilton of Dalzell, a Hamilton relative, while the Duke himself was the Honorary Colonel-in-Chief of the 6th (Inniskilling) Dragoons. The connection was therefore a close one and he acquired a wonderful selection of animals. Dr Warren of the Natal Museum in Pietermaritzburg was helpful – as were people in all four provinces. At times he was a little worried about the task: 'The London Zoo is using the King's name as a stalking horse to get animals on the cheap. So, I shall have some trouble. Smuts was pretty good-natured and laughed about the thing so suppose I shall be able to carry on.' There was also the question of his taking on such a mission while still being employed by the Transvaal government. He nevertheless applied for six months unpaid leave, and asked that the government consider re-employing him at the end of that period – provided that he had sufficiently recovered his health.

Cissy constituted a major family problem at the time. Her husband had died and she had returned to Britain with her daughter, Peggy, who suffered from Downs syndrome. As she still did not get on with their father, James thought he would put some interest into her life by taking her with him to South Africa when he went to make arrangements for the King's Collection. She proved to be a great nuisance and thoroughly spoiled the experience for him. She was, he said, 'the most impossible person. [I am having] the worst time travelling with her. . . . What a sister to have! If she'd be civil, I'd help her. I've had a lesson that will last a long time.' Without any sorrow, he saw her return to Kirkton at the end of the enterprise. But in 1913, trouble was once again brewing. '7 January: Letter from the Colonel. Cissy had one of her attacks again. Rushed out in the rain and had to be fetched by attendant Payne. It is really awful and I suppose some day she will go right off her head.'

After the King's Collection had been delivered, James decided to return to the Sabi Game Reserve. The job was still his: he had not resigned, only taken his long home leave and extended it in order to arrange the King's wildlife collection.

Making the decision to return to South Africa had been a difficult one, but ironically, not long afterwards, the year 1912 saw his greatest achievement of the period: the publication of his book *Animal Life in Africa*. It seems that Theodore Roosevelt had first put the idea into his head when they met in East Africa. James delivered the manuscript to Heinemann, who was keen to publish and soon produced proofs. *Animal Life*, at a cost of eighteen shillings, appeared to wide acclaim. The foreword was written by Theodore Roosevelt himself. In the preface, James makes clear what he wished to achieve. He was aware of the numerous books on the wild animals of Africa, which included personal adventures, sporting narratives and scientific works. But he had long felt that there was a gap in the literature and that interested people needed 'in condensed form some account of the life economy of the animals which he finds around him'. The emphasis was therefore on the habits of African animals, and how they interacted with each other and with their environment. This was highly unusual for its time and marked a watershed in the literature. The book begins with general chapters on the 'Great game of Africa', their destruction, and then the effort to preserve them. The chapters that follow are on various groups of animals: hoofed mammals, elephant, different kinds of antelope, carnivores, birds, reptiles and fish. The book concludes with hunting aids and hints on African travelling, transport notes, and also contains a long appendix on game laws. Stevenson-Hamilton took an environmental political stand right from the beginning of the book when he countered the arguments which were used to denigrate game reserves.

All the reviews were extremely complimentary. They appeared in more than fifty South African and international newspapers and magazines – amazing publicity for a South African book. The *Times Literary Supplement* of 2 May 1912 praised the book highly and acclaimed Stevenson-Hamilton's achievement in making a new profession out of being a 'warden'. It noted that more than the prevention of poaching was needed in such a man:

> No University can train him for it, or grant a certificate of competence; and hitherto the selection of game-warden has been to a certain extent fortuitous. It is no secret that in some colonies appointments have been made which turned out unsatisfactory, but in the Transvaal, the right selection was made at the outset and the triumphant success of the experiment may be largely attributed to this fact.

James was referred to as a 'first-class scientific naturalist, an accurate observer, and a thoroughly sympathetic animal lover . . . Let it be added that he shows himself possessor of a style which is vivid, graphic and withal scholarly, and it will be realised that a book of unusual fascination is the result.' Indeed, the book 'embodies the proper spirit of the compleat game warden'.

Dr William Hornaday, the influential president of the New York Zoological Society, said 'You have written what is positively the greatest wild animal book that ever came out of Africa! In its splendid combination of high-class game protection and natural history, it strikes a new note and goes into a class by itself.'[18] *Animal Life* was indeed a pioneering work in literary and natural history since it combined first-hand observations, ecology and adventure. The publication of the book also marked a milestone in the development of protectionist philosophy. Since the mid-nineteenth century, when the first steps to save wildlife were taken in the Transvaal, people had come to think differently about wild animals. The idea of Africa as an unconstrained and untameable Eden, in which the protection of individual species was paramount, belonged to the past, and Stevenson-Hamilton publicised this fact in a measured but fascinating way.

*Animal Life* combined rationality with romance in a manner not previously achieved. Fantasy still had its place, and descriptions of the magical world of the solitary, permanent white inhabitant of the game reserve were much enjoyed by readers. Life among the 'denizens of the wild' was romantic, even akin to living in paradise. Tales of everyday life in the outdoors, exploring, observing, camping, dealing with poachers, enlivened throughout by the excitement of a dangerous lion or a crocodile encounter, made Stevenson-Hamilton's book extremely popular. Serious and useful observations of wildlife were indeed made and communicated to readers, while the notion of a courageous person enduring privations in taking care of his charges fed the market for romance.

# 8

# 'Biggest War in 100 Years'[1]
## England and Gallipoli
## (1914–1917)

THE ERUPTION OF the First World War confronted James Stevenson-Hamilton with his first major life crisis since he had left the army after the South African War. From 1902 he had been comfortable with the fairly loose connections which he had enjoyed with his family, friends and events in Britain. Although the romantic notion of Empire, with which he had been brought up, linked mother country and colonies in an inextricable matrix, another kind of politics, the politics of Commonwealth, of nurturing bonds between independent political entities, increasingly began to dominate twentieth-century thinking. Stevenson-Hamilton had not thought about colonial nationalism as being in any way different from being British. Now, for the first (but not for the last) time in his life, he was obliged to choose and make a decision which indicated where his loyalties lay.

In July 1914, when war was imminent, Stevenson-Hamilton received a letter from the War Office to say that a general mobilisation was planned and that, as a reserve officer, he had been appointed to a 2nd Division cavalry regiment. His world was suddenly shattered as he contemplated what a return to active military life would entail. His inclination was to go back to England. Where would he be most useful? The game reserve could not be neglected and running it was obviously his first duty. But, he decided, 'I cannot bury my head in the Sabi – I could never hold my head up again.' There was no one he could talk to. On 8 August he wrote: 'The papers don't really tell much. Worried about what to do. Am I a fool to go? What course should I follow? Do they want my services here? If no, then should I apply for leave and go home and get taken in on one of the reserve regiments?'

Believing that he should make some contribution to the war effort, he decided that his first step should be to visit Pretoria and find out more about current events. He handed over the administration of the game reserve to the provincial authorities and badgered friends, such as Eddie Rooth, the prominent Transvaal politician, for information. James still did not know in

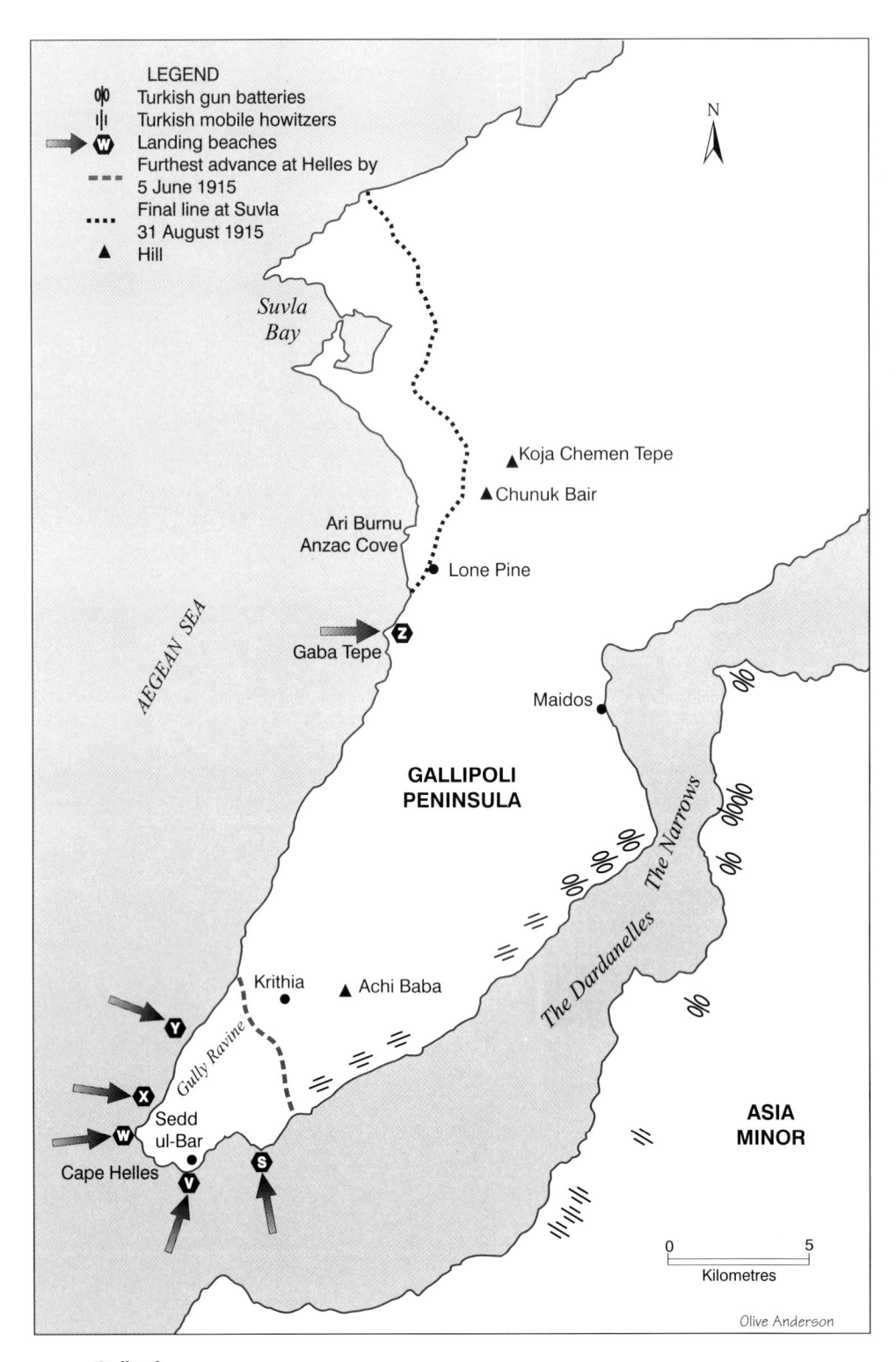

*Gallipoli.*

what capacity he might be most useful. On 21 August he met with General Smuts and other government officials and was offered a senior position in military intelligence in South West Africa, then a German possession and the obvious initial military target for South Africa's forces. It was tempting, but the main arena of war was in Europe, and Britain was directly threatened – and vulnerable. The warden confided to his journal, 'I would much rather go home and soldier.' He was, after all, a trained and experienced cavalryman, not an intelligence officer. But he remained agonised by the decision for many weeks afterwards and could not get his dilemma out of his mind. He was well aware of how generous it was for Smuts to have offered him a position and he was immensely glad to be held in high esteem by such an eminent man.

In the event, Stevenson-Hamilton's dutiful decision to return to Britain inaugurated one of the most unhappy periods in his life. Although he might have found something in his old regiment, he thought he might do even better. His greatest effort was expended in trying to persuade Colonel Fitzgerald, Lord Kitchener's secretary, to find something for him, and his father also wrote to influential people in this regard. After more than a month of whiling away the time, Stevenson-Hamilton finally learned that he was to be made Brigade-Major of the Notts and Derby Mounted Regiment, at that time stationed at Holt in Norfolk. Stevenson-Hamilton soon came to hate the Brigadier-General, Paul Kenna V.C., passionately. The relationship was a total disaster and for many days, very unusually, James was unable even to confide to his journals the depth of the psychological trauma which he was experiencing. If Dauncey had made him disillusioned and angry, Kenna's power to demoralise him was even greater. Perhaps if they had met under different circumstances, Stevenson-Hamilton might have liked and even admired Kenna, for he had a most distinguished personal, military and general record. An outstanding horseman, Kenna had seen service in many parts of the Empire, commanded prestigious regiments and was made aide-de-camp to the King. Among his many honours, he had been awarded the Royal Humane Society's Certificate and even the Victoria Cross after the Battle of Omdurman in 1898.[2]

It is difficult to conjecture what went wrong between Kenna and Stevenson-Hamilton, for the latter does not make it explicit. Perhaps, as far as Kenna was concerned, Stevenson-Hamilton was a mere gamekeeper from some far-flung colony who had been foisted on him by higher authority. The only account Stevenson-Hamilton ever gave was after Kenna had been killed at Gallipoli in August 1915. When he heard about the battle, Stevenson-Hamilton wrote:

> When we heard in middle of August of the last disaster at Suvla and the death of so many of the old Yeomanry Division, I must say my sorrow was tempered so far as my late General, Kenna, was concerned. I had a very thin seven months under him as his Brigade-Major. Since, I have realised that he was really quite mad and irresponsible, and it was a very good thing he was killed before he had the chance of getting his men cut to pieces unnecessarily . . .

While he was stationed at Holt, Stevenson-Hamilton tried to escape whenever he could. He spent New Year's Day of 1915 with his dear friends, the Lindsay-Smiths, at Ashfold. One of Helen's sons, Algie, was 'missing' and the worry being experienced by such a special family affected James greatly. He lunched with his Barotseland friend, Robert Coryndon, in February and later also with his brother, Olmar, and his wife, cousin Gwladys, who were in England on six months' leave from India. He also saw some of his old regimental companions, and near Aldershot he stayed with his regimental comrade, Jackson – 'Jorrocks'. But this made him perseverate unhappily: 'I wish now that I had stuck to the reserve [of officers] where I should have felt myself more useful trying to help the old regiment in various ways.'

Stevenson-Hamilton's escape came when orders were received to leave for Egypt as part of the Mediterranean Expeditionary Force. Stevenson-Hamilton was only in Egypt from May to July 1915, but it was long enough to convince him that he did not like it. There was little effective work for him to do, for the main purpose of the military occupation of Egypt was to cope with the many thousands of sick and wounded soldiers who streamed into the hospitals of Cairo. He therefore asked for another position: 'Since there appeared no hope of cavalry being sent to Gallipoli, I applied for a vacancy of Assistant Provost-Marshal and . . . found myself in July 1915 with the Lowland Division at Helles.' In this way began Stevenson-Hamilton's involvement in one of the most famous and most controversial battles of the First World War.[3]

The Gallipoli campaign still stirs the imagination of military historians. Certainly, from the Allies' perspective, it was one of the war's most spectacular failures. But there were achievements too: a military diversion in favour of Russia, a probable delay in Bulgaria's entry into the war, and the immobilisation of a large body of Turkish troops. To this must be added its importance in the national mythology of Australia and New Zealand – whose troops bore the brunt of the fighting. When it was devised, Gallipoli was to be the brilliant prelude of a movement which would close with the triumphal march of the Mediterranean Expeditionary Forces into Constantinople.

After a series of disasters, at the beginning of June 1915, a new offensive was launched. It was evident to all that if Gallipoli was to come into Allied hands, massive reinforcements were needed. This was the stage of the Gallipoli campaign when Stevenson-Hamilton arrived with the 52nd (Lowland) Division.[4] In his new job as Assistant Provost-Marshal, Stevenson-Hamilton was based at Cape Helles in the south. His responsibilities involved patrolling communication trenches, controlling water points (troughs and wells), dealing with sentenced prisoners, and interviewing enemy prisoners on behalf of Intelligence. When he first disembarked at Cape Helles it was midnight:

> All was very dark and still. All one could make out was a whitish escarpment of high lying background. A star shell goes up. Then, out of the silence and the darkness comes one solemn, deep 'boom'm'. At a minute's interval follows another and then another. Then silence again. It was very impressive and reminiscent of, and giving rise to, much the same feelings as are called up by the distant roaring of a lion in the depths of the lonely African bush.

When he described his landing, he wrote:

> This particular beach is known as 'W' (Lancashire Landing) and is a mass of stores of all kinds, mingled with tents. Some of the more permanently installed people live in sandbag shelters on a ledge half-way up the cliff which bounds the beach, but the majority dwell in tents on the beach itself and just take their chance. Nearly every tent is more or less shell torn; but the fellows say that as there is no rain in summer practically, it does not matter.

Stevenson-Hamilton soon found his way about, often walking around in the early hours of the morning, when it was

> nice and cool and very quiet. No guns and not much sniping. The trench labyrinth is extraordinary ... When you have climbed up from W beach ... an extraordinary sight reveals itself. Behind and below you is the crowded and busy beach ... [while] in front of you lies a great open undulating plain ... The foreground of this plain resembles nothing so much as an overturned ant hill. It is all dug up into channels of trenches, and is one seething mass of men, mules and carts, and horses and mules, all on the move and changing like the bits of glass in the kaleidoscope which used to amuse us when we

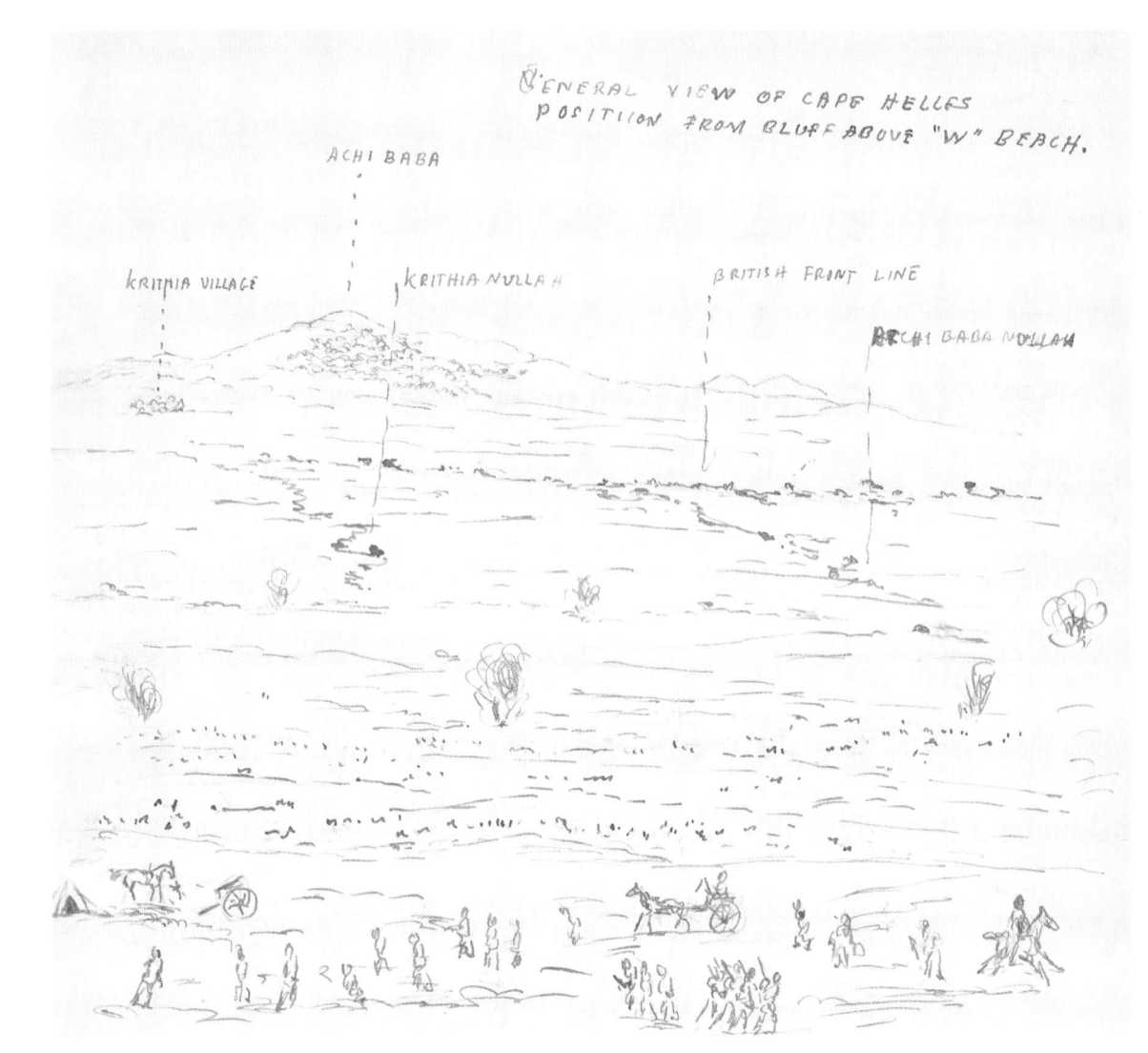

*General view of Cape Helles.*

(Labels on sketch: GENERAL VIEW OF CAPE HELLES POSITION FROM BLUFF ABOVE "W" BEACH. ACHI BABA; KRITHIA VILLAGE; KRITHIA NULLAH; BRITISH FRONT LINE; ACHI BABA NULLAH)

were children. Amid this apparently confused mass burst at intervals of a few seconds or minutes . . . shells of all kinds fired from the commanding ridges of Achi Baba . . . The amazing part to the newcomer is the apparent indifference with which everyone regards these shells. A mule occasionally breaks away, or a man may dodge when a shell comes close to him, but the others hardly even glance round. . . . In one case a man . . . was walking along the road when a shrapnel burst right over him, and the bullets struck the road like whips, knocking up the dust all round him. He was hit by one in the hand, stopped a moment to look at the wound, and then quietly pursued his way, tying a handkerchief over the place as he walked. No one else took any notice.

There were other awful impressions. The entry for 26 July reads:

> Very hot and [there were] inconceivable swarms of flies, and a mixed odour of dead men and chlorate of lime, the former the more pungent and penetrating. There are several trenches full of half-buried dead Turks, and hundreds of the 52nd Division killed in the big attack of 12th and 13th July are lying about unburied. Here and there a foot sticks up through the floor of a trench . . . The ground out in front between us and the Turks is covered with dead bodies, which are mostly quite black with the ribs showing white.

As for his work, because 'there is practically no ordinary crime here, one's job is a varied one and one is generally sent for when the proper person is not available for any old thing. In an action the Police are supposed to picquet the communication trenches to keep stragglers from getting down. But the whole thing is a bit hazy.' Before a 'cannonade' of 6 October he was to 'put up notice boards with new names of streets on them and [get] back before the ball commenced' to enable people to get from one end to the other of the trenches and to find their way during battles. He was also doing general staff work and acting as a general Camp Commandant: '[I] sit in the Staff dug-out compiling returns, writing orders and War Diary for three hours every morning. I know something of the general position.' He appreciated the insights this gave him, but he was made all the more apprehensive by what he came to know. 'We are as a force gradually fading away. Every day 150 men are evacuated sick and wounded from the Peninsula from this Division alone . . .'

During August the final big attack took place. Although the landing at Suvla Bay was initially successful, the Generals hesitated when they could have given the order to move further inland. Compounding the problem, the reinforcements did not advance soon enough, and remained too close to the beach. Although some sixteen thousand men left Anzac Cove and headed for Koja Chemen Tepe, the Turks managed to hold the high ground. The New Zealanders approached the stronghold of Chunuk Bair, and some even caught a glimpse of the sea on the other side of the peninsula. But from then onwards, for many reasons, the attack turned into a shambles.

Stevenson-Hamilton, of course, heard all about the northern attack, and on 12 August he wrote: 'The main attack north of Anzac which raged all Sunday and Monday seems by the cessation of the gunfire to have come to a full stop . . . The delay is giving Turks time to dig in. . . . Bad weather approaching too. I don't like it, and think the attack should have succeeded at once to be of any use.' On each following day the attack was renewed, but the initiative was eventually lost and the Turks were able to drive them off. Stevenson-Hamilton concluded: 'I suppose this will read as one of the worst bits of one of the worst carried out enterprises in British military history.'

The troops in Gallipoli tried to make some sense of what had gone wrong. Stevenson-Hamilton's opinion was as follows: 'The fact is that this kind of thing is not so much the fault of individual men or battalions, as of a system which insists on pushing absolutely raw and untrained troops into a general action, in which they lose over half their effectives and three-quarters of their officers, including all the best ones.' Death in battle was only one way to meet one's end; illness was possibly even worse. In the unbearable heat, the

> trenches were like ovens; the grass had long since withered and vanished and the hot wind stirred up the dust . . . On the limpid sea the corpses of horses and mules floated stiffly . . . Ashore, the bloated loathsome green flies [were] swarming hideously in the latrines, filling every trench and dug-out and covering the food, they were responsible for a virulent form of dysenteric diarrhoea – generally known as 'the Gallipoli Trots' or the 'Gallipoli Gallop'. All the men had gaunt sunken faces, and were unable to escape from one another or from the horribly unsanitary conditions which prevailed.[5]

By the end of August some of the worst illnesses were abating as the evenings became cooler. But, as Stevenson-Hamilton wrote, winter brought problems of its own:

> Prospects none too bright; will stay here for the winter . . . Now the position seems to be that we can't advance and can't leave without a disaster, so we must just stay where we are. We then have the choice of living underground up to our necks in water, or living above ground, a constant mark for shells. . . . Here conditions are in some ways worse than Flanders, because, their spell of duty over, the men have no safe dry billets to come back to rest in, but only rough dug-outs which at present are protected from the fierce sun by inadequate waterproof sheets, and later will be waterholes. Constant shelling and nothing to do. The whole thing has been an appalling muddle of politicians, soldiers and sailors from the start. One would like the true history of these things to appear alongside the official dispatches . . . The men are discouraged by no fresh blood coming out to them, and so take every chance of getting away . . . A jolly nice jumble it all is . . . This

sort of thing one expected in a Gilbert and Sullivan comic opera or in 'Alice through the Looking Glass' but not in what by some is considered to be a serious war.

The major head to roll after Suvla was that of Ian Hamilton. By 16 October the troops all knew that Hamilton was to be sent home and that General Munro would be coming in his place. 'Hamilton's farewell order very flowery as to be expected and the usual stuff.' But at the end of October, James was complaining that they were not getting much news, and 'in this campaign, we have learned that no news, or scanty news, usually implies bad news. They are always quick enough to tell us anything encouraging, often heavily embroidered.' He, like all the others, was very unsure about what was going on: 'Wonder what will be the outcome of the changes. They can't expect to gain much by keeping us here.' They were all beginning to realise that something had to be done: either immense reinforcements must arrive or otherwise they would have to cut their losses and withdraw. But under the circumstances of the exposed beaches, retreat was difficult, perhaps even impossible.

At the end of October he wrote: 'My dug-out is quite dry, but the poor fellows in the trenches had a bad time, with no shelter and run down as they are. Luckily they are Scotch and like the cold better than the heat.' Gallipoli in winter was bleak and windswept and storms were frequent. Heavy rain lay on the ground. Nothing was absorbed and there was no run off. Deep liquid mud was everywhere, mixed up with rubbish and the remains of dead soldiers. There were helmets, old tins and bits of equipment, like 'a very dirty old Boer encampment as we used to find them in the South African War'. One storm destroyed almost the entire harbour. Some men drowned, blizzards and snow claimed the lives of others and thousands suffered from severe frostbite. Stevenson-Hamilton's wells were all covered with a thick layer of ice. Like thousands of others he suffered from ailments such as lumbago and rheumatism because of the damp and the cold.

Early in December it was decided to evacuate Gallipoli. On 8 December the secret order was given after the Cabinet's approval had been secured. Stevenson-Hamilton was ecstatic: 'Great news of the day is that Anzac and Suvla were abandoned last night . . . Best thing we have done for a long time; good staff work.' On 29 December formal orders came to evacuate the Cape Helles area, with final embarkation from beaches W and V. On the next day Stevenson-Hamilton was, like everyone else, packing up the heavy stuff, and by 31 December it was 'an open secret that a general evacuation is intended'.

*Stevenson-Hamilton's dug-out.*

By 10 January 1916 Stevenson-Hamilton was in Mudros, having played his part in this difficult process. So carefully had the evacuation been planned that the Turks were ignorant of what was happening within their sight. Everything not taken away was destroyed – even the dug-outs. Once at Mudros, rumours about what nearly went wrong kept tongues busy. Apparently the navy did not sent the correct kind of craft and even treated those who came off the peninsula rather badly. Stevenson-Hamilton commented: 'The man who said, "We have three things to contend against at Gallipoli: 1. the Navy, 2. Sickness, 3. Turks, in importance of order named" was about right.'

    After Gallipoli there was a problem about what to do with all the troops evacuated from Turkey. Certainly many could go to France, but the Suez Canal was still a vulnerable area and there was some evidence that, although the Turks had failed once to secure it, they might renew their attack. They were certainly massing troops in Palestine and Syria. After a fortnight at Alexandria, Stevenson-Hamilton returned to Cairo as Provost-Marshal in the Egyptian Force with the rank of Lieutenant-Colonel. Two months later he was transferred as Camp Commandant to the General Headquarters of the Mediterranean Expeditionary Force at Ismailia, where he spent four months. It was not a pleasant interlude. He described it as 'pure wash-out. Watching for officers breaking the rules.' He soon began to chaffe under the inactivity of a staff position. Stevenson-Hamilton yearned to do something more worthwhile and more active than church parades in the searing heat, beating off the flies and conveying messages between senior staff. Too much of his time was spent riding and dining and listening to the gossip and acrimony between the Egyptian forces and the British. He had little time to spare for his senior officers, although they were all extremely influential men. He considered them 'notoriously unimaginative, which is, of course, our national failing', and was back in the kind of subservient position that he always hated.

Stevenson-Hamilton had a temporary respite during September 1916 when he returned to Britain for a month's leave. Again he sought out the South African High Commissioner in London, but again there was nothing constructive for him. There was the usual round of family and friends to be seen and enjoyed. He joined his father at Kirkton and saw his sister Cissy again. There was plenty of entertainment and it was a great pleasure once again to see the Lindsay-Smiths at Ashfold. But despite the outward gaiety this was not a relaxing month. The tension between his father and sister was mounting. They disliked one another intensely, and hardly ever spoke. Because of the uncertainty over family matters, Stevenson-Hamilton thought that he ought to be at home. He considered applying for a transfer to Britain, but he also wanted to spend time in France and to see out the war in some military capacity. No one knew how much longer the war would continue. James sent in his application for a transfer either to France or back to South Africa but, after a fortnight of uncertainty, he received a cable 'saying "disallowed". Anyway, it settles my mind and I can't kick myself for not having tried.' He had to return to Egypt.

The voyage from London back to Port Said was pleasant enough: 'some astoundingly pretty girls on board', but Egypt was wearily predictable: 'Bedlam as the ship arrived.' Everything was much the same: the heat, the boredom, polo, sailing, and the irrational military structure which had led to such bitterness between the various Near Eastern commands. The number of senior Generals and their intense jockeying for position and internal rivalries were disconcerting, and Stevenson-Hamilton found it difficult to pander to them. There were really too many commanders in Egypt and the confusion of the 'trinity' of Generals was increasingly counterproductive. Stevenson-Hamilton rather cockily denigrated them in his journal, clearly loathing his role as their toady. He felt that some of their orders, including that to wear boots and breeches all the time in the dreadful heat, were 'ridiculous'. He may even have made his opinions publicly known. In the middle of November, Stevenson-Hamilton apparently pulled down a flag without permission. He had done so before as he felt that it 'advertised GHQ [General Headquarters]'. But, he told his journal, this had 'Offended the Great Ones. Will be on the carpet tomorrow.' Indeed he was, and he was in agony over it: 'On the carpet ... my age. Can't ruin my army career. ... The real trouble is that I won't lick their boots.'

Stevenson-Hamilton felt stifled by the protocol and pettiness of headquarters and chafed against the politics of military command. He wanted to remain 'useful' to the war effort, and returning to South Africa – or leaving the army – was impossible while war was on. He had already been refused a transfer. Consequently, he decided to ask to leave Egypt and to be seconded into the civil service of the Sudan, which had been depleted of its senior officials, who, in joining the army were leaving the civil administration in a chaotic state. At first he was not allowed to go, but by 30 November, he was pleased to note: 'They have decided I may go to Mongalla.'

Troubles seldom come singly and it was at about this time that more problems came into his life. He received a visit from Olmar and learned 'dread things. Gwladys deceiving him [Olmar] for years with Gunner Meecham ... He bears her no ill will, simply feels utterly crushed and broken. She had *written* to tell him.' Perhaps Stevenson-Hamilton's feelings were compounded by the fact that he was fond of his cousin, and had even fancied her once upon a time. It is likely that he felt as betrayed as his brother – for she was, after all, 'family'. All the awful memories of his father's unhappy marriage, of the meaning of family were uppermost in his mind. 'I have never knowingly seen a human being in such agony before', he wrote of his brother's misery, 'and it makes one mad against this wicked woman.' It was the last time that he saw Olmar, who died of cholera in India in 1919, still with a broken heart.

Life had suddenly taken a turn for the worse. At the end of the year he recognised his anxiety and at Khartoum he wished that he might have the '... gift of taking things as they come'. He saw that he had made heavy weather of life's upsets, but even so he recognised that this situation was 'not as rotten as 1915' when he had been on the beaches at Gallipoli. As 1917 commenced Stevenson-Hamilton sailed down the Nile towards the Sudan.

# 9

# 'Truculent Dinka Clans'[1]
## The Sudan
## (1917–1919)

THE TIME THAT Stevenson-Hamilton spent in the southern Sudan, from December 1916 until September 1919, was productive, peaceful and interesting. Events of the war were certainly worrying and he anxiously kept abreast of them, but they seldom intruded directly into his personal world. His job in the Sudanese civil service as an Inspector (District Commissioner) suited him perfectly. Within a month or two, Stevenson-Hamilton realised that he was back in familiar terrain. He had a task to do and he was happy once more. 'I am dropping back into the way of African veld life again, am used to the discomforts and am much more contented than in civilised surroundings.' He had, of course, no idea of how long he would remain in the Sudan, for this depended on the duration of war and whether or not he would continue to be needed. Stevenson-Hamilton took his administrative duties seriously and performed them responsibly and competently. In addition, he offered constructive advice as to how the Sudan and Mongalla province might be more effectively governed and took an active interest in improving the game protection laws of the country. He did some mapping, planned a book, and collected material for a number of articles. 'The Dinka country east of the Bahr-el-Gebel', appeared in *The Geographical Journal* in 1920 and was illustrated with a number of his own photographs.[2] He also wrote 'Field notes on some mammals in the Bahr-el-Gebel, Southern Sudan', in the *Proceedings of the Zoological Society of London*, 1919. By the time he left, Stevenson-Hamilton received enthusiastic testimonials from all the influential people he had come to know and he had been mentioned in dispatches and awarded the Order of the Nile.

Although mail was slow and intermittent, Stevenson-Hamilton did not lose touch with his friends. He had letters from his game rangers in the Sabi Game Reserve which filled him in on what was happening there. Helen Lindsay-Smith also wrote to him and he corresponded with Robert Coryndon, at first in Basutoland and later in Uganda. Coryndon's reply to Stevenson-Hamilton's initial letter must have taken him aback for it read:

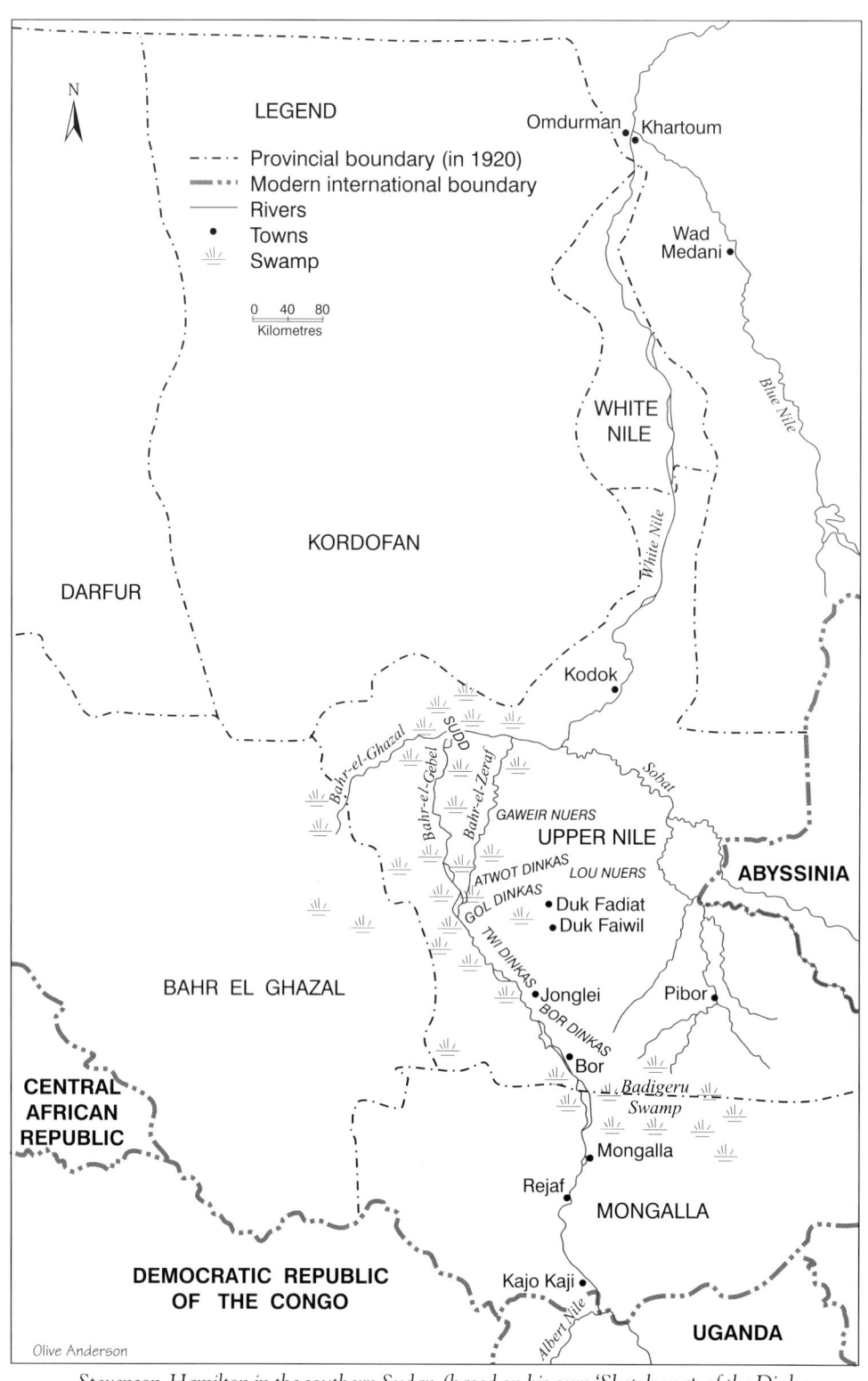

*Stevenson-Hamilton in the southern Sudan (based on his own 'Sketch-map of the Dinka country', 1920).*

'How dare you write to me – you are, or ought to be dead – I heard you were blotted out like so many others in Gallipoli! Indeed I passed the news on, as one does, and we all said "poor chap" and recounted your virtues.' The journal entry notes: 'Coryndon seems quite aggrieved about it.'

Stevenson-Hamilton soon came to appreciate that there was far too much red tape jamming up the smooth working of the Sudanese administration. He was critical of the low status of the white (British) officials and what he believed to be pandering to the Egyptians. He also made the observation that the Sudan had 'terrific prospects for agriculture'. 'Under a less bureaucratic government', he noted, 'it should soon be a rich and self-supporting country.' His other first impressions related to Bor, the district he had gone to administer: 'It is a beastly station', he had heard from the Governor, R. Owen. At one level, he soon came to agree. The Sabi Game Reserve was a 'health resort in comparison with this. Flies, mosquitoes, swamp.' 'Could not get up at 5 a.m. as planned', he wrote in June 1917, 'because mosquitoes were too bad. They were a bit better at 5.30 but by then the big biting sheroot flies had joined in. This is an awful place.'

Geographically the southern Sudan was not at all like the desiccated South African landscape to which Stevenson-Hamilton was accustomed. Landlocked at the upper reaches of the Nile River, the whole spectrum of life was determined by the riverine regime. The economy, politics and society of the southern Sudan were regulated by the Sudd, that 'dreary dead level of reed and papyrus swamp [extending] to the uttermost horizon with nothing to break its depressing monotony'. The enormous flooded area was often up to a metre deep, filled with abundant supplies of nutritious fish but also choked with a dense floating vegetation which impeded all water-borne traffic for long periods of the year.[3] Livestock was the basis of the southern economy as well as the core of its socio-political organisation. In times of flooding the precious long-horned cattle, which represented wealth, social obligations and aesthetic and religious assets, were moved onto higher sandy outcrops on which a little shifting cultivation could be done. Without sufficient dry ground to support large numbers of people and livestock, groups fragmented. In the dry season, when the mud, that 'mass of glutinous porridge', had been baked by the sun into 'the consistency of brick',[4] the pattern was reversed. Larger groups then made use of the more abundant grazing areas. Wildlife also migrated from high to low ground depending on seasonal conditions.

When the level of the swamp was highest, humans and domestic animals sought refuge on the ridges, the *duks*. On these outcrops of high ground there were trees and fresh water could be obtained from natural reservoirs.

Heat and standing water brought their concomitant diseases: endemic cerebral malarial fever, sleeping sickness and dysentery, to name but a few. Outbreaks of 'cerebro' were common, particularly in the extremely rainy year of 1918. Prevention in the form of 'a gargle of permanganate and a snuffle of formalin' were given out to people queuing in line by the doctor. Illness was politically inopportune too, and Stevenson-Hamilton wrote: 'Diseases: wish they would cease, [the local people] always think the government has sent them.' Wildlife and domestic stock were also affected and Stevenson-Hamilton was witness to hundreds of dead and dying tiang.

It was not long before Stevenson-Hamilton had familiarised himself with the ways of the pastoral economy of the area and its people. Unlike the predominantly Arab population of the north, the southern population comprised interrelated groups of Lou (or Lau), Dinka and Nuer people. Many centuries previously these Nilotic Negroid people had intruded in small groups into the southern Sudan, probably seeking pasture-land. Although they eventually came to inhabit a large territory, their fragile vulnerable economy, nomadism, flexible group size, lack of internal cohesion, and an absence of external threats did not require the creation of any centralised institutions.[5] Communities were frequently at odds with each other, and officials often found it very difficult to disentangle the intergroup feuds which usually concerned livestock. Stevenson-Hamilton was fascinated by these people as he had been by the African culture of the Transvaal lowveld. He enjoyed collecting their oral traditions, learning their language and trying to understand their religion and their attitudes to life. He generally asked people about times 'very long ago' and was curious about where they had come from, where they had first settled and where the old settlements and cattle holdings were. All in all, he concluded – very much in the colonial jargon of the early twentieth century: 'Notwithstanding all their defects, it is impossible to help liking the Dinkas. Individually they are delightfully irresponsible and invariably cheerful, quick to appreciate sympathy, and I think, for Africans, remarkably grateful for small kindnesses ...'

Mongalla, the province to which Stevenson-Hamilton was posted, had come to mark the tribal boundary between the Dinka and the Nuer of the Upper Nile Province. In an already complex situation, a defined border and what appeared often to be overt Mongalla governmental support for the Dinka against the Nuer, made effective government difficult and small-scale revolts became widespread. Accomplishing effective control meant putting an end to the endemic intergroup conflict. A number of complex factors created these conditions of ongoing violence, but the formal government response was uninformed and very often ineffectual, as Stevenson-Hamilton

*View from terrace, Kajo Kaji.*

realised. There was, in essence, no real policy except to impose order by ruthlessly suppressing all resistance.[6] The official view was that the 'pacification of the southern Sudan was forced on the government by the turbulence of the people themselves'.[7] Despite close ties between the Dinka and Nuer, their obsession with livestock and resistance to authority led – as it did in many other parts of Africa – to conflict over cattle ownership and access to pasture. The circle of raiding and counter-raiding was difficult to break. Indigenous leadership structures were not fully understood by the British administrators. Patterns of vengeance, whether over livestock or women, were also sometimes misconstrued. To complicate matters further, a distorted picture of the traditional clan position was often deliberately fed to officials in order to promote particular interests.

Issues were exacerbated because provincial borders did not coincide with the traditional lands of specific clans and divided groups were discontented because administration on one side of the line was different from that on the other. Stevenson-Hamilton was unusual for the time in recognising that there was little wisdom in defining tribal boundaries and trying to keep people separate. They were linked by co-operation as much as by conflict, and boundaries only intensified the latter. He felt that a single administrative district in the region would be preferable, but personal rivalries between the Governors of the Upper Nile Province and Mongalla made this impossible. Without exception, all groups resented paying tribute, particularly when people felt that the British could not defend their tax-paying subjects against forays from enemies. Losses were recouped by raiding, and defiance of the government led to a renewal of local feuds. The position also worsened when some groups supported government initiatives not for the sake of justice or peace but only in order to capture cattle for themselves.

At the time of Stevenson-Hamilton's arrival, three columns were sent out to retaliate against the annihilation of a government patrol which had been despatched to support the Dinka against a massive Lou raid into Bor territory. Stevenson-Hamilton was active in containing this raid and other eruptions of violence. From January to May 1917 he joined the Lou-Nuer patrol with Major Bramble, District Inspector of the Upper Nile Province; in May 1918 he raided the Atwot Dinkas; in July that year he 'peacefully penetrated' the Gaweir Nuer country; and in May 1919 he 'punished' the Aiwil clan of the Alit-Twi Dinka. All of this was accomplished during years of exceptional Nile flooding, which made travel extremely difficult and complicated the confiscation or appropriation of livestock.[8]

But most of Stevenson-Hamilton's stay at Mongalla did not involve the excitement of battle. The bulk of his time was spent attending to routine matters. He was a little nonplussed when he discovered that he had to give his approval to and sign documents which were written in Arabic and to take the word of his chief clerk, Issedin Effendi, a Druze from the Lebanon, or his Ma'mur, the Egyptian Mohammed Effendi, as to their contents. He began to learn Arabic, listing useful words and phrases. In the cooler months he travelled widely into all the corners of his district, meeting the people and trying to learn as much about them as he could. He found many of the far-flung administrative outposts neglected because the British staff had been withdrawn and then remembered that his own Sabi Game Reserve might well look as derelict.

Unable to return to South Africa while war continued, James gave a great deal of thought as to how he might better administer the southern Sudan. He compared it with the position in South Africa, noting that the 'whole system here is so different . . . that it gets on my nerves'. He complained that the 'whole province would be efficiently run by two white officials and a few clerks'. He confessed himself at one point, 'bored stiff' – which he never was in the Sabi Game Reserve – and resented the fact that the swamps constrained him from travelling around. It did not take him long to realise that Governor Owen 'does half an hour's work a day. Bad for the country financially and demoralizing for white officials themselves. [They are] thoroughly incompetent when they leave and have to do real work.' He was at times appalled by the rough justice meted out in his province and eventually Owen was removed because of his ignorance of the atrocities meted out in his name and his public indifference to a dreadful murder. At the beginning of 1918, as Owen was making plans to leave the province, details of his corruption were beginning to surface. Stevenson-Hamilton discovered that Owen had been giving elephant hunting licences to his friends and subordinates in exchange for favours. He felt a measure of unease over the fact that such a man was not being removed in public disgrace, but that he was instead being appointed governor of the western oases in Egypt, with his headquarters at Luxor, and on a salary of £1 000 per annum until the war ended.

Apart from the vagaries of their behaviour, Stevenson-Hamilton found the racial mix of the southern Sudanese officials fascinating because they were quite different from blacks in South Africa. In South Africa there was no middle group of educated coloured people to fill the roles which the Egyptians or northern Sudanese did as Ma'murs and clerks. The racial order was, for this reason, more complex in the Sudan, and the differences between black and white were less clear-cut at these levels. The pastoral Dinkas and Nuer might, however, be compared with the tribal Africans in South Africa. On the one hand, Stevenson-Hamilton believed that Sudan officials did not understand the differences between black and white. On the other hand, when he sat down (as he generally did) with all the effendis to dinner, he wondered what would have been said had this happened in segregationist South Africa. Another occasion gave him the opportunity to write what he thought about the practice of having a local mistress, a common practice among single male administrators at that time. When he was back at Bor in March 1918, a 'comely wench' was brought to his attention after a Nuer dance, and those who offered her doubtless thought that he would be interested. He wrote afterwards: 'But the rule in these matters which I have always followed is a sound one, I think (although it is a generally understood and accepted practice all through tropical African even among officials) that it does no good to prestige.'

Turning fifty is frequently an occasion for reflection and, on his birthday in 1917, he wrote:

> My 50th birthday. A shocking affair. I don't believe I look anything like it as I am only just beginning to get grey at the temples, and I have got a small bald patch which has not increased much of recent years. But it is an awful thing to contemplate; the more so that one's life is not settled yet.

*A Nuer dance.*

Now that he was well into middle age, he was beginning to know himself better. In March 1918 the new Governor of Mongalla arrived to take over from Stevenson-Hamilton, and the latter wrote: 'Northcote wants me to stop here as Inspector [but] I know now well that the root of all evil to me is the second place.' At the end of March, after Northcote's installation, Stevenson-Hamilton returned to Bor as Second Inspector, 'Nominally running this district for a year but first time reins in own hands.' This was what he preferred. Back at Bor, he began to think again about administrative procedures and why they were not effective in bringing harmony and prosperity to the district. He did not think the assistance he received from the Sudanese or Egyptian officials was helpful: 'each equally dishonest and each equally set on deceiving the European officer and exploiting the native'. About the local people, he wrote:

> These tribes are badly neglected. Bit more attention from British inspector on the spot might have obviated all the raiding etc. over the last ten years. Sudan district official is usually young, devoid of administrative ability and intent only on drilling police and shooting elephant, or, if keen, becomes a bureaucrat and thinks the only work is office work. Cannot administer anything successfully from a little

affair like this, up to the British Empire, properly without going about and knowing things from your own personal experience.

He had time on his hands and tried to find out everything he could about the Bor district, seeking out its remotest parts, and even going to places and villages which he believed he was the first white man to visit. He got to know the people while collecting tribute, doling out gifts and supplying medicines. He felt that 'If Inspectors had been less tied to the river and less fond of going on leave, there would have been a very different state of things today.' He was extraordinarily thorough in seeking 'personal experience'. He could also appreciate by this time that it was impossible to separate Dinkas from Nuers, despite their interclan feuds and despite the fact that often the 'Nuer assumed air of conquering Prussians over the Dinka'. They spoke one another's language easily and fluently and accepted the authority of one another's chiefs. '[They] cannot be divided', he noted, 'although it looks good on paper. Can we wonder that government are regarded merely as robbers and the punitive expeditions merely as cattle raiding razzias?' Stevenson-Hamilton wrote a number of sharp reports to suggest improvements and to comment on how matters might be better handled.

The major benefit of the southern Sudan for Stevenson-Hamilton was that he was back among African wildlife. The Sudan has been important in game protection history because of the issue of ivory extraction in this region which had galvanised the game protection fraternity into action in the early years of the twentieth century. In the Sudan, British enthusiasm for game-saving was soon evident. The Preservation of Wild Animals Ordinance was drafted in 1901. Significantly, unlike South Africa, a distinction was made between 'natives of the Sudan' – which included civil servants stationed in the country – and visitors. More privileges were accorded to the former. Within a few years, there were a number of game reserves, the most important of which was that of some forty thousand square kilometres, bounded by the Blue and White Nile, the Sobat River and the Ethiopian boundary.[9] This legislation, together with the appointment of A.L. Butler as Game Superintendent,[10] would seem to indicate convincing official support for the protectionist programme. There were, however, tensions and contradictions from the outset. What most bothered imperial conservationists, the Society for the Preservation of the Wild Fauna of the Empire in particular, was the virtually unbridled liberty to hunt obtained by the white officials in the Sudan. 'Natives' generally captured wildlife by unsophisticated methods and were consequently not very destructive. In addition, many indigenous communities in the Sudan were not hunters by tradition and the field was thus left open to officials.

Stevenson-Hamilton was an official and thus enjoyed hunting privileges. He took every opportunity which came his way, and even regarded his 'raid' and 'punishment' expeditions as chances to obtain game. He killed Nile lechwe, white-eared kob, Tora hartebeest, tiang (topi), Mongalla gazelle (a race of Thomson's gazelle) and many other species. But the particularly rewarding new experience was that he had access to elephant, which were almost extinct in southern Africa at this time. The conditions under which elephant were hunted in the southern Sudan were laborious and Stevenson-Hamilton detailed some of these in his separate notes entitled 'Successful elephant hunts'. Here is a sample:

> Found Jonglei completely under water and it is waist deep for miles inland ... During the night elephants were heard and news of their whereabouts arrived early. I was not particularly keen about going out after them, but as Lawton was very anxious to do so, we started off at 7 a.m. in the big felucca, with the Ma'mur (Ibrahim Effendi) and Kameel Effendi; some police and Dinkas accompanied in dug-out canoes. After having proceeded for two miles up the khor, the water shallowed and we had to get out of the felucca and into dug-outs. I went with the Ma'mur in one and Lawton in the other one; we each had several Dinkas to paddle and pole. Pushed about for several hours among the swamps and through trees, reeds and papyrus and water three to four feet deep. At last heard the elephants close, and coming to the edge of a reed belt, sighted them on the other side of an open piece of water about 200 yards away. There were eight bulls, all standing immersed up to their bellies in water. We manoeuvred the canoes to within about 100 yards, when they heard something and began to move off slowly. I fired at once at the biggest one ... Followed them up as fast as possible and fired at the biggest that was left, killing him dead with one shoulder shot, and as the rest disappeared, hit a third. They then got into long reeds and we could not follow.

On another occasion he took off his boots and 'waded in. It was hard work as I had to wade all the time through liquid mud over my knees, with many water holes into which I repeatedly fell, and three wide channels to cross waist deep.' As a resident officer, he took advantage of the wartime provision which doubled the elephant ration for each £6 licence holder from two to four, and sold the ivory profitably. While part of him was glad to hunt elephant and to obtain ivory, he also felt repelled by it. After observing an elephant plucking a big bunch of grass and playing with it with his trunk,

Stevenson-Hamilton noted how he then 'flogged himself under the belly and on the sides to kill the flies. He also used his trunk to scratch himself behind the ears. It feels rather like murder killing such intelligent beasts.'

As soon as he arrived in the southern Sudan, Stevenson-Hamilton became active in game preservation matters. As was his custom in South Africa he kept meticulous observations on the wildlife he encountered (including birds, reptiles and fish), noting favoured ranges and habitats, the relative abundance or scarcity of certain species, and morphological and colour variations. He also studied the legislation applicable in the Sudan and corresponded with influential and interested people on the issue.

Owing to the enormous cultural and developmental gulfs between the two countries, the issues facing wildlife conservation in the southern Sudan were very different from those which Stevenson-Hamilton had known in South Africa. Nature protection in South Africa was growing in national importance, and notions that wildlife was an asset, and an aesthetic or cultural 'heritage' rather than a marketable commodity, were fast gaining ground among whites. By contrast, new conservationist ideology had not yet penetrated into the southern Sudan. There were still great expanses of state land which supported large herds of elephant, and sustainable exploitation (which was motivated by the revenue which ivory yielded) rather than protection remained the dominant philosophy. Governmental support for game protection was far less in the Sudan than it was in South Africa, where the prime minister's office was well disposed towards the programme and where it was, indeed, in the forefront of fresh initiatives despite the war. In the Sudan, in 1914, when A.L. Butler retired from the Game Preservation Department, he was not replaced: wildlife preservation became moribund and the department was subsumed into the Forestry Department.

However, despite a low local profile, the international protectionist fraternity recognised the contribution which Stevenson-Hamilton could make while he was in the southern Sudan. He had been out of South Africa for so long that – just as he had done in 1910 – he began to consider the possibility of leaving. The Transvaal provincial authorities had been in touch with him wanting confirmation that once the war was over he would return to his duties. Again he was being given a choice and, as always, he began to worry about what course of action he should take. He was suspicious of the approach by the province. Was it part of a plot to get him to resign, he wondered, thus absolving themselves of the responsibility to pay out a pension? He felt that they were insensitive to the fact that a war was on, and that he certainly could not return until he was officially demobilised. But he admitted that he was uncertain about what he should do.

He hankered after South Africa, and felt that he preferred it to Britain. He also needed the income as things would be financially difficult in post-war Britain. From his friends in South Africa he heard about the rising tide of Afrikaner nationalism and feared for his position as warden of the game reserves if such Afrikaners were to become politically more powerful. He had also been told by Wolhuter how inefficiently Fraser, the acting warden of the reserves, was running them and wondered whether he was up to the task of rectifying years of incompetent administration. To complicate his decision further, there were aspects of Sudanese administration that he really enjoyed. In addition, he felt that he was appreciated, to the extent that he toyed with the idea of remaining in North Africa. However, he put off any final decision and wrote a 'non-committal answer' to his Transvaal employers.[11] In 1919 the Zoological Society of London supported his tentative plan to stay on in the southern Sudan as game warden. Of special interest at the time was Stevenson-Hamilton's innovative scheme to make the enterprise self-funding and less dependent on state money and control.

He also had ideas about policing the ivory trade, the corrupting power of which he had personally experienced. While in the Sudan, he worked on an article which appeared (using the obvious *nom de plume* 'Sabi') in 1921 in the *Journal of the Preservation of the Fauna of the Empire*, under the title, 'The preservation of the African elephant'. Blaming Europeans for the elephant slaughter, he recognised the role that the 1900 Convention had played in assuaging consciences and trying to regulate elephant destruction. But he did not hesitate to criticise the British colonies in Africa for upholding protectionist laws only when convenient for them, and for using ivory extraction as a political tool. He spoke out strongly against unsporting and cruel methods of killing these 'formidable denizens', particularly the method of 'ring-fencing'. He predicted that the uncontrolled greed for ivory, facilitated by official neglect and avarice, would result in the extinction of the elephant in Africa. His proposal was to 'impede', if not actually 'fend off this destruction' by adequate and well-policed elephant sanctuaries, by regulating the size of slaughtered elephant and by closely monitoring licences. And he had learnt at first hand the vagaries of official attitudes towards licences. He advocated that ivory extraction should be an international issue and managed at imperial, not local, level.

As he did when engaged with the Dinka and Nuer clans, Stevenson-Hamilton tried to find out everything he could about the various forms of wildlife in the Sudan and to study them closely. He always had his field glasses and natural history books at hand. He was sure that he found a genet which was different from the South African species, and was fascinated by the bats, which came pouring out by the hundreds from holes in the trees on some of the *duks*. He even undertook some experiments to see how much movement or colour was required before an antelope would take notice. He tried to find out more about the vegetation and wrote to the Director of Woods and Forests in Khartoum, giving a list of the trees around Bor. He sent specimens, described what grew in the region, provided him with the Arabic or Dinka names, and asked for genus, species and English names. Soon he was suggesting to Khartoum that part of Bor – a strip of about fifty kilometres on either side of the river – be made into a game reserve. This suggestion impressed Sir Lee Stack, then Governor-General, and he promised to support the proclamation of a 'preserve, whatever that is – it sounds like jam'.

Stevenson-Hamilton had agreed to continue in his post when the war ended but by early 1919 he had changed his mind. His district had been well run and he had enjoyed the work, but there were rumours that the Temporary Inspectors were to be replaced by permanent staff, and he did not want to apply for such a post. In addition, his recurring bouts of malaria were wearing him down and although it was tempting to remain, it was really time to pursue something else. His decision to leave the Sudan may possibly have been affected by the rebellion in Egypt in March 1919. When the Egyptians realised that their protectorate status would be extended after the war and their dissatisfactions were not redressed, violence erupted. There were signs even after peace had been restored that the disputes had not been settled and that another revolution, perhaps one including the Sudan, was imminent. Having survived the First World War so unhappily, James may well have wanted to avoid getting involved in another conflict. In February 1919 Stevenson-Hamilton informed his superior that he wanted to go on leave for three months from June and then retire from the Sudan Government Service and the Egyptian army. When the news got out, he received some excellent testimonials and letters attesting to his abilities. This seems to have pleased him, for the documents are tucked into his journals.

Stevenson-Hamilton's homecoming was dismal. A general strike on all the British railways was paralysing rail transport and this made getting to London difficult. It also reminded him of the growth of socialism and the erosion of the power of families like his own. Once in the capital city, he returned to his lodgings at 35 Duke Street, only to find that they had been converted into offices and that

> Old Weeks, the landlord, left bags and baggage in February taking all my stuff with him and leaving no address. So here I am stranded in

this filthy climate, no clothes except the tropical ones I am wearing. Cannot write to anyone as no postal service at present. Hyde Park given over to food distribution. What a country! . . . Everything has gone wrong, whether in public matters or private affairs. [The] Rag has no sugar and no rolls. There are fewer newspapers than at the Turf Club in Cairo. Awful prices, 1/3 for a whisky and soda, 1/- for a cocktail.

Worse still, the Cavalry Club, the 'Rag', itself was very changed. 'A *lady* secretary!', James exclaimed. Service was slack, and his suitcase was mislaid through inefficiency.

He went to investigate his pension and war gratuity, finding that 'it all takes a long time'. He received a depressing letter from the Sudan which intimated that the revival of the Game Preservation Department was unlikely because of the cost involved. Disappointed at the news, Stevenson-Hamilton thought it perhaps best to return to South Africa and 'to carry on there, meantime putting in an application for Game Preservation in Sudan when vacant. Sudan more interesting than South Africa and closer to England.' But he soon had second thoughts about being closer to England, writing, even after the strike was over, that it is 'a disgusting country to live in nowadays. Cold, bleak, uncomfortable and expensive.' The only highlight was his visit to Ashfold to see Helen Lindsay-Smith again: 'She is now about 48. Wearing wonderfully. Better than her 30-year-old daughter. She's an absolute marvel. I have known her for 28 years.'

James was always at his worst when trying to make up his mind. After the war many people were unsettled and many careers had been disturbed, and Stevenson-Hamilton was a case in point. He had a number of choices and to all of them he could adduce arguments for and against. He could have returned to South Africa, but he had had a long break from the Sabi Game Reserve and now that Olmar had died, he was anxious not to neglect his father. Remaining in Britain would have enabled him to care better for family interests, and in fact he tried hard to find something in Britain to further his wildlife career. He went down to Tring to admire Rothschild's excellent zoo and spent a great deal of time at Rowland Ward. Perhaps there was employment for him in that line? He gave a talk at the London Zoo on conditions in the southern Sudan and a lecture at the Royal Geographical Society, and lunched with Buxton, the leading preservationist, then 'close on eighty, but good'. But when he talked about southern Africa to Edward Pennefather, his old friend from Pietermaritzburg days, he was tempted back into some kind of military life. 'I manage things badly,' he complained. 'Allenby seems to think highly of me, and I am leaving just as he takes over.'

One unpleasant family task in London was to sort out Olmar's will. There had been a son, Vivian, who had been born of the marriage between Olmar and Gwladys. Because this boy was now the only Hamilton heir, James felt a double responsibility for him. James insisted that he would only pay for Olmar's son's education if his mother, Gwladys (then living with Alan Campbell Ross, her second husband) had nothing whatever to do with her son and gave up her role as joint guardian. As she did not contest this arrangement, she seems to have been happy with the idea of losing her only child. James thus agreed to care for Vivian and to educate him in a suitable manner. Quite unused to children, James tried to get to know young Vivian and to take an interest in his welfare and his future. He went to meet the child, who was then 12 years of age, at Houghton House near Carlisle. Vivian was staying there with the hospitable Margaret Broadhurst, a widow who had lived in India and whose large house provided a sanctuary for a number of children whose parents were abroad. A week or so later, he went to Stancliffe Hall, Vivian's school, and afterwards wrote: 'Vivian came in later. Like Olmar, rather nervous, not quite a stammer. Thankful to see little of his mother [Gwladys]. Clarke says thick mentally, but works... glad I saw the boy, am much pleased with him, though he is no "smasher".' A few weeks later he saw Vivian again at Houghton House and tried to be a good uncle by playing soldiers with the child. He does not record what happened or what the youngster did, but by 3 January he had concluded that 'Vivian is not a good egg.'

James also went up to Scotland, and on 31 October he visited Fairholm. He recorded: 'Trees grown up. Cannot see Larkhall. Awfully nice; long to be able to live there, but uncertain times...' He remained torn between his love of Fairholm and an equal love of South Africa. However, something had to be done about getting better value out of the Scottish properties, and Thomson, the family lawyer, advised selling Kirkton in order to obtain funds. The economy of Scotland was at this time extremely depressed but, while money and employment were in short supply, land still fetched good prices. But selling Kirkton would be 'epoch-making' as Stevenson-Hamilton put it, and his father was adamantly against it. Stevenson-Hamilton himself had reservations, but from Thomson he learnt that 'I have now a free income of only £700 per year. Cissy gets £400 and Olmar's boy about £200 for education. Obvious I cannot live here on £100 per annum. But don't like the idea of getting rid of Kirkton.' Other Scottish aristocrats took the opportunity of ridding themselves of property. On 8 November Stevenson-Hamilton visited Hamilton Palace which was about to be demolished; its contents would be auctioned by Christies.

Stevenson-Hamilton noted that the family pictures alone went for £52 000 and commented how 'Angus, late Duke, went through money. [Even] in 1882 many of the best things had to be sold.' It was a lesson in how not to conduct financial and family affairs.

Stevenson-Hamilton had returned to Britain only to find that everyone leant on him for support. Family, friends, and acquaintances all sought his help. The responsibilities were enormous, and there was no one who could understand what this meant for him. Sometimes this must have seemed like an intolerable burden. He spent Christmas at Kirkton with his father and Cissy and went again to Fairholm. It is 'a mess', he declared. 'Must find a tenant. Cissy is in trouble again. Seems I keep everyone going – as long as I am not married I can help family and friends.' His sister was a real problem. Without prospects, instead of befriending her brother, she lied to him and he told his journal that she was a 'bit touched' and that 'I am hurt by her abusing me.' Apparently she frequently took out her frustration on her elderly father and James even feared for the old man's safety because of her violent tempers.

It is hardly therefore surprising, given these depressing circumstances, that he finally decided to return to South Africa. Firstly, although he did not yet admit it openly, he could not stay away from the Sabi Game Reserve. He spoke of being 'bewitched' by it. It was his creation – perhaps the only great achievement he was truly proud of. In South Africa he not only had a secure job; he also enjoyed a considerable reputation, and his prospects were far brighter there than they were in Britain. And, of course, everything would be cheaper. In December he began to make arrangements to return to South Africa and negotiated the details of his back pay and his passage out.

# 10

# 'An Imperishable Monument'[1]
## Founding the Kruger National Park
## (1920–1930)

THE DECADE OF THE 1920s was probably the most significant and rewarding in James Stevenson-Hamilton's life. Professionally, the years were marked by the establishment of the Kruger National Park – that 'imperishable monument' as his American friend Dr William Hornaday, called it. But if James's outward life was satisfying, his inner life was a turmoil. He had reached the age of 55 in 1922 and was therefore nearing retirement. When he had returned to London from the Sudan at the end of 1919, it had struck him like a blow how much Britain had changed, but things in South Africa were also not the same after the end of the war. The 1920s saw alterations in the political scene and a rise of intolerant Afrikaner nationalism, developments which Stevenson-Hamilton viewed with alarm and despondency.

Although he wished it were otherwise, the wider socio-political scene had an impact on Stevenson-Hamilton. Having dedicated his creative endeavours to his game reserves, he strongly believed in their lasting worth. He began to think that the only way of entrenching their existence was to have the reserves taken out of the hands of the Transvaal Province (his own employer) and placed, with legal security by way of an Act of parliament, under the control of the national or central government. The issue got its first public airing in the Legislative Assembly of the Transvaal in 1907 when a member mentioned that the Transvaal game reserves could, one day, become like Yellowstone, the national park in the United States.[2] Stevenson-Hamilton was already thinking along the same lines, and he raised the matter with his Het Volk friend Eddie Rooth on 27 May 1909 when Union was under discussion. The journal records '[they are] prepared to make game reserves a national affair but I doubt if they will be able to . . . [it needs] Smuts to carry it through . . .' The achievement of this object must have been daunting to Stevenson-Hamilton because he generally avoided politics and politicians, and the prospect of garnering backing, of lobbying, of endless meetings and the idea of getting involved was anathema. But, he could also appreciate that all his efforts would be brought to nought if the game reserves were to be deproclaimed, a process which could be achieved with a mere notice in the *Provincial Gazette*.

After his period in the Sudan and five months thereafter in England, Stevenson-Hamilton was back in South Africa in March 1920 to resume his wardenship of the game reserves. He sailed from England to Cape Town and as he passed East London, he thought – as he always did – of his romance in 1888 with Hilda Browne. He never forgot her, and wrote of remembering that 'memorable parting 32 years ago as vividly as ever'. Perhaps it was the influence of those ancient romantic memories that stirred the following comment in his journal at the same time: 'Mrs Clarke on the ship. Could have made a fool of myself. Idle flirtation – she does attract me most awfully.' But he did not succumb to the charming Mrs Clarke and diligently spent his time on board typing out his South African War journal.

Back at Sabi Bridge his spirits lifted immediately and soon Britain and even Fairholm were far from his mind. At the end of March 1920, he wrote of the area, 'it does take hold of me more than anywhere I have ever been'. He seems not to have minded many of the matters which required his attention after an enforced absence of seven years. There were meetings in Pretoria and Johannesburg to acquaint himself with political changes, for Prime Minister Louis Botha had died in 1919 and had been replaced by Jan Smuts. He spoke to mining people, civil servants and friends in an effort to familiarise himself with what had happened in his absence.

Before long, Stevenson-Hamilton was settled back into the routine of game reserve life. There were plenty of files which required his attention, and piles of correspondence that needed answering. He felt these tasks to be more onerous than he remembered, perhaps, he mused, he was getting older, or perhaps the reconstruction after years of 'neglect' while he was away, was the problem. But his journals at this time are generally replete with the wonder of it all and a strong sense of joy in his surroundings. 'Weather and climate here is perfect. Sunshine and dry . . . the bougainvillaea is beautiful . . . a gorgeous day which one might well call perfection.'

While it was agreeable to be back in his favourite place on earth, there were some worrying elements. When Stevenson-Hamilton had left for the war, it was not at all clear that his reserves had a successful future. Certainly the idea of transforming the two reserves, the Sabi and Singwitsi, into a national park was gaining ground. Smuts was in favour, but his support was not sufficient on its own. In many quarters there was little enthusiasm for the retention of game reserves and even open hostility began to appear. Mining was followed by secondary industry and commercial farming, and South Africa was set on a course of becoming an industrial society in which game preserves had little place.

The Rustenburg Game Reserve was the first to go. Landowners had protested against it at the time it was proclaimed in 1909 for it included private land, but in the end the involvement of the warden, P.J. Riekert, in the 1914 Afrikaner rebellion, his unpopularity, dereliction of duty and ignorance ended the reserve's existence when a proclamation to this effect was published at the end of 1914.[3] The Pongola Game Reserve in the south-eastern Transvaal was also affected by the changing times. The Minister of Lands argued that using state land for settlement was a far higher national priority than the continued existence of an ineffective game reserve. And so, by Proclamation 1 of 1921, the life of the Pongola Game Reserve was ended. Game reserves were deproclaimed in the Transvaal, in Namaqualand in 1919, Gordonia-Kuruman in 1924, and Umfolozi in 1920.

Wildlife outside of game reserves received its worst blow in the 1920s. An outbreak of nagana (sleeping sickness) among the domestic stock in Natal – the only province in which wildlife was still abundant in the rural areas – evoked an over-reaction in the form of calls for the destruction of all wildlife in South Africa. Nagana had disappeared from the Transvaal and Natal with the outbreak of rinderpest in 1896, and leading entomologists had speculated that because so much wildlife had died from the rinderpest, it was the lack of a game host which had been the critical factor in eradicating the tsetse fly. When nagana recurred in Natal after an absence of more than a decade, the burgeoning numbers of wildlife within the Natal game reserves were held responsible.[4] The provincial and central governments provided finance and other resources to assist agriculturalists in culling almost all the wildlife of Zululand to curtail the nagana epidemic and massive slaughter occurred. In Swaziland, too, game reserves were abolished and there was wholesale extermination of all wildlife.

Even Stevenson-Hamilton's own game reserves were not free from attack. As Union loomed around 1910, Stevenson-Hamilton had been warned that wildlife protection would became a party political issue. He did not have to wait long. In 1911 neighbouring white farmers cast covetous eyes upon the grazing potential of the south-western part of the Sabi Game Reserve and they presented a petition to the new provincial council asking that this portion of the reserve be deproclaimed and opened for grazing.[5] Reluctant to alienate the farming vote and also mindful of the drought conditions which prevailed at the time, J.F.B. Rissik, the Administrator of the Transvaal, allowed the grazing concessions in the game reserve, although he did not countenance deproclamation. Stevenson-Hamilton spoke to Smuts about it – he was 'dead against Rissik's scheme of grazing' – but there was nothing that he could do.

A larger threat than permits for winter grazing came from the need to find new areas to settle white farmers. After Union the central government considered the Sabi Game Reserve for this purpose. The completion of the Selati railway line had given access to a part of the eastern Transvaal hitherto poorly served by communications, and in 1913 the Department of Lands (central government) asked the Transvaal provincial authorities to excise the portion of the game reserve adjacent to the railway line. Political rivalry between the national and provincial governments saved the day, and the province refused the request.[6] In 1916 the Department of Lands tried again, but was rebuffed once more.[7]

The avaricious Department of Mines was also staved off. This was another central government department which considered that the game reserves were merely 'sentimental objects' which were far too large.[8] The Department of Native Affairs entered the fray because the Natives Land Act of 1913 had been passed and land for 'native reserves' had become a priority. Before he left the country in 1914, Stevenson-Hamilton was successful in warding off these attempts to reduce or deproclaim the two reserves, and he actually had them extended. The Sabi and Singwitsi Game Reserves were not contiguous: the northern boundary of the Sabi Game Reserve being the Olifants River and the southern boundary of the Singwitsi Game Reserve being the Letaba River, there was thus a substantial gap between them. Although Stevenson-Hamilton had the authority to protect wildlife in the intervening region, the area did not formally become part of the reserves until the situation was rectified by proclamation in 1914.[9] While no doubt congratulating himself, at least on this achievement, Stevenson-Hamilton was well aware that nature itself seemed to be conspiring with the politicians against his reserve. Between 1912 and 1916 recurrent drought and the consequent lack of breeding habitats for the vectors of horse-sickness and malaria created the impression that game reserves were indeed agriculturally viable and not as 'worthless' as had originally been thought.

The only way to secure the long-term future of the reserves was through nationalising them. But how to go about it? In February 1913, Stevenson-Hamilton formally broached the subject with the Provincial Secretary of the Transvaal writing of a wholly state-owned, 'permanent game sanctuary'.[10] He also corresponded privately with the Administrator about the matter. He soon realised that there was a difficulty with mutual understanding of what a national park really was. That same year, 1913, his journal records:

> Rissik talked about not wanting to keep countless thousands of animals. None of those final arbiters know anything about it. They seem

to want a deer park, ignorant of the fact that wild animals without huge – not big, but huge – areas to exist in, will deteriorate and die off, besides which they lose their customs and become different animals and thus lose all their interest for science. I am about fed up.

While Stevenson-Hamilton was dealing with the Administrator of the Transvaal and the provincial council, it was imperative also to persuade the national government that the game reserves were worthy of national asset status. Moreover, as the owner of state land, a considerable amount of which comprised the game reserves, its own interests were directly affected. There were some encouraging signs. As early as 1914 the matter of national game reserves was being informally discussed at high levels of government. In May 1914, Smuts, then Minister of Finance and Defence, had asked to be kept informed of game conservation matters in the Transvaal[11] and in November he had written directly to Rissik:

> ... there appears to be a grave risk that the future of the Reserve may at any time be imperilled by the establishment of cattle ranching in that area ... it would be a thousand pities to endanger the existence of our South African fauna. It has been suggested that the best way of obtaining the object in view would be to constitute a portion of the existing reserve as a National Sanctuary on the lines of similar institutions which exist in the United States and in other parts of the world, and set it aside for all time for the purpose. ... If you agree generally with my views, I think the first course to adopt is to appoint an impartial commission to go over the ground ...[12]

Smuts was Stevenson-Hamilton's most important ally. But, the warden knew politicians were not to be relied upon because practical matters, particularly where voters and elections were concerned, often intervened. Something needed to be done to set the formal process in motion. It began with a debate on the question of a national park in the Transvaal Provincial Council in June 1913, when the member for Soutpansberg, T.J. Kleinenberg, announced that the 'the time has arrived when the Sabi and Singwitsi Game Reserves should be nationalized and that the Union government be urged to take the necessary steps to accomplish this'. At the time there was, however, no debate, nor was there again until 1915 when a motion was introduced in the council by S.H. Coetzee, the member for Lydenburg, asking the Administrator of the Transvaal to urge the Union government to reduce the area of the Sabi Game Reserve.[13]

While Stevenson-Hamilton was away at war he corresponded with a number of people in South Africa, and was therefore aware of what was going on. He heard that, on 6 April 1916, a Commission of Inquiry into the game reserve position had been appointed in line with Smuts's suggestion. When the commissioners began hearing evidence (their report was published in August 1918) the warden was not there to direct proceedings, but the Commission had access to his comprehensive reports and correspondence. News from South Africa in this regard was not encouraging. In April 1917, a letter from game ranger Harry Wolhuter warned Stevenson-Hamilton of the detrimental evidence given by a number of the farmers along the Crocodile River in the south whose crops were frequently ruined by marauding wildlife.

The most significant outcome of the Game Reserves Commission was on matters of protectionist philosophy. In this respect, the Commission was 'not a little struck by the uselessness of having these magnificent reserves merely for the *preservation* of the fauna', and advocated a different stance – in fact, the 'creation of the area ultimately as a great national park'. For the first time, the objectives of and arguments for a South African national park were provided and the Commission recommended that '. . . greater facilities should be offered to scientists, naturalists, and the general public to make themselves acquainted with a portion of their country which should be of the greatest natural interest' because of its wilderness, which 'owing to the advance of civilization, [is] now rapidly disappearing and must eventually disappear altogether'.[14] When Stevenson-Hamilton returned to South Africa the Commission's report had been published but no progress in the direction of a national park had been made.

As the warden settled back into his daily routine at Sabi Bridge, he was aware that poor administration might jeopardise the chances of nationalising the game reserve. Fraser, the warden of the Singwitsi, had been brought to Sabi Bridge to take charge while Stevenson-Hamilton was away at war and the reserves had been seriously neglected while in his care. Administrative matters were in a shambles, white staff had been reduced, and control over African staff and poachers had been lost. What little infrastructural development there was, by way of roads and buildings, had not been maintained. It was a chaotic situation. Stevenson-Hamilton's impression was that 'there has been a general retrogression, bringing the state of things now obtaining back to about the position occupied in 1904'.[15]

The warden was unfortunate in not receiving very much help from the game rangers in his employ. Of the old guard, only the hard-drinking Duke was a comfort, 'I always feel well when he is here . . . [It is] a pleasure

*In this posed portrait Sergeant Judas Ndlovu apprehends an armed poacher.*

to talk to him when he is sober.' He also liked De Laporte, for at least he accepted responsibility and was an efficient acting warden. He missed Healy, killed in East Africa, who, despite the problems of his private life, could be relied upon for support. There was also Harry Wolhuter of whom James later became really fond, recognising his outstanding qualities of hospitality, gentleness and loyalty. But in the 1920s the relationship was not close, and

Stevenson-Hamilton was critical of Wolhuter's avoidance of responsibility, accusing him of paying too much attention to his own farming practices. And when Wolhuter was ever obliged to help he left things in a 'proper muddle'. Stevenson-Hamilton also felt alienated from Wolhuter who, with the fervour of the 1920s and the rise of Afrikaner feeling, admitted to his boss that he was 'three parts Dutch – he doesn't think it necessary to be English any longer'.

While Stevenson-Hamilton had been absent, four new rangers were appointed. For the first time two of them were Afrikaans and all were a different calibre of person from those he had appointed in earlier years – young adventurous people of British or colonial military background. Despite their foibles, the old rangers could be trusted, the new ones could not. In the north was J.J. 'Kat' Coetzer who had replaced Fraser when he had retired in 1920. Stevenson-Hamilton did not like Coetzer from the start. Not only was he a 'gasbag' who fabricated stories about his past, but he had left his previous employment with the Department of Native Affairs 'under a cloud'. Piet de Jager, stationed at Rolle, was no better, 'swindling the African police', noted Stevenson-Hamilton. Then there were rangers Brent and H. Brake. Brake was 'no good . . . only worse and as nervy as Brent'. Brake's case was sufficiently serious to be brought up before the powers in Pretoria. 'There must be good men somewhere', lamented the warden. Stevenson-Hamilton was cautioned about his employment of L.H. Ledeboer in 1921, the person who had been responsible for the establishment of the Singwitsi Game Reserve in 1903 and who once knew all the famous old hunters in the Transvaal before joining the notorious Bushveld Carbineers during the South African War. 'I think a good choice', wrote James, 'Neergard, the Witwatersrand Native Labour Association official says a bit lazy, but does not drink.'

It is probably not surprising that the quality of ranger personnel was so low, for theirs was a hard life. When Ledeboer contracted pneumonia, Stevenson-Hamilton described how, in a leaky hut, Ledeboer's wife had to nurse her husband as well as look after her sick baby. There was no hope of getting any medical attention, nor even the most ordinary invalid comforts. Ledeboer recovered, but ranger William Lloyd, 'a regular little wild man of the woods' did not. He died in November 1922. And yet, despite these hardships and dangers, the job of game ranger was then, as it is now, very much sought after. To many people it seemed adventurous and exciting to live among wildlife and the duties of patrolling one's 'section' and managing a small African staff did not appear to be onerous or demanding. In March 1923, there were 241 applications for one vacant post, 'Mostly duds, poor whites and biltong hunters. About ten outstanding.'

There were wider problems which claimed Stevenson-Hamilton's attention. On his return in March 1920 he was faced with different conditions in South Africa from those he had left in 1914. As soon as he got off the ship in Cape Town he heard 'gloomy stories' about the changed political situation and how the country was 'rapidly being "dutchified"'. A general election was held in the month that he arrived back which, with the greatly increased Afrikaner power which was recorded in the votes, changed the face of South African politics irrevocably. The Nationalist Party under the leadership of J.B.M. Hertzog won the majority of seats in the House of Assembly (44), obliging Jan Smuts and his South African Party with only 41 seats to rely on support from the fiercely pro-imperial Unionists.

The reason for the electoral upset had much to do with the strong imperial connection which Stevenson-Hamilton and many others valued so highly. After Botha's death, Smuts had replaced him as prime minister and there had been growing political tension between Smuts and the Afrikaners. Smuts's role at the Treaty of Versailles and in founding the League of Nations had drawn admiration in Europe and in Britain and among the English-speakers and British population in South Africa, but it was not seen as something to be proud of among Afrikaners. Smuts's imperial work had alienated them and they strongly believed that the time had come to cut South Africa's ties with Britain and to fight for self-government. These developments led to increased tension within South Africa – 'racial tension' as it was referred to at the time.

With the growing power of the Afrikaners, Stevenson-Hamilton feared that the 'biltong hunters' in the Transvaal Provincial Council would abolish the reserves and thus end any progress that had been made towards garnering support for a national park. But as well as Stevenson-Hamilton, major catalysts in pushing the national park process forward were the land companies which had allowed their lowveld farms to be included in the game reserve area in 1903. As time passed and circumstances changed, these owners argued that they could not exploit the value of their farms because they had signed agreements with the game reserve authorities giving up their hunting rights. The contracts between the Transvaal colony and the landowners had initially covered a five-year period and were extended for a further five years in 1908. After the expiry date of 31 March 1913, the contracts were renewed for just one year, during which time the province promised to formulate a definite policy as far as the future of the reserves was concerned.[16]

But even two years later the province had done nothing in this regard, and the Transvaal Land Owners Association suggested that a way around the problem would be to arrange an exchange of land with the government so that the farms in the reserve would revert to the state and the game reserve, in consequence, could become wholly state-owned.[17] But as talk of creating a national park increased, the companies were adamant that they would not be donating their farms to the government for this purpose, but would hold out for the highest possible price on them.[18] In terms of the game reserve legislation they could make use of their farms, but not kill any game on them. The companies argued that the presence of wild animals made it impossible to use the farms, for the antelope would eat any planted crop, and lion and other predators would kill any livestock. But Stevenson-Hamilton and others realised that the area was totally unsuitable for crops or ranching, and that the companies were merely trying to hold the government to ransom.

When he returned in 1920, Stevenson-Hamilton spent a great deal of time visiting Pretoria, lobbying the provincial authorities, meeting with the various national government departments and generally trying to speed things along. Together with the land companies, there were other interests which needed to be taken account of, and it seemed a wise course of action to have a full and public discussion of the matter. Towards the end of 1920 the warden met senior government officials, and the Secretary for Lands introduced him to Deneys Reitz, another Boer fighter from the South African War, then Minister of Lands – 'an excellent fellow – sympathetic', recorded Stevenson-Hamilton.

A round-table conference to try to agree on a strategic plan of action was held on 25 February 1921. There was no opposition to the idea of a national park. But, if there was general agreement in principle there was considerable dissension when it came to practical matters, in particular, how large this national park should be. Most debate revolved around whether the Sabi Game Reserve, the southern reserve which was being hemmed in by commercial farming and a growing local African population, should be reduced. Even Stevenson-Hamilton conceded that the western part of the Sabi Game Reserve could be taken over by the Department of Native Affairs, there being 'no great objection from a game preservation point of view',[19] although he subsequently confided to his journal that 'I cannot bear to contemplate it.' Ultimately, the conclusion reached by the meeting was that a considerable amount of land in the western Sabi Game Reserve would be excised, much of it for Africans to settle on. But a further advantage would be that many of the private farms that had hitherto been part of the reserve would be excluded, thus reducing the number of exchanges or sales which the government would have to pay for. It was also agreed that the Department of Lands would negotiate to acquire all the remaining privately owned land in the reserve.

No sooner had Stevenson-Hamilton got to grips again with his game reserve affairs, sorted things out, and become up to date on administrative issues, than he returned to the Sudan. Before he left he had committed himself to going back to draw up game legislation for that colony. The reason Stevenson-Hamilton had accepted this task was that he did not realise just how entranced he would again become with the Sabi Reserve and had wanted to keep his options open. Typically, he could not decide what to do. His mind went back and forth over the problem. All of 1921 he mulled over where his future lay. He was worried that the national park project might not succeed in the face of land company demands. He poured his heart out, as always, in his journal: 'I am absolutely down to zero again about going away. The longer one stops, the harder it is . . . [Here I am] happy and busy and sheltered from all the horrid things that make the world so unhappy at the present.' As it often did, the crisis of decision-making brought forth cogitations on what he had done with his life. Had it all been worthwhile? With hindsight, he thought he could see what had gone wrong at every turn and his lack of confidence returned. 'I feel I haven't climbed in the world like my contemporaries. The Sabi "witched" me away from the world. The Sabi is a courtesan and her delight kept me in dalliance so that I never climbed as I might have done . . . now I am too old . . .'

Probably for the first time in his life, he had someone to share his thoughts and worries with, for his half-sister Adela, with whom he had become acquainted in Cairo during the war, was in the Sabi Game Reserve on a visit in the first half of 1921. Adela needed a change from life in Britain and a housekeeper was needed at Sabi Bridge. It was not often that the warden had guests to stay, and his usual routine was 'early to bed and early to rise'. Visitors were a pleasant interlude. On one occasion when a visitor who had been a Corporal in the north-west Canadian mounted police at Klondyke told amusing stories and they listened to the phonograph, they stayed up all night, fortifying themselves with coffee and hot soup. 'I never dreamed that I should see the day when I would sit up all night at Sabi Bridge!' was the warden's response.

Adela's company was not as convivial, and the journal is full of Stevenson-Hamilton letting off steam about her, for he could not allow her to see his frustration and annoyance. The journal entries begin rather mildly, 'Adela seems to feel the heat. A quaint person and thinks herself a man-hater – most amusing.' But soon the comments have a great deal more force: 'Charm of the old life completely gone now. I found it mainly in the liberty which one has from being alone . . . Women are very selfish but the worst is they are unaware of it. They think they are helping, but they're a damn nuisance.' The brother tried to interest her in hunting, and she proved proficient at shooting francolin and guinea-fowl. She even shot a lion. But her presence hampered the warden's work. To cap it all, she lost her diamond tie-pin in the veld. He was, however, beginning to see what the problem was and to become more understanding by May. 'She would like to be a mother really. Afraid of men, that's why she persuades herself that she dislikes and abuses them.'

Perhaps he did her a disservice describing her in this way, for it was indeed a rare well-bred young woman at the time to be out hunting lions, diamond tie-pin primly in place. His opinion of her certainly improved when he discussed the Sudan dilemma with her. He carefully explained that it was being said that it was 'a pity I intend going just at the time of the nature sanctuary being established, but this is more and more in the dim and distant future. In any event, it will be emasculated and small.' He was amazed when he told Adela about his difficulties that 'she gave me quite a sound opinion'. They continued to talk along these lines, and by the end of June, James was confessing 'I have an admiration for her character now that I know her.'

It was at this juncture that Stevenson-Hamilton left the Transvaal to spend his leave in the Sudan drawing up game legislation as he had agreed to do in 1919. It crossed his mind once more that he should make his future there rather than in South Africa. He arrived at the end of 1921 and just weeks later he had had enough. This time he was not stationed in the southern Sudan but in Khartoum with the designation 'Superintendent Game Preservation Department'. He did not arrive with a particularly good grace, 'My first impression is that I don't like the place and that the work will not be quite in my line.' Just the following day he wrote, 'I see now I made a bad mistake coming here. It is more than an anticlimax.... This place is the limit. I am bored to tears and wish I hadn't come.' But he wanted to do justice to his project – 'A reputation matters.'

He had done what he had been asked to do by way of new legislation at the end of December and prepared to leave. He was not sorry to go. He had three months' leave in Britain and, reading his journal of that time, one can well appreciate why South Africa was so alluring. Only a few days after arriving in Britain he was in the thick of family affairs. His father was ageing, his sister was a great problem and there was Vivian, Olmar's son, then 14, who was not turning out as well as Stevenson-Hamilton had wished. In Scotland that February, he had the usual meeting with the family solicitor, who took a 'dim view of the future'. Fairholm, his precious house, was also little source of joy, although it was 'not so bad considering that no one has been living there for the past year'. But the roof leaked and the 'trees do not hide the awful village of Larkhall'. Stevenson-Hamilton needed to think about a possible future for himself in Britain. It was clear that once he was sixty, even if not before, he would have to retire, and he would have to make a change. One possibility which presented itself was that he should return eventually to London to run the Zoological Society and this was discussed. But his heart was not in it, and he concluded that it is 'a bore wanting to be in two places at once'.

By March 1922, when Stevenson-Hamilton returned to South Africa from the Sudan and his period of leave in Britain, the national parks issue was still unresolved. The warden was despondent that while the various government departments were beginning to reach agreement and prominent politicians were buying into the scheme, things were being protracted by the greediness of the land companies. By 1922 the major role-player was the Transvaal Consolidated Lands Company which had by then bought out most of the other landowners in the Sabi Game Reserve. Matters came to a head when the Company appointed a manager, A.J. Crosby, and instructed him to plant crops and maintain a livestock herd in order to force the government into action. He was also told to 'begin shooting the game as a test of rights'. This he did, right in front of Stevenson-Hamilton with whom he was on good terms. The warden reported him and a summons was issued for illegal destruction of game and a court case ensued.

It is not clear whether this case had anything to do with it, but by November 1922 a compromise between the government and land companies seemed assured. Prime Minister Smuts then announced his firm intention of introducing legislation for the establishment of 'a National Park and Game Reserve' during the parliamentary session early in 1923.[20] By then so great had the difficulties in connection with the eastern Transvaal game reserves become for the government that the more ambitious scheme Smuts's government had at the time to start a number of national parks throughout the country – the Kalahari, Addo in the eastern Cape, Zululand, the Drakensberg and the Orange Free State – was shelved as being too contentious to put before parliament.[21]

Throughout 1922 Stevenson-Hamilton had had a foreboding that the national park would never happen and that his reserves would be abandoned and sunk into the history of South Africa without trace. He was in a difficult position. He was not a full-time lobbyist who could spend extended periods softening up the politicians to his view. His primary function was to run his reserve, and it required a great deal of attention after its wartime neglect. He was out of communication much of the time. Occasionally a rumour made its way to the game reserve, only to worry him all the more. In addition, he was hamstrung by the fact that he was a civil servant of the provincial government, and in this capacity not permitted to speak publicly on political matters (which is what the national park issue was) nor to get involved in national legislation or show support for any national political cause.

He was therefore obliged to work behind the scenes, writing letters, attending meetings when he could, speaking privately to people to try to win them over to his point of view. In June 1922 he wrote a long memorandum to Reitz, the Minister of Lands, explaining to him the ideal of making the game reserves like the Yellowstone National Park of the United States. Reitz seems to have been impressed by Stevenson-Hamilton's thinking and legislation was prepared in draft form. By 9 December Stevenson-Hamilton believed that the 'National park idea will go through, but under provincial council.' He was, of course, wrong, for by then the land companies had become obdurate and the whole process of an on-site land inspection was needed.

The year 1923 began on a depressing note. All the efforts of the past few years seemed to be in vain. The politicians were immobilised by the land companies and, in addition, the government was afraid of the considerable opposition which the introduction of the Bill would excite in parliament. Were draft legislation to be thrown out at the start of the debate, they knew that reintroduction at a later stage would be impossible. Politically, 1923 was a momentous year in South Africa. In April, Hertzog's National Party entered into a formal electoral pact with the Labour Party and the real fear existed – correctly as it turned out – that in the next election Smuts would be out of power. His popularity among important sectors of the South African public was waning in these years and his violent solutions to the Bondelswarts Rebellion in 1921, Bulhoek, and the Rand Strike of 1922 destroyed his reputation in certain quarters. For much of 1923 the government was emasculated and the national park issue, never a top priority, was given scant attention.

In that year the South African Railways began operating a tourist service called the 'Round-in-Nine'. Over a period of nine days, various points of scenic or historical interest around the country were visited. Part of the railway route went through the game reserves on the Selati Line and Stevenson-Hamilton persuaded the railway authorities to make a stop for a short while:

> I don't think anyone was more surprised than the railway authorities when they discovered at the conclusion of the first tour that the short halt in the game reserve was, to the majority of the passengers – mainly townspeople from Johannesburg – by far the most interesting and exciting part of the whole trip. Later it was agreed that more time in the reserve should be spent by the tourist train, and it was further arranged that a ranger should travel on it, and at each halt take the passengers for a little walk in the bush. The camp-fires, too, became a great attraction; the people sat round the huge blaze, alternately singing choruses and shivering with delight at the idea of being watched, from the dark bush close at hand, by the hungry eyes of beasts of prey . . .

All this was grist to the publicity mill which was needed in order to persuade parliament that a national park would be welcomed by voters. At the end of 1923 the western game reserve land was transferred from the reserve to the Department of Native Affairs. Stevenson-Hamilton lost a large piece of the Sabi Game Reserve, and although he hated the idea he felt it was in a good cause as it would facilitate the introduction of legislation in the 1924 parliamentary session.

His regular allocation of three months' home leave to Britain – December 1923 to March 1924 – came at a bad time. It was a tense period as far as the national park issue was concerned and he was still unsure of what to do with his life once the status of the park had been settled. He was, after all, almost sixty and retirement loomed. So he set out for Britain with a heavy heart. But aboard the *Windsor Castle* his spirits lifted because it was one of the happiest voyages to England he had had in years. Two attractive women took him under their wings and he enjoyed the attention immensely. One was Princess Marie Louise, granddaughter of Queen Victoria, and the other was Mrs Frances Ingram of Cape Town. In London Stevenson-Hamilton kept up the acquaintance with the Princess, who invited the warden to dine with her at her home. 'If anyone a month ago had told me I should be driving a Royal Princess about London alone!' he exclaimed to his journal. He was flattered by her attention: she even remembered to send him a 'valedictory wire' before he returned to South Africa and he confided to his journal, 'I really like her very much now I am used to trotting around with royalty! . . . Really, I do think the lady rather likes me!'

But he was in Britain for a more serious purpose than 'trotting around with royalty', enjoyable though it was. He needed to try to find suitable employment when the game reserve was eventually nationalised and his job terminated either by retirement or his replacement by another official appointed by the Union government which would succeed the province as the controlling authority. The most likely work prospect in his retirement was the joint secretaryship of the Zoological Society of London and the Fauna Society, the renamed Society for the Protection of the Wild Fauna of the Empire which Buxton had founded in the early years of the century and which was still going strong. The committee was putting pressure on him to give a definite date and, of course, James did not want to commit himself, not knowing when the national park might see the light of day. He certainly did not want to leave South Africa before the matter was finalised because he knew how helpful he could be to the national park effort and it would consolidate for posterity all the work he had put into getting the game reserves onto a sound footing since 1902. But later he accepted the London position, having been persuaded at a committee meeting which he attended. He was not really looking forward to the job and lamented that it would be more attractive, 'if I were only married to someone suitable'.

If future employment was one matter seemingly tied up satisfactorily; his family was a far greater hurdle. His cousin, Mary de Segundo, daughter of his mother's younger sister, Anne, felt sorry for him, 'How I wish you had a nice wife', she wrote around this time, reminding him in this letter that Cissy was 'hopeless, all her time spent on self-pity. I suppose you, Gracie [Mary's sister] and I are the only ones who really love Fairholm.' And love it he did. He visited the house with his father on 29 December while snow lay deep on the ground. What would become of Fairholm in the future he wondered? 'Vivian has no interest in it. Of course, I ought to be married and have children. It is a dear place, every nook is familiar.' On this visit, Stevenson-Hamilton came to realise that his sister was mentally unstable, abusing her father and threatening him with violence. There was nothing for it: Cissy was removed by the local doctor to a mental asylum. Soon the son pronounced, 'The Colonel is looking better.' They went to the Hamilton parish church together, looked at the Fairholm family graves and spoke about happier times and precious people of the past.

When he returned to South Africa bad news awaited him. The Nationalists had won the general election and there was a new Minister of Lands, Piet Grobler. But while Stevenson-Hamilton was delighted to learn that Grobler was keen to continue the work of the previous government as regards a national park, there was another problem: 'Percy [Greathead] has beaten us.' There it was – the land companies had wrecked the scheme. Years of effort had been wasted.

In time, Stevenson-Hamilton came to believe that the land companies' delaying tactics may have been for the best. At the time he was devastated, but in *South African Eden* he explained the situation as follows:

> There had not yet been nearly enough propaganda in the country and the public was far from being awakened. I feel pretty certain indeed that had the Act then gone to parliament, it would have emerged in so mutilated a form as to be not fully effective for its purpose. The whole thing had been pushed on in a hurry, largely on the enthusiasm of the minister concerned [Deneys Reitz], and there had been no time, by a widespread press campaign, to get the politicians and the public into the right frame of mind.

Stevenson-Hamilton was pleasantly surprised when he called on Piet Grobler towards the end of 1924 to find that he strongly believed in the national park scheme. But it was certainly ironic that as 'a Britisher' who was fearing for his future in an Afrikaner-dominated South Africa, Stevenson-Hamilton should find an ally in a grandnephew of President Kruger. Grobler and other National Party politicians were able to utilise the national park for their own ends and thus took up the idea with enthusiasm. While Smuts, Reitz and others had come to the national park idea as naturalists or sportsmen, Grobler and his party favoured the national park for what it would do for Afrikaner nationalism. The election platform of the National Party was the promotion of Afrikaner interests and values. Soon, Afrikaans rather than Dutch would be recognised as an official language. South Africa would get a new flag to replace the Union Jack, a new anthem instead of 'God Save the King', and the constitutional link with Britain would be re-evaluated in favour of more South African independence. Soon Afrikaner culture was being promoted and Voortrekker leaders were elevated to the status of national heroes, as were the presidents of the former Boer Republics and their republican sentiments were being revived.

Thus the foundation of the national park took place at the same time as clear demonstrations of an aggressive, though perhaps still nascent, Afrikaner nationalism, and a search for a white South African national identity. National parks in other parts of the world – the United States and Australia for example – also came into being for reasons related to the promotion of national feeling.[22] Indeed, national parks appear to be connected to a certain stage in a country's cultural evolution and serve to weld together different groups within it. That this is true of South Africa in the mid-1920s can be seen in the groping for a common identity between English-speaking and Afrikaans-speaking whites. Their collaborative creation of a national park

*Advertising poster for the Kruger National Park designed by Harry Stratford Caldecott.*
*(The poster reads: Accompany South African Railways to the Transvaal Game Reserve: the most unique sanctuary for wildlife in the world. Visit your national park.)*

played a role in the process of unifying these two culturally different, but economically converging, groups.

As soon as he came to appreciate that the new government would not destroy the national park initiative, Stevenson-Hamilton continued his efforts to bring the scheme to fruition. He could do nothing personally about the land company negotiations but Grobler did. Although concerned that compensation money was a problem, Grobler took a firm stand and managed to locate enough suitable unoccupied land in the Transvaal which the owners accepted in exchange for the game reserve farms at the end of 1925. It may well have been that the landowning companies realised that the Pact government, with its lack of sympathy for Johannesburg business interests, would not negotiate any further and that expropriation was a possibility. It has also been suggested that some land companies, particularly the Transvaal Consolidated Lands Company, were disillusioned with the Smuts government and happier to co-operate with the National Party.[23]

Where Stevenson-Hamilton could make a contribution was in the campaign to change public opinion in favour of wildlife protection and national parks. He had already done much to educate the public through his book, his many articles, and his willingness to assist journalists and other writers with material about wildlife and the game reserves. In August 1925, however, he met the ideal partner in the publicity venture, the artist Harry Stratford Caldecott, a South African, but Paris-trained landscape artist of merit. In August 1925 Caldecott visited the warden at Sabi Bridge on an assignment from the South African Railways to paint posters to advertise the 'Round-in-Nine' tours. The two men liked each other at once. They had the same intellectual interests, they played chess and spoke about interesting subjects – and began a friendship which lasted until Caldecott's untimely death a few years later.

Caldecott, almost single-handedly, orchestrated a massive national press and publicity campaign in order to consolidate public opinion on the side of the national park. If anything, his efforts erred on the side of idealistic over-enthusiasm, and Stevenson-Hamilton at one time warned him not to 'exaggerate too much' or people would tire of the propaganda and actually be repulsed.[24] Once started, however, publicity was self-generating.

What the new park would be called became a priority as the popularity of the idea grew. Stevenson-Hamilton said that it was Caldecott who came up with the idea of calling it after Paul Kruger. In *South African Eden* he was diplomatic in his recall:

> We were talking of the early beginnings of the reserve and I was show-

ing him a copy of the first proclamation of 1898 signed by President Kruger. He looked hard at me and 'catching on', I said at once, 'Of course you are right, that is the obvious name – "The Kruger National Park"!' Few would be willing to oppose the founding of an institution linked with the name of the great president and one felt that much of any possible opposition would thus automatically collapse.

In December 1925 Stevenson-Hamilton wrote to H.B. Papenfus, a Transvaal politician whom he was later to know very well as a member of the National Parks Board, that the 'Kruger National Park' would be an excellent name 'and would carry an atmosphere with it [that was] attractive and highly popular'. He asked whether this suggestion could be relayed to Grobler.[25] Privately, Stevenson-Hamilton was less tactful and he wrote the following to Caldecott in a letter: 'The man who *really* was responsible was R.K. Loveday ... but the "Kruger stunt" is I think of priceless value to us, and I would not for the world do aught but whisper otherwise...'[26]

A few years later, in writing to his friend Abel Chapman, who had in 1901 been the first to suggest that the entire eastern Transvaal boundary would make a suitably large game reserve, Stevenson-Hamilton expressed his regrets that Chapman's name was neglected. Chapman replied:

> Never you worry, my boy, that they cut out my name... it was, indeed, a 'brain-wave' of yours to put old Kruger first and foremost and keep the Rui-nek [Red neck – Briton] in the background. Besides, neither you nor I seek kudos – all we want in this world is to safeguard our dear old friends the wild beasts – and that, by Jove, you've done more effectually than any man living or dead.[27]

Chapman was, of course, correct. All Stevenson-Hamilton wanted was that the national park come into existence, never mind what it was called. In fact, the political ploy worked well to gain the support of 'poor whites', landless rural Afrikaners, in particular. Not all, however, were as pleased with the opportunistic suggestion and the 'South African National Park', or even the 'National Milner Park' were suggested instead. As a relative of Paul Kruger, Grobler had no reservations about the name (indeed, it was politically advantageous to him).[28] Invoking the name of the president certainly touched the right emotional chord at the right time.

On 30 May 1926, the National Parks Bill passed its first reading and was drafted into law on 11 June. Stevenson-Hamilton's journal that day – he was in Pretoria – reads as follows:

## 'An Imperishable Monument'

*Unveiling the plaque to Paul Kruger (1933). Piet Grobler is speaking and Hilda Stevenson-Hamilton (who married James in 1930) stands in front of the South African flag.*

Cross called up from the office and told me I could see Grobler at Residentie Hotel . . . He has got the excellent idea that the whole National Park emanated from him . . . In fact, all the people who have had anything to do with it, think 'they alone did it' and it is well it should be so. What a quaint old world it is. Between me and this page, I do believe that it is only my humble self and the way I have consistently worried everyone that has kept game preservation going in the Transvaal since 1902 and worked it up again from the moribund condition I found it in [in] 1920 when I came back, until it reached its present robust stage. But being only a damned foreign Scotchman, of course, the less one dwells on this, the better . . .

Suddenly it was clear to James – who had so often wondered whether he was on the right track – that he had accomplished his life's work. The year 1926 saw the Kruger National Park a practical reality although much had to be done before roads and accommodation were improved and tourists could be encouraged to come. But equally important were the changes in environmental thinking which were embodied in the game reserve's new status, changes which Stevenson-Hamilton had spearheaded. The physical environment, to which Stevenson-Hamilton was so closely tied, was given consideration, and not just the wildlife which lived in it. The old attitudes of the turn of the century and the views of museum collectors and hunters, such as Selous, were outmoded, and the warden had done much through his own publicity and writing to alert public opinion to the link between wildlife and its habitat – what is today called ecology.

While delighted at the attainment of his ambition for the park, Stevenson-Hamilton did not fancy the prospect of carrying on as warden under the thumb of a committee of superiors, interfering with his work and telling him what to do. He doubted that there would be a real role for himself to play in the new park, 'If I thought I could add to the scope of the reserve by staying on, I would. Make it as well known as Yellowstone . . . But main thing is not to acquire personal notoriety but to have accomplished an object which one has long striven for and the only catastrophe would be to see it ruined now.'

He thought it was time to leave and he planned accordingly, advising the government that he was considering retirement. He was due for long leave and decided to return to Britain to consider his options. As he looked over his old diaries and packed he was despondent. His father, about to turn 88, had been ill for about three weeks, and Stevenson-Hamilton headed for Kirkton first. He realised at once that his father was near death: 'He wants a simple funeral, with no one there, and to be buried next to Eliza. I am glad, it shows that marriage to mother was the real one, the others merely asides.' It was a sad and lonely time, with the responsibilities of being the Laird of Fairholm weighing heavily: 'It is pathetic to see the Colonel. My own future is insecure. No one except me is interested in family heirlooms . . . Only in the old days was handing things over from father to son something permanent.' The following day his father died.

Sorting out his father's possessions was traumatic. James went through Fairholm and Kirkton with his half-brother Leyland, sorting and burning papers, and making lists of furniture. Not only did they not know where their things were, or what belonged to whom, but when the lawyer arrived with the legal papers, James was dismayed, 'I am handicapped by not knowing anything about estates etc. Everyone in the neighbourhood regarded father as the laird and me the ordinary successor. I am a stranger to my own land and this is in no sense my home. I don't have one, except Sabi Bridge.' He needed a sense of belonging, and Fairholm seemed no longer to supply it.

At the time of his father's death, James had begun his job as Secretary of the Fauna Society, but within a month he was disillusioned. The dark, dull days of a London winter played their part but so did the work itself. He began to fantasise about returning to South Africa, and letters from friends, such as Leonard Gill, Director of the South African Museum in Cape Town, telling him to come back, did not help.[29]

The year 1927 began with a short trip to the Alps. This pleasant interlude contrasted with the journal entries on his return: '18 January: Back at work. Dull and rain at intervals. 19 January: Zoo all day. Dull and cold.' The following day a breath of South African sunshine arrived in the mail. The National Parks Board wrote to ask him to return as warden of the Kruger National Park. He accepted the position by cable, stating that he was not going to treat the job as permanent, otherwise 'the place will again get hold of me'. He was indeed 'bewitched'.

By May 1927 he was back at Sabi Bridge after paying his respects to the National Parks Board and to various politicians, including Smuts, then leader of the opposition. The first Board meeting on 2 June was a great success. For once, the gods seemed propitious, but a disaster was lurking. From mid-June Stevenson-Hamilton began complaining about 'feeling like nothing on earth', but he was used to the regular recurrences of malaria. But on 16 September he was so ill and short of breath that he had to obtain medical attention. His journals tail off during this period because, for the first time since he had scarlet fever at the age of five, James was seriously ill. He was taken to the Arcadia Nursing Home in Pretoria and underwent an operation for empyema, a pleural abscess. The recovery period was a long one, but he was well cared for by Sister Ruth Baber, later to become a family friend, 'a charming and capable person'. After a month in hospital he was discharged and stayed with friends in Pretoria until the end of November.

He resumed his duties but was not feeling quite right. Ideas of mortality haunted him, and he felt that he just could not cope. As 1928 began, he started to think that perhaps he should retire (he was then sixty) or at least take a long spell of sick leave. He was worried about who might take his place at the helm of the Kruger National Park because he wanted it to be in capable hands. A former top police officer, Elliott Howe, was suggested. He might be suitable, thought Stevenson-Hamilton, because 'it will be easy for Howe to deal with a Board of heavyweight amateurs, full of a sense of their own importance and belief in their own wisdom'. There is a strong sense of desolation pervading these journal entries, the sadness of finally ending the most significant era in his life. Despite the newspapers reporting his retirement and congratulating him on a successful career, in his inner self he was torn:

> Everyone knows now about my going and who is taking my place. But I still eagerly and pathetically cling to the notion that I shall end my days here . . . Getting more miserable about leaving this place. This is my life, now I have burnt my boats. Formerly I cherished the idea of getting married, but I am too old now.

As he took Howe around the park and showed him the ropes he realised, 'I am making a huge mistake by leaving – broken-hearted. I have had everything here. They would have kept me another ten years and I chuck the whole thing to go to England which I hate. I have done it this time and no mistake. I lie awake at night and wake before dawn, thinking "What a fool".' Even as he was packing he wrote to the Board on 28 April saying that he would be willing to return after a year's long leave. Arriving back in England he wrote, 'It is a nuisance having no home, I feel like a lost dog.' He returned to his Fauna Society job, only to find that his replacement, C.R. Hobley, was doing extremely well. 'I need not have come back,' he muttered.

This was a decade in which a number of women impacted on Stevenson-Hamilton's life in a way which had not previously happened. He mentioned marriage occasionally in his diary, a thing he had not done before. He was still drawn to attractive women and always took notice of them. There is the occasional entry such as 23 February 1924, 'Pretty woman. Noticed wedding ring and retired.' On 6 July 1928 he had lunch with Margaret Broadhurst. Vivian's education had been completed at school at Uppingham and at Sandhurst, and in 1926 he had been commissioned into the Gurkha Rifles, so he was off Mrs Broadhurst's hands. There was also a further connection in that Ellen Chambers, another 'ward' of Mrs Broadhurst's, was to marry Claude Graham, a friend of Stevenson-Hamilton's from White River. In addition, something of a friendship had developed between James Stevenson-Hamilton and Margaret Broadhurst and it was convenient to stop at Carlisle for a visit to Houghton House on the way to or from Scotland. On 4 August James did just that and it turned out to be the most momentous day of his later adult life, for there he met Hilda Cholmondeley, whom he was to marry two years later. Hilda was then 27, 35 years younger than James. She came, as James would have put it, from a 'good family'. At the time of their meeting, James did not record what he thought of the pretty, but large (she was extremely tall, much taller than James) young woman, full of adventure and zest for life, with the nickname of 'Chum'. He probably did not think about her particularly again, even though he may have considered her attractive and charming. After all, he was old enough to be her father – older, in fact, than her own mother – and he was used to women mothering him and fussing over him as he regaled them with stories of lions and other game reserve adventures. But Hilda was different. She was fascinated by his life among the wildlife of Africa and determined to see more of him.

James had no plans to return to South Africa and after meeting Hilda spent about two months in Scotland before taking up his Fauna Society job. As for Fairholm, he wrote, 'Pity I cannot live here, the place looks lovely. This may be the last time a Hamilton lives at Fairholm. . . . Dear old Fairholm. Memories flood back. Sad to see it fallen from its former glory. Wild ducks on the river. Larkhall boys in the woods.' He installed his wildlife trophies in the house, put up pictures, and did up the dining room so it 'looks like I remember it as a child'. Then he went for a walk; the 'face of the land had altered' and there was a 'dreadful and constant menace of the surrounding black country' and the tentacles of the coal industry, that 'deadly enemy of the land' creeping ever closer to his home. So despite his 'cheerful memories' at Fairholm of the Colonel in his younger days and his wish to end his days at Fairholm, he had, in fact, reached the conclusion finally that 'My heart is, I suppose, really in Africa.'

Perhaps it was the slightly derelict house, the surroundings marred by industrial development and the nostalgia of the past which prompted the journal entry about his heart being in Africa. But more likely it was the meeting with Hilda Cholmondeley and her enthusiasm for African animals – she was an artist – that renewed his desire for the sunshine of Africa. He lunched with Hilda in London on 16 October and they 'did the old reptile house' at the London Zoo. That evening over dinner Margaret Broadhurst told him that she and Hilda were planning to visit South Africa to see their friends Claude and Ellen Graham at White River, a cousin of Hilda's in Colesberg, and to tour around to see something of the country generally. Meetings between James and Hilda became fairly frequent over December 1928 and January 1929 as they discussed South Africa, and he gave her a copy of *Animal Life* and his diary of lion hunts to read. Before long his feelings for her had to be acknowledged: 'She is a dear, only she is much too young, and I am too old and now too unwell.' He talked to Margaret Broadhurst about his dilemma, 'Told her about my heart ailment etc. and she is sure to pass it on to Hilda C. and just as well the latter should know.' With nothing resolved he saw them off on board the *Llanstephan* for South Africa on 31 January 1929.

Hilda and Margaret were on their way to South Africa but Stevenson-Hamilton was not. What was he to do? Stevenson-Hamilton was in touch with the National Parks Board in South Africa and it seemed that Howe was doing well as a temporary replacement, 'I really think he is now a much better man for the job than I am. He is fifteen years younger, more energetic etc. I am simply living on my reputation now.' But Howe wanted to move on because he had problems with his pension and Stevenson-Hamilton's year of long leave was up. James's retirement was not yet formalised and the possibility existed that he could change his mind and return to the Kruger National Park if the Board would have him back.

'A decision, but as soon as I make one, all arguments of the other side show themselves. Wrote out a cable saying I shall return but will sleep on it.' Next day, 'Sent off my cable. Relief to have got it off my chest.' For a while he was unsure quite whether the National Parks wanted him back or not, but it seems that they did and on 25 June he was writing, 'Back at Sabi Bridge after another permanent parting. It seems to be my lot to be bound up with this place.' His sense of purpose as warden of the Kruger National Park was probably renewed by the fact that Hilda was there. 'Chum and I love South Africa,' wrote Margaret Broadhurst. When, in July, Mrs Broadhurst left to return to England, Hilda stayed. She was living in Johannesburg, painting the animals in the local zoo and she wrote regularly to the warden. Even if *he* had not, she had certainly decided that he was the man for her. But perhaps, by then, he had too, for they wrote to one another almost every day. By April 1930 she was buying clothes for him ('two suits from Stuttafords at 10/6 each') and was teasing him about passing her off as his 'great-niece', whenever she was visiting him at Sabi Bridge, a description which some visitors saw through immediately.[30]

Hilda's mother, it seems, was not happy about the 'great-niece' ploy and on 8 July 1930 a letter from Ina Cholmondeley arrived which threatened to 'kybosh' everything. Hilda considered returning to England but, in fact, they decided to get married. On 12 August they were in Johannesburg seeing James's financial advisers and a marriage agreement was drawn up. The pair then visited a home for abandoned dogs, where they bought a wedding present for themselves – nine dogs, at a cost of one shilling each:

> An expensive trip. H. and I marked it by getting married at the Registrars; it came as a considerable shock to both of us afterwards. It is a rotten way I suppose to treat the most important event in my life and I have dodged it for so long. It is just about the only thing I have not done.

## 'An Imperishable Monument'

His first birthday as a married man was a memorable one, 'present and cake for the first time in more years than I can remember. It is rather queer starting all this sort of thing at my age.' He was also thinking of starting a family at once, and when he felt a little ill a month later he wrote, 'feeling rotten and giddy. Shooting pains in the head. Keep out of the sun and not drink liquor. Suspect that [is] what a doctor would say and charge five guineas for saying it. Make codicil to will. It would be a bore if I pegged out at this juncture before I could get a family . . .'

Hilda left for England in December and James met up with her in February. For the family's sake there was another wedding ceremony in a pretty little traditional church in Dorset. Once in Britain he saw his tax adviser who told him not to sleep at Kirkton or Fairholm, even for one night, for that would constitute domicile and make him liable for £1 000 in tax. 'A nice country this to come to!' was James's response.

# 11

# 'The Guardian Spirit of the Low-veld'[1]
## The Kruger National Park and Retirement
## (1930–1946)

AFTER THE WEDDING CEREMONY in Dorset James Stevenson-Hamilton returned with renewed enthusiasm (and an energetic young wife) to get the national park in South Africa on a sound footing. Having once been virtually a solitary figure in the eastern Transvaal lowveld, he was now surrounded by people and he had a good number of social and professional obligations. He had a family to keep him company, and there is no doubt that he received great support and sustenance from Hilda and their children, Margaret (born 1931), James (born 1933), and Anne (born 1935). Hilda revelled in the lifestyle of wife of the warden, making the most of every opportunity to go out into the bush. She was an accomplished hostess and her home was often filled with guests, but she far preferred being out with her gun walking in the veld. There was the extended family as well, particularly Hilda's mother, Ina, and Hilda's two sisters, Lettice and Ethel. Professionally, Stevenson-Hamilton's solitary circumstances altered too. In order to carry out its function as a public national park, tourists had to be cultivated and encouraged to visit the area. The park had to be administered with their needs in mind – roads, camps, shops, petrol stations, and other infrastructural developments had to be built and serviced. For all of these, the warden was responsible. But Stevenson-Hamilton was now accountable to a superior body – this he dreaded more than anything. If there was an aspect of his later life which caused him anguish – although it never marred his dedication to working in the Kruger National Park – it was his relationship with members of the National Parks Board of Trustees.

In all his dealings with the outside world, Stevenson-Hamilton was a thorough professional. While he was certainly not afraid to have his say on issues he believed to be important, he kept to the ways of the civil service, or the army, never openly criticising his superiors. The National Parks Act had taken wildlife conservation out of the hands of sportsmen and old-style game wardens and projected it into the mainstream of South African politics. Placed under the general supervision of the Minister of Lands, national parks were

*Skukuza rest camp (c.1929).*

not constituted as a government department, but were subject to control by the Board, a statutory body representing state, provincial and private wildlife conservation interests. The Board was required to 'control, manage and maintain' all aspects of South African national park policy, and consequently had considerable power.[2] During meetings, Stevenson-Hamilton could argue his case, present his reports and make his viewpoints known, but ultimately he had to abide by the decisions of the National Parks Board. He disliked this intensely for he came to think that the Board interfered too much in the minutiae of his job. In many respects he was correct, because Board members were amateurs and not qualified to provide any nature conservation direction. They consequently busied themselves with administrative and petty detail. There were no defined portfolios and membership of the Board increasingly became a political reward. The warden complained that certain members made nuisances of themselves by being unnecessarily argumentative, or gave support and then buckled under pressure.

By the mid-1930s, Stevenson-Hamilton's journal recounted personal jealousies and even 'wars' between Board members, and an atmosphere of 'lies and scandals'. He detected coteries which were either for him or against him, and during the 1930s he frequently felt that his job was threatened.

In many respects, this was ironic. For many years, he had toyed with the idea of leaving, and had actually accepted other employment from time to time. However, now that he had entrenched himself so happily at Sabi Bridge with a family to keep him company, the thought of leaving increasingly became anathema – the prospect of slow physical and mental decay appalled him, and he also knew how much Hilda enjoyed their way of life. But Stevenson-Hamilton's persecution was not a figment of his imagination, even the chairman of the National Parks Board admitted in 1941 that there was a deliberate attempt to oust him.[3] The seasoned politician Reitz also deprecated the faction fighting and intrigue which characterised the operations of the National Parks Board of Trustees.[4]

It is somewhat strange to think of a man of seventy years of age wishing to hold on to his job. In truth, Stevenson-Hamilton did realise that he could not be there for ever and that at some stage – although later rather than sooner – someone would have to succeed him. But he was determined not to let his hard work go for nought and be followed by an unsuitable successor who did not think the same way he did and whose values about wildlife and the park development were different. Stevenson-Hamilton himself favoured Dr Arnold Schoch, senior law adviser to the government and the man who had drafted the National Parks Act. As a lawyer – Schoch obtained a doctorate in law from Leiden University – although certainly a competent person with an interest in wildlife, it is not at all certain why Stevenson-Hamilton thought him so eminently suitable as a replacement. But in April 1938 Schoch became seriously ill, and any chance of his being tempted by the warden's job evaporated.

The power struggle between Stevenson-Hamilton and the Board had its origins in the fact that the National Parks Act did not define the precise organisational responsibilities and administrative structure of the parties involved. When the Kruger National Park was in its infancy, Stevenson-Hamilton and his small staff could cope adequately with visitor and wildlife management affairs. Later, however, when the success of the park was demonstrated by the many thousands of visitors who demanded sophisticated facilities, and when other national parks were established, some kind of head office and formal administrative bureaucracy was required. This Stevenson-Hamilton – so used to running his game reserve efficiently and without interference – resisted.

Lying at the nub of the difficulties was politics and, in particular, the changing politics of South Africa in the 1930s. Although after losing the 1924 election many thought that Jan Smuts would soon be back at the helm, this proved not to be the case. The 1929 election was a bitter one and Hertzog was returned to power, stronger than ever. But there was a fusion between the parties of Hertzog and Smuts (into the United Party) in 1934 as a result of the circumstances of the Great Depression – when it seemed advantageous for the major parties to co-operate for the greater good of the country rather than to fight each other. Until 1939 Smuts was therefore the junior in the partnership with Hertzog as prime minister in what was often a fragile relationship. In those years, Afrikaner nationalism became a vibrant political doctrine and many of the segregationist policies which were to find full expression under apartheid in later years appeared on the statute books. As far as external affairs were concerned, throughout the decade the imperial link was loosened as South Africa was set on the road to full independence as a sovereign state, free from what many considered interference from Britain. It seems that, when one comes down to it, Stevenson-Hamilton and the Afrikaner nationalists on his Board of Trustees and among his staff were simply not compatible. He was, as he put it, 'the wrong class' in Britain and the 'wrong race (British)' in South Africa. But, having said this, he was – as were so many others at that time – extremely patient with Afrikaner aspirations, feeling that they had got an unfair deal out of their defeat during the South African War.

Stevenson-Hamilton certainly admired Smuts because he was a statesman on a world scale who had combined a love of his Afrikaner heritage with a love for Britain and Europe. A further, perhaps stronger, reason for Stevenson-Hamilton's attachment to Smuts was that he had supported the game reserves from their earliest days and had also supported Stevenson-Hamilton personally, to the extent of offering him a significant position during the First World War. Stevenson-Hamilton also admired Louis Esselen, secretary of the South African Party after 1919 (until 1941) and Smuts's confidential adviser, who was able to cope well with the ageing politician. When Esselen died in March 1945, the warden thought it a tragedy, 'the worst thing that has happened in my recollection in the country, the park and the board. He was Smuts's right-hand man and a steadying influence behind the scenes. Now we are thrown to the wolves.'

The 'wolves' were, in the main, staunch Afrikaner nationalists, determined – as Stevenson-Hamilton thought – to undermine his position as warden and replace him with a man of their choice. A short while after his retirement in 1946, this is precisely what they did and in time the National Parks Board and the National Party had extremely strong links.[5] In Stevenson-Hamilton's time the power of the Broederbond was increasing. This was a secret organisation with the explicit aim to see Afrikaners in positions of authority everywhere, with Britons (and even English-speaking South Africans) tossed aside. This was the group which saw Smuts more and more as a tool of British imperialism.

Not being a political animal himself, Stevenson-Hamilton did not think any politician was a really 'nice' person. But ultimately it was a clash of two cultures. The meticulous British cavalry officer versus the more casual man of the veld; the sophisticated gentleman versus the egalitarian republican. When Stevenson-Hamilton attended a Board meeting in 1940 at the Kalahari Gemsbok National Park in the northern Cape, he remarked that he felt like a foreigner because the only language spoken was Afrikaans. And yet James could speak the language, having been a star student at the Pelham Institute in 1932. It was not only the language which separated them, but a cultural gulf as well.

However, it is difficult to identify Stevenson-Hamilton's political outlook, for he had maverick tastes in politicians, believing that it was the man who was important, rather than the political platform. His strangest friendship was with Oswald Pirow, whose family background was German and who had studied law in Germany before the First World War. On his return to South Africa Pirow had become involved in National Party politics, in 1929 becoming Minister of Justice in Hertzog's cabinet. But Pirow's particular claim to fame is that he maintained strong links with Germany, meeting – and admiring – Adolf Hitler. The friendship between a person who was a declared enemy of Smuts as well as a dedicated Afrikaner nationalist and Stevenson-Hamilton would in itself have been unusual, but Pirow was also a neo-Nazi. Stevenson-Hamilton loathed Hitler and Nazism believing that 'a curtain of darkness and bloodshed [was] descending on the world' heralding the end of the British Empire he held so dear. It may have been just Pirow's love of wildlife which brought the two men together. Pirow wrote a number of books about wild animals and the South African landscape; Hilda illustrated some of them, and James wrote the introductions.[6] Stevenson-Hamilton knew all about Pirow's views and was concerned by them, but nonetheless commented, 'Pirow will always have a warm corner in my heart though politically he is ploughing a strange furrow. We don't discuss politics ... we talk about lions – a nice safe subject.'

Stevenson-Hamilton's relationship with his Board of Trustees and the unresolved question of supreme command within the Kruger National Park impacted on the game rangers as well as their warden. The rangers knew about the tension among their superiors, and some even exploited the situation by going to the Board behind the warden's back. They also had disagreements and infighting among themselves which the warden was often hard-pressed to resolve. At times Stevenson-Hamilton was not sure how to handle his staff, and complained that he and Hilda heard only rumours, never anything he could tackle in the correct managerial manner. It is quite possible, though, that the staff's responsibilities were hard to define, and it was difficult to check up on their daily activities as they were stationed in remote parts of the park far from the warden's eye. Certainly, a number were lazy or did not care for Board property as properly as they should. Stevenson-Hamilton admired them for what they were prepared to do, remarking when Duke died in March 1934, what a wonderful ranger he had been, and how he had a remarkable ability to cope with hardships – even self-imposed ones. Although Stevenson-Hamilton generally got on well with his rangers, he really did not like Ranger Louis Steyn, who had joined the park in 1929, and who was later to become park warden in 1954. Stevenson-Hamilton alleged that Steyn stole from Africans, by not giving them receipts and that in the end, when the transaction was queried, it was the white man's word against that of an African. The warden also had to guard against being caught out in indiscretions himself. For example, Steyn had complained about Hilda wanting to join him (Steyn) in shooting lion, with 'some justice in my opinion', wrote the warden, although Hilda, 'whom I indiscreetly told, is furious'. Without doubt, the ranger who was closest to Stevenson-Hamilton and upon whom he relied most was Harry Wolhuter. When Wolhuter became ill in July 1943, Stevenson-Hamilton was extremely worried because 'if he were to die I don't know what I would do'.

In the 1930s the warden and his rangers had not only their regular routine of old to discharge, but immediately the park was proclaimed it proved to be one of the most successful tourist destinations in the country. Tourist regulations evolved in response to practical circumstances. At the outset, no visitors could be allowed into the northern part of the park owing to the lack of roads and amenities. The threat of malaria and the fierce summer thunderstorms led to the decision in 1931 that the Kruger National Park would be open only during the winter months. All the rest camps were soon quite inadequate as visitors poured in by car and by rail. There was no administrative machinery to take bookings and therefore no means of knowing how many visitors would arrive to demand accommodation and services. There were only a few huts so most people camped in tents and did their own catering. Sometimes game rangers offered accommodation in their homes to tourists who were hard-pressed. At the camps, bad behaviour was frequent: drunkenness and loud noise from gramophones and radios spoilt the wilderness experience for many. Caldecott had warned Stevenson-Hamilton of 'vulgarization . . . rubberneck waggons and tourists',[7] and when a tourist used one ranger's personal toothbrush on a visit to the park, vulgarisation seemed

*Stevenson-Hamilton with Wolhuter at the Lindanda tree – site of the latter's escape from being killed by a lion (in 1903). Wolhuter was seriously mauled but managed to kill the lion with his sheath knife.*

a most appropriate description. When the visitor season closed each year Stevenson-Hamilton was glad to have some peace and to have his liberty restored.

The huge number of visitors necessitated a growing infrastructure to provide for them. The perennial shortage of money meant that the provision of accommodation usually lagged far behind visitor demand and there were frequent complaints of overcrowding, a lack of facilities and poor conditions of hygiene.[8] The staff at the park were unable to manage all aspects of visitor care, and experiments were made with private contractors, the employment of gate officers and ticket formalities, as well as the construction and design of rest camps and accommodation. Complicating any permanent development strategy was the fact that because most of the Kruger National Park was open only during the winter season, it was thus difficult to offer permanent employment and to take care of accommodation facilities when there were no visitors around.

*Tourists camping out in the Kruger National Park (c.1930).*

Stevenson-Hamilton played a role in these arrangements, although it was the side of running the national park that he enjoyed the least. He was excellent at writing reports meticulously, keeping records and correspondence up to date, and presenting accounts. But he also regarded himself as a guardian of the national park, not merely as engaging in its exploitation. He himself was, for example, responsible for retarding visitor services. He was determined to provide a wilderness experience for visitors to the Kruger National Park and he fiercely resisted any attempt either to upgrade accommodation or to provide entertainment, even of an educational nature. In 1930 he was appalled that Board member Papenfus could suggest allowing dancing and gramophones at rest camps and he even dismissed the showing of instructive wildlife films and lantern slides at the rest camps as unnecessary entertainment. Because he held the view that the Kruger National Park was not a recreational outlet, Stevenson-Hamilton considered that camps should be functional, efficient and minimal, the main aim being to provide the ambience in which to savour wildlife and nature. 'Luxury' mattresses, for instance, rather than coir, were not stocked even in 1939, and electric light at Pretoriuskop was also regarded as unnecessary because too many improvements would over-civilise the park. No stranger to physical hardship himself, Stevenson-Hamilton wrote that all tourists wanted was comfort at night with adequate catering and camp arrangements. Despite these inadequacies, most visitors were neither deterred nor dissatisfied: in 1940, soon after the beginning of the Second World War, more than 22 500 visitors came to the Kruger National Park.[9]

One cannot analyse the life of a man in South Africa without raising the question of how he related to the Africans around him. He admired the qualities of endurance and courage in his 'native police' as he did in his white game rangers. Stevenson-Hamilton was not romantic about Africans. In fact, many of his ideas on how to treat Africans are sharply criticised today and regarded as anachronistic, out of step with the shared humanity of the modern world. For example, he believed strongly – perhaps it was a relic from his military days – that corporal punishment was a legitimate method of punishment. He had his reasons in that he thought that youngsters became contaminated by contact with other hardened criminals in prison. 'Flogging' he saw as a practical solution to the problem of discipline, being a visible and humiliating punishment but one which did not endure.

He was also paternalistic about Africans – he would have been very unusual to have had notions out of context with his time on the issue. But in the course of his work as Native Commissioner within the game reserves he had opportunities to learn about the African way of life. He had an excellent sense of the strengths of African society, even when compared with his own. In 1920, for example, after finding some rock paintings in the Sabi Game Reserve and reading G.W. Stow's, *The Native Races of South Africa*[10] on the San Bushmen, he wrote that it was a sad tale of lies and brutal injustice. 'How could such extermination be called the progress of civilisation?' he demanded.

He had grudging personal compassion even for poachers:

> Gave old Mbonboni six months for poaching and three for escaping from custody. It is against the grain and I have great sympathy with the old man as a sportsman, but he is such a desperate enemy of the game ... Of course, I sympathize far more with native poachers than most of our sordid, murderous white men ... they get off much lighter than the native does.

He was also forbearing to the 'wild man', Sifomise, who was probably deranged and wandered naked around the game reserve robbing the African rangers. Unusually for his time, Stevenson-Hamilton appreciated the value of traditional healing, and after a female African healer had cured one of the 'police' for £5, he wrote, 'Serves to confirm my formed opinion that, apart from surgery at which they are quite good too in a rough way, that in arts of medicine, native African doctors are quite equal – in some ways, superior – to our own.'

But he was also critical of the African 'mind', saying that the African 'fails lamentably when plans needing foresight are to be made and ideas of what the other side will do [are needed]. Perhaps it is just as well for the white man that the African, being his superior in courage, activity and most moral qualities is only lacking in cunning.' When Hertzog's Pact government of the mid-1920s was planning its segregationist policies, Stevenson-Hamilton could see the future repercussions: 'Nothing but the prospect of trouble regarding natives for the next generation. They are exploited; have no justice and are never given a fair show. That's how the natives see it.' Stevenson-Hamilton appreciated in 1938 that 'South Africa has been carried on the backs of a. the natives, and b. the mines. and there is no b without a.'

In his journals the warden freely criticised his white game rangers and there are also frequent criticisms of the Africans. In fact, he was more closely associated with the African staff on a daily basis, for he had always a group of 'police' and servants around him. The journals are filled with comments about the men, his 'troops' in many respects. At times they forgot items, they were stupid, they absconded, or drank, or in other ways did not perform their duties properly. But he also could give credit where it was due. Njinja Ndlovu, 'Ginger', the senior African assistant, 'has a wonderful head and notices everything. To think that such men are considered to be inferior to the low dogs, almost imbecile, Europeans as Afrikaners one meets', and could sympathise when Ginger 'says he does all the work here but gets paid like the others. A just complaint.'

In September 1940, Stevenson-Hamilton handed the bronze medal of the Royal Humane Society to Sinias Nyalunga, one of the rangers who worked for game ranger Hector McDonald (who had replaced De Laporte in 1929 at Crocodile Bridge) for saving a woman and her baby from the flooded Crocodile River at the risk of his own life. The warden observed that it was the first medal to be bestowed on an African though he knew that many had deserved it, but 'no one bothers to recommend a native'. He also mused on how his white game rangers related to their African staff, commenting in 1940 that Ranger Tomlinson was 'always worrying about what the natives think of him; he has the inferiority complex of those who have been mixed up with native women. They look for "cheek" and this leads to lots of injustice.' He found some of these interracial sexual unions tragic, and noted in 1942 that a local storekeeper who had a black girlfriend was found out, and because this was now a punishable offence, had shot her and then himself.

Many of the labour intensive tasks of the game reserve were done by prison labour which the warden and his rangers organised. The mining industry attracted illegal immigrants into South Africa, particularly from Mozambique. The system which seems to have operated in the game reserves was that the illegal work-seekers were either arrested or reported themselves as trespassers to Stevenson-Hamilton, as the Special Justice of the Peace, and then consequently received a fortnight's imprisonment, this being the appropriate sentence for the offence.[11] When their sentence ended, the men were given what was known as a 'pass' – permission which entitled them to seek work in the Transvaal. These prisoners were not incarcerated while serving their sentences but laboured instead in the game reserves on road-making and similar tasks.

In addition, the relationship between the Kruger National Park and its African neighbours was not a happy one. In 1933, Stevenson-Hamilton played a role in dispossessing the Makuleke community of their territory between the Levubu and Limpopo Rivers. The game reserves and the Makuleke and Mhinga people in this area had long been uneasy neighbours, and in 1912 several Makuleke villages under Mhinga in the northern part of the Singwitsi were excised, thus reducing the game reserve area. But as the Tsonga population increased over the years, so the people spilled over into the game reserves with an increase in poaching and other illegal activities within the park's boundaries. In the early 1930s the proposal was put forward by Stevenson-Hamilton and the National Parks Board to evict the Makuleke and move them on to land further south which would be excised from the park for this purpose. Relocating the Makuleke was not, however, a simple matter because the Department of Native Affairs took the side of the Makuleke and refused to give its permission.

In order to circumvent the Native Affairs Department, in 1933 the provincial authorities declared the district to be the Pafuri Game Reserve and then gave it to the warden to administer. Makuleke's 'location' was surrounded by this reserve, although excluded from it. A stalemate followed because the Native Affairs Department continued to oppose any translocation of the Makuleke community. Indeed, so unfair did the situation appear to be, that even National Parks Board secretary H.J. van Graan, pleaded with Board members:

> Is it wise to take this step in view of the reputation of the alleged

> suppression of native races? It is obvious that Pafuri is better agriculturally than the dry piece of grazing land we offer in exchange ... frankly, I foresee in this gain of today, if we acquire the Pafuri, the future germ of destruction of the whole Park.

Van Graan was ignored and the impasse continued until 1952, when the Board returned the Pafuri Game Reserve to provincial control, explaining the situation as unworkable.[12]

When the Kruger National Park was opened to visitors in the late 1920s Stevenson-Hamilton would probably not have objected to African tourists. But under his Board the warden did not have a free hand, and visitor access for Africans was restricted. In 1932 Gustav Preller recorded his distress that Indians were using the same camp as whites, an incident which Stevenson-Hamilton dismissed tongue-in-cheek with the comment that he had thought that they were Portuguese.[13] Once when the Japanese *chargé d'affaires* was visiting, the warden wrote, 'Pray God these fatheads do not treat him as "Asiatic".' As segregationist policies became more rigid, the National Parks Board determined to replace all African skilled labour with whites. Stevenson-Hamilton was appalled, believing that 'good natives' were far better workers than 'poor whites'.

When it came to ecological considerations, Stevenson-Hamilton feared that the national park would become like a zoo – a large zoo admittedly, but a zoo nonetheless. He feared that visitor requirements would take precedence and that wild nature would be the loser. He set out his goals as follows:

> The first object of the park should be to educate the public in the rudiments of natural history; to show people what the wild animals of their country look like, and how they act in their natural state, free from the terror of man. It should also cultivate a spirit of sympathy with them; to let it be realized that wildlife is more admirable alive, and in their natural setting – themselves in fact – than converted into the rags and bones of hunters' trophies, or confined, listless prisoners, behind bars. As town populations increase and urban industries develop, life generally grows more and more artificial and it will no doubt become correspondingly more interesting – as well as scientifically valuable – to have retained one spot where nature remains unspoilt ... But, in addition to its above popular objects, a wildlife sanctuary supplies the most favourable ground whereon may be sought the answers to many riddles of natural history, since the indigenous species

are there permitted to live their natural lives unhampered by artificial aids and restrictions. Full answers to the various questions which suggest themselves cannot be expected now nor perhaps at any time; a certain amount of artificiality is inevitable in any region where man is present, however firmly he may restrain his hand, and however honestly he may endeavour to leave nature to herself. But in the Kruger National Park there exists the opportunity of getting nearer the truth than is possible perhaps anywhere else in the world today.

Apart from visitors, Stevenson-Hamilton resisted the presence of scientists. One must remember that in the 1920s and 30s there was no such thing as an ecologist or even a discipline such as wildlife management. The main reason why Stevenson-Hamilton distrusted scientists was that his experience had been with entomologists and zoologists, and he had personally witnessed that it was thanks to them that the wildlife of Zululand and Swaziland had been exterminated because of the supposed link between wild animals, tsetse fly and nagana. He also had to argue against those who wanted to exterminate lion in the Kruger National Park. When the national park was proclaimed in 1926 Stevenson-Hamilton stopped any killing of lion. Not only did visitors love them, but antelope populations had increased to such an extent by that time that there was no need to control predator numbers. However, in the drought conditions of the 1930s the antelope herds thinned and National Parks Board members and many of the game rangers (not Stevenson-Hamilton, who felt that nature could take care of herself) wanted lion hunts to begin again. From the rangers' point of view, selling lion skins, skulls and fat brought in a small private income and lion stories provided good tourist material.[14]

Throughout his life, Stevenson-Hamilton was working towards a way of expressing the links between wild animals and their environment. Part of him was in the old-fashioned mould of population dynamics, but he also linked vegetation and animals in an ecological manner. He thought about these things deeply, and every day of his life was filled with observations and thoughts in an engagement with nature of which he never tired. He was not just a 'penitent butcher'. Like Aldo Leopold in another context, Stevenson-Hamilton was trying to articulate an ethic of respect for nature, and he consistently argued against its manipulation and management for any purpose whatsoever.

Since James Stevenson-Hamilton's time the arguments for and against management practices in national parks have waxed and waned. The scientific managers eventually won the day in the Kruger National Park, and

Stevenson-Hamilton would have been horrified had he lived to see herds of elephant being monitored by helicopter before being 'culled' in their family groups. But so too would he have been appalled when, in Tsavo National Park in Kenya, ideas of leaving nature to take its course resulted in the destruction by far too many elephant of their entire habitat and thus threatened their continued existence in the region. No doubt he would have been practical in this matter, as he was in so many others, but what he was arguing for essentially, was the right of animals to be respected on their own terms and not to be regarded either as the trophy of the hunter or the trophy of the scientist. Bullet or dart needle were the same to him – it was the idea of control which was anathema.

Nature had a sanctity of her own, and a sanctuary was the way of preserving this special quality:

> The ideal wildlife sanctuary should aim to be fully and accurately representative of the particular area, as it may have been before man had progressed sufficiently to disturb its ordered arrangement. All indigenous species of fauna and flora ought to be represented. The introduction of exotic types of either should be religiously avoided. They introduce a discordant element, and, even should they succeed in assimilating themselves with the environment, they will generally appear incongruous, conferring an air of artificiality on the whole. Only by keeping such a place perfectly natural may the student acquire true knowledge, and the ordinary visitor a real education in natural history . . .

Stevenson-Hamilton saw his job as warden as a managerial position, its core functions to deal with human resources, administrative and developmental issues. He did not consider that training for the position of warden or that of game rangers needed to encompass specific qualifications in natural history. In his time, this would have been zoology, rather than the broad applied science of ecology which had not yet come into its own. In the Kruger National Park early game rangers came from the ranks of former hotel- and storekeepers, railway foremen and storemen, as well as junior civil servants. In common with other senior conservationists of his time, Stevenson-Hamilton actually preferred this kind of man to any naturalist. He believed that the desirable traits of rangers were physical strength and energy, reliability, a knowledge of 'natives', bushcraft, horses, firearms and agriculture and, preferably, the absence of a wife. University degrees were unnecessary, he thought, even detrimental, because they led to specialisation, whereas a ranger's knowledge ought to be broad and diverse: 'It is best that a man pick up his biological knowledge direct from the face of nature, unhampered by previous prejudices and preconceived notions.'[15]

Despite his views on formal qualifications in zoology being inappropriate for national park management, Stevenson-Hamilton also decried amateurs who interfered without any knowledge of what they were talking about. In this regard, the Board members were problematic, suggesting in 1930 that lechwe, a tropical water antelope, be introduced into the park.[16] Gustav Preller enjoyed bird-watching and thought there were too few birds when he visited the park. Without producing any evidence, he said that this was due to jackals destroying fledglings, and he persuaded his fellow Board members to instruct Stevenson-Hamilton to exterminate jackals throughout the national park.[17] J.G. Ludorf had a craving to see springbuck and blesbuck in the veld around Pretoriuskop, although there were no records of these species ever being there;[18] and in 1939, W.A. Campbell, under the influence of the Kenyan Game Department of the time, advocated that grass and fruits from Kenya should be imported to provide additional feed for the wildlife of the Kruger Park.[19] It was this kind of tampering with nature which Stevenson-Hamilton argued strongly against. And yet, in 1939 Stevenson-Hamilton was pleased to have a scientist on the National Parks Board, Dr R.A. Bigalke, director of the National Zoological Gardens in Pretoria and a highly respected zoologist.

Occasionally Stevenson-Hamilton himself dabbled in 'science', only to have it backfire badly. In the late 1930s there was a serious outbreak of foot-and-mouth disease among the substantial number of livestock being kept by the warden, game rangers and African 'police' in the Kruger National Park. The story which Stevenson-Hamilton does not tell in detail in *South African Eden* (although he refers to it) is of how Hilda's and his experiments to see whether foot-and-mouth was transmittable between wild animals and domestic stock nearly led to disaster. On 28 December 1938 he recorded that Hilda wanted to see whether impala contracted the disease. But at once, he could see the dangers – even the ruin of his life's work – because if they did get the disease then all the wildlife in the national park might be destroyed. They told the veterinary institute in Pretoria what they were doing, but immediately Hilda had put the diseased animals in a pen with the impala, she too was in a state. In fact, the animals died from a contagious sepsis and the disaster was averted. The lesson concerning tampering with nature had been learnt once more.

In the 1930s Stevenson-Hamilton's reputation as one of the most knowledgeable experts on wildlife was secure. He had a high reputation because of his wardenship of the Kruger National Park – none of the other South African national parks had even approached it in importance. He was also on the radio in May 1937, in one of the first international broadcasts from South Africa. He, and Hilda in particular, also enjoyed making films and were among the very earliest producers and photographers of wildlife movies. Many of their films were shown in South Africa and in Britain and were accompanied by a talk, usually given by Hilda. Stevenson-Hamilton's high profile was also due to his talent as a writer and the fact that he could project educational material in an entertaining way. *South African Eden*, his memoirs which first appeared in 1937, has already been extensively quoted, and it demonstrates a wonderful mix of personal anecdote, exciting wildlife adventure, landscape description, and philosophy of nature. Prior to this, his success with *Animal Life in Africa*, which appeared in 1912, has already been mentioned as a significant milestone in the wildlife literature. In 1929 he published *The Low-veld: Its Wild Life and its People*, also a pioneering work. This is an interesting book which was acclaimed in its time, even reprinted in 1934, but which is seldom mentioned today. It is a regional history of the lowveld, combining one part geology (Smuts's suggestion) and vegetation, a second part dealing with animal life, and a third comprising African habitation of the region. It is fashionable now to decry the inclusion of Africans with landscape and wildlife as patronising and demeaning because it places them with the 'natural history' rather than the 'cultural history' of Africa. But attitudes and ethics change over time and this was not Stevenson-Hamilton's intention. He wanted to bring to the public's attention, as he had done with the wildlife, what considerable interest there was in looking more carefully at African culture and society.

Marriage to Hilda in 1931 changed the focus of James Stevenson-Hamilton's life. At last he had someone to confide in, and his journal entries became less introspective, less burdened with history, less literary, shorter and more factual. He still needed his diary as a record of his life, but it was not his only companion. Hilda shared all his professional as well as his personal concerns. It is clear that she set her sights on the warden because, although she had never been there when they met, she loved Africa and its wildlife. In fact, the main thing James told his friends about her was that her 'name was Hilda Cholmondeley and she likes chasing lions'.[20]

Hilda was a strong personality. She spoke with a gentle voice, but she had definite ideas. Apart from lions, she was passionate about art and she continually painted and drew, her strong visual sense giving James new insight. She also refocussed James into South Africa and into the present. His affection for Fairholm was not extinguished, but it was less intrusive. Marriage gave him other priorities. Hilda had not come with a dowry, and although James had a good income from his employment and his Scottish properties as well as investments in Britain and South Africa, he was past retirement age and the expense of a wife was a worry. Moreover, a baby was on the way immediately and Hilda did not take her pregnancy well. On 7 November Hilda went into the White Lodge maternity home, and James occupied himself by pacing about with Lettice, his sister-in-law who was staying with them: 'Hilda so plucky and cheerful, makes people like Dr Adams who don't understand think that she is not in pain.' But the physical pain was nothing in comparison with the emotional distress at producing a daughter rather than the hoped-for son and heir. They called her Margaret, but referred to her as 'Marmosette' or 'Bombie', and they were soon totally absorbed by her. They had decided for the sake of Bombie's and Hilda's health that over the hot summer months when fever was at its most prevalent, mother and child would rent accommodation from the Wolhuters at Mtimba, higher up on the plateau near White River. Every weekend James joined his family – it was a two-hour journey – and he was always glad to see his baby daughter looking cheerful and happy. The first family Christmas was in 1932 and James wrote, 'Cannot remember having such a good time since I was seven years old.'

While Hilda was staying at Mtimba she and James wrote to each other every day. Their letters were loving, domestic, teasing and practical. Many contain lists of household items to be bought when James was in Pretoria or Johannesburg for meetings – these he underlined in red so as not to forget them. Margaret was gaining weight, Lettice had a cold, a short note about nothing in particular, or just a loving note. Did the Board meetings go well? Was having a nanny too expensive, should they give her up? There are moths in her brand new jodhpurs, she has designed a bird-bath, she is sorry to hear that the meeting went badly but proud of what she read about him in the newspaper, and Bombie cut a double tooth.

James was entirely happy with domesticity. When they were separated he was lonely, and sent a telegram saying, 'Aye, but I'm longing for my ain folk.' He sent her copies of his journals to read so that she knew what he had been doing and he shared all his professional troubles with her, greatly valuing her advice and support. He described his birthday in October 1933: 'Now I am settled in life these annual events don't worry me so much as formerly, and inundated as I now am with presents and congratulations from darling Hilda, I feel as I used to when I was ten years old . . . I certainly don't deserve all this.' By the end of 1932, Hilda was pregnant again and suffering from morning sickness. On 21 May 1933 their son James

Christopher was born: 'Splendid for Hilda. Another girl would have broken her heart.'

There was talk about a third child in order to complete the family. Stevenson-Hamilton was glad that he had not left the Kruger National Park in 1926, 'I would be sitting grousing in the windows of the Rag today among the other old gaffers.' Instead, he had a challenging career, a vivacious and attractive young wife who revelled in the kind of lifestyle they shared, and two young children.

The year 1935 was, by contrast, a dreadful one. In February, Bombie was ill. On 13 May the eagerly awaited third child was born. It was a girl and Hilda was again bitterly disappointed. After the birth, Hilda herself was unwell and James was sure that the cause was her psychological distress. Hilda wrote to him, 'I am so frightfully sorry only to have produced a girl . . . Poor little Caroline Anne. She may be the best of the bunch but she is having a rotten start.' On 24 July there was a desperate call from Pretoria, Bombie was extremely ill. Three days later she was unconscious in the Arcadia Nursing Home, but James could not stay in Pretoria and he and Hilda had to keep in touch by cable and letter. These exchanges and the journal entries are agonising to read as Hilda and James were tortured by the slow loss of Margaret. Hilda was still weak from phlebitis and pleurisy; Anne was an infant; and Jamie was a boisterous two-year-old.

Within two weeks of Bombie's illness the parents knew that she was likely to die. And were she to live, Margaret would certainly be brain damaged, for she had a form of encephalitis. As news of Bombie's rallies and decline reached the warden at Skukuza, as he battled with the Board, his rangers and the tourists, he was overwhelmed with admiration at how Hilda coped with the crisis. At the end of August, Hilda was already mourning for Margaret, 'It is much nicer to think of her as a sort of Peter Pan of the Game Reserve, never to get any older.' On 25 October the dreaded telegram reached Skukuza. It was 'not a shock', James confided in his journal, 'but a realisation of what a sore thing it is to bear'. There was a cremation the following day. Christmas 1935 came and with it 'missing Bombie. Hilda burnt a candle in front of the casket . . . Though one distracts oneself, sometimes I waver. I cannot believe I will never see her again.'

Early in 1936 Hilda decided to send the children away from the tropical climate to Fairholm to be cared for by her mother and sisters, and James agreed. They had leave due in the year and thought that the time had come to sort out Fairholm and to think, perhaps, of living there themselves after retirement. In August 1936 they were in Scotland. The family time at Fairholm was busy, nostalgic and fun. Larkhall was not growing and the coal pits

*James with his children, Jamie and Anne.*

had closed – the rural atmosphere was returning. Workmen were brought in to repair the house and install electric lighting. All the boxes which had been in storage were unpacked, and twenty-two bottles of 1870 wine were found, five of a 1865 claret. On 14 September they discovered the buried ruins of an old house near the oak tree, probably the first Fairholm house on the property. Stevenson-Hamilton was well pleased with his house and grounds, particularly now that he had a son. Nephew Vivian, who would have been his heir had Jamie not been born, was in total disgrace having stolen a number of items from Fairholm and had a reputation for drinking and womanising. The uncle was implacable, 'Now I would see him dead in a ditch with the utmost pleasure.' James felt betrayed, because he thought that Vivian had much to be grateful for.

Leaving the children in England, James and Hilda took an aircraft (for the first time) back to South Africa and were together in the national park by November 1936. Living at Skukuza, James and Hilda were able to spend more time together, sharing their days, sorting out the house, reading, and even 'typing out my 1890 journal. I don't like myself much in those days.' At the beginning of 1938 as the situation in Europe became tense, Stevenson-

Hamilton began to worry about impending war in Europe. He dreaded the prospect of Armageddon again. While he had been unencumbered by direct dependants during the First World War, he and Hilda were worried about the children who were at Fairholm with their grandmother and aunts – the distance between South Africa and Scotland was great and it would have been dreadful for the family to have been separated for the duration of a long war.

In May 1939 Hilda's mother returned to South Africa with the children and everyone was reunited. But while Stevenson-Hamilton could bring his children out to be with him, he could not do the same with Fairholm. With many large houses in Britain becoming public buildings, he dreaded the thought that Fairholm could become a shelter for slum children, or that the Country Council might site a sewage farm on the property. He raged to his journal on the subject, but tempered his outbursts with the sad thought that he might never see Fairholm again. At the outset of war and while conditions of conflict made him unable to maintain his links with Fairholm, he began to feel that he had betrayed his trust with the house by being absent from it for so long. Things would never be the same again, more so when he received a cable in April 1940 to say that his sister, Cissy, had died. Now that both his brother and sister had died, and he himself had a male heir, the lineage seemed secure and Stevenson-Hamilton began seriously to consider disentailing Fairholm. The necessary papers arrived and the process was set in motion. In 1942 he heard that all land would be taken by local councils and he was extremely depressed at the prospect. It was a 'point of honour not to abandon the family place after nearly five hundred years passing from father to son'. He felt uneasy about it all, but still very possessive. In 1944 he heard that the 'Boy Scouts want to take over Fairholm. The mere mention makes me gasp with fury.'

When war was declared in September 1939 there was little that could be done from the Kruger Park. Almost every day Stevenson-Hamilton made some comment in his journal about the progress of the war and his thoughts at that time. For the duration of the conflict, the warden and his rangers were on the alert to monitor any suspicious Germans coming over from Mozambique. There were plenty of rumours, but nothing materialised. The Stevenson-Hamiltons' friendship with Pirow and their acquisition of a radio started tongues wagging in the lowveld and Hilda and James were accused of being German spies. Gossip is a powerful weapon in a small community and the radio was confiscated. Stevenson-Hamilton wrote immediately to Esselen and to a number of Board members and soon the wireless sets – which had been confiscated from all the rangers – were returned.

## 'The Guardian Spirit of the Low-veld'

For much of the war the Kruger Park was closed to tourists and sources of funding dried up, but there was still much to be done. The Board continued to hold regular meetings, and reports and other documentation were required. Stevenson-Hamilton was put onto a commission in 1945 to investigate a new national park in the Limpopo River valley, called Dongola. He had wanted to get out of it but had to go to Cape Town for the hearings.[21] At home there were plenty of visitors; the house always seemed full of them, 'as bad as the tourist season' was one of Stevenson-Hamilton's comments.

Underlying all the anxiety about the war and the children, this period was dominated by the fear that retirement could not be delayed forever. There were signs of becoming elderly that even James could not ignore. He was well into his seventies and complained of being cross for never having quick sharp comments when he needed them. He found the effort of giving evidence at the 1945 Dongola commission very trying and tiring. On one occasion, quite uncharacteristically, he alighted from the train at the wrong station and almost missed his connection to Cape Town for a meeting. A 'good Samaritan' gave him a lift, but James neglected to ask his name and had to put an advertisement in the newspaper in order to contact him and thank him. He was in trouble with Hilda too, for not remembering something she had apparently told him about.

News eventually that war had ended caused great jubilation at Skukuza. The family cine of Fairholm was brought out, which the children always liked. But James was not feeling his best, he was suffering from pneumonia. When the doctor, and even Hilda, suggested that perhaps the job of warden was becoming too strenuous, James rallied. But he could not hold out forever and soon there were rumours that he would be asked to leave. Black emotions descended and the reality of parting from the Kruger National Park began to impress itself on him. For one thing, he had no home in South Africa apart from the national park and he worried about where to go. And, feeling that it would be better to be dead than useless, what would he do with himself? But he could not stave off the day indefinitely and, at the Board meeting at the end of July 1945, it was agreed that he would leave the park on 30 April 1946 and take six months leave on full pay thereafter. Two of the oldest rangers, including Harry Wolhuter, would leave at the same time.

Telegrams and letters began flooding in once the news was made public. His friends and colleagues sent good wishes on his retirement and many visitors who had been to the park wrote to thank him for his hospitality. There was a suggestion that the park should be renamed in his honour. There were tributes to his success in arousing South Africans to cherish their wildlife heritage, not only by creating the park but also by his numerous publications.

Despite the accolades and tributes, for Stevenson-Hamilton it was an awful prospect. He and Hilda had to find somewhere to live, they were unsure about Fairholm – Hilda was not keen – and did not want to burn their bridges in South Africa. They had been talking about finding land close to White River alongside Longmere Dam, an area close to a number of their friends. There were farms for sale, but the Stockley's was too expensive, and the Bairstow's, unattractive. 'Clinker' Willis's seemed the nicest, but Mrs Willis was initially not keen to sell and only relented in January 1946. Stevenson-Hamilton was also worried about having enough money to live on – pension funds not being mandatory in those days – for Hilda and the children were still young and would need support for many years. A number of people took up the question with the Board and the government.

Stevenson-Hamilton began the long task of going through and sorting old letters and papers. He spent most of his time writing copious and detailed instructions and notes for his successor, trying to entrench his thinking into future policy. He could not bear to think of another in his place and listed the ideas he had tried to achieve and how he had gone about these. In fact, both he and Hilda were pleased with the replacement warden who had been found. He was Colonel J.A.B. Sandenbergh, an airforce man. Stevenson-Hamilton's last days were blighted. He wanted to avoid any farewell party, and Sandenbergh passed on the message, so there was none. On 20 April he went out for the last time to shoot impala for rations. It was a fiasco – not only did he miss many shots, but a tourist saw the lorry full of dead carcasses. To make matters worse, Hilda was in hospital in Barberton. On 30 April 1946 his journal records, 'Last day as warden. All intriguing and bad feeling latterly. I had to make a speech of sorts but nearly wept.' A career of more than forty years in wildlife protection had ended.

As warden of a highly successful and well publicised national park when he retired, Stevenson-Hamilton was a famous figure, well known not only in South Africa, but also abroad. He had received two Honorary Doctorates in Law, one in 1935 from the University of the Witwatersrand, and the other from the University of Cape Town in 1945. Their citations were fulsome tributes to what he had achieved in promoting wildlife protection in South Africa.[22] Stevenson-Hamilton was also the recipient of a number of prestigious medals, including that of the Fauna Society in 1940 and the Coronation Medal in 1953. There was, however, one accolade which he would dearly loved to have had – a knighthood or other British honour. But in the new South Africa of the 1920s, he was ineligible for these. In the family archives there is a letter dated 4 January 1929 from Smuts – then leader of the opposition – to Stevenson-Hamilton (his letter has not survived) which reads, 'Yours of 7 December duly to hand. I note and can fully appreciate what you say about Honours. At the same time, the matter presents great difficulty in view of the Resolution of our House [of Assembly] four years ago . . .' He was referring to the fact that at the parliamentary sitting of February 1925 it was decided that no British citizen living in South Africa would be eligible for the conferment of titles or other British honours, as such were in conflict with the 'spirit of a new country'.[23]

# 12

# 'Little Benefit to Living after One's Work is Done'[1]
## *After Retirement*
## *(1946–1957)*

TWO DAYS AFTER LEAVING the Kruger National Park, James Stevenson-Hamilton was writing about how difficult it was to be an ordinary citizen going about the business of shopping or collecting the mail. Part of his despondency about retiring as warden was his fear for the future of the Kruger National Park without his strong guiding hand behind it. But he thought that perhaps he could take an interest in the wider system of South African National Parks and be of sound influence in their development. In June 1947, he was welcomed onto the National Parks Board to replace an outgoing member, but only a year later at the time of the National Party election victory, he received a curt note to say that his membership would be terminated. In 1950 Stevenson-Hamilton was awarded the title of Warden Emeritus of the Kruger National Park, but as he was not included in any events or decisions the title was an empty one.

In the absence of Stevenson-Hamilton, the Kruger National Park changed in two ways. Firstly, the 'man of action' was displaced almost at once by the professional scientist as pacesetter of the park. Influential in this respect were Sandenbergh, the new warden, together with a number of Board members, especially Dr R.A. Bigalke, director of the National Zoological Gardens. A scientific division was established, and in 1951 a professional biologist was appointed. Scientific record-keeping was started, surveys of fauna and flora were executed, exotic vegetation was cleared and soon considerable stature became attached to those scientists who managed and studied wildlife. By 1957 the motto of the National Parks Board had become 'management by intervention' and culling excess wild animals became the order of the day. There are many arguments for and against the wilderness philosophies of Stevenson-Hamilton and the interventionist tactics of his successors. There is a strong viewpoint that with fencing the park (the western side was fenced in the 1950s) and with population and development increase on its borders, the vastness of the wilderness contracted so that leaving nature to its own devices was just not a practical proposition. Moreover, the birth of wildlife management as a scientific discipline which resulted, has been an important international contribution from South Africa. In addition, it must be remembered that even today there remain very large sections of the Kruger National Park which are out-of-bounds to tourists. Thus although visitor numbers have continued to expand, places of undisturbed peace for wildlife still exist. But from Stevenson-Hamilton's point of view, the wonder of nature – its romance – had taken a back seat with scientific management, as wildlife numbers were manipulated by scientists, as visitor demands were heeded, and as an air of modernity permeated the Kruger National Park.

Secondly, with the change of South African government in 1948 when D.F. Malan's National Party won the election, there was strong Afrikaner affirmative action and a denigration of everything British. Even before the election, Stevenson-Hamilton heard that the National Party was agitating for a republic and many of his fellow English-speaking civil servants were pessimistic about their future in South Africa. As Stevenson-Hamilton had suspected, very close bonds were developed between the National Parks Board and the government after 1948 and they were to affect the ethos of his park. One seminal policy of the incoming government – indeed a reason for its electoral success – was to minimise the country's international and imperial connections. Former Prime Minister Smuts was a victim in this regard in Parks Board literature, and so was Stevenson-Hamilton.

To anyone visiting the park, Stevenson-Hamilton's accomplishments were undeniable – it would not have existed without him. But much was done either to minimise, even deny, his achievements, or to have him share them with Afrikaners. His book, *South African Eden*, was ignored in park publicity material, even though it was the only book about the Kruger National Park in print at that time.[2] Moreover, he was even vilified as being unsuitable for his task: 'it would have been difficult to conceive of anyone seemingly more ill qualified for the job. He was a Scottish aristocrat and trained British officer.'[3] Piet Grobler, Nationalist Minister of Lands in 1924, into whose lap the already well advanced national park proposal fell, was given equal credit with Stevenson-Hamilton.[4] In the early 1950s a scandal consumed the National Parks Board and the Kruger Park. Financial and other administrative irregularities were uncovered. It seems that Sandenbergh had not been a successful warden: he was even a disappointment to Stevenson-Hamilton who considered that he had compromised the accomplishments of many years of hard work. Not only did it become increasingly evident that Sandenbergh's talents as an administrator were overestimated but he also became enmeshed in political machinations and accusations of corruption and drunkenness into which there was a detailed inquiry, 'the Hoek Commission'. Indeed, although full details of Hoek's inquiry were never made public – although it was very much in the public interest to do so – its findings were used to transform the administration of the National Parks Board into an all-Afrikaner bureaucracy.[5]

From friends and acquaintances who came to his home and from the occasional visit to the park, Stevenson-Hamilton heard all the rumours. The retired warden did not like what he heard: the interference with nature, the corruption, and the political machinations. The entire infrastructure he had spent his life constructing, seemed about to fall. Even the staff was about to be emasculated, perhaps even moved out of the park, and all power would vest in the officials in Pretoria. He concluded that 'there is little benefit to living after one's work is done'. Wolhuter, who often visited and with whom all the memories of more than forty years could be shared, agreed.

Among his own friends, of whom there were a great many, Stevenson-Hamilton was treated as the prominent wildlife protectionist that he was. He was still acclaimed and many people recognised his fame and accomplishments. In January 1955, two young men came up to the house, 'apparently they just wanted to have seen me'. A movie company asked him for information of animal habits, and he was glad that they had not asked the park biologist. At a meeting in Nelspruit he was referred to reverentially, but remarked that he could not hear all that was said and hoped that he looked appropriately grateful for the compliment. He was put on the governing body of the Sabi Sand, a privately owned consortium of game farms adjacent to the Kruger National Park, ironically the area excised from the game reserve in 1923 which had then belonged to the Transvaal Consolidated Lands Company. But there were more hurts than accolades. In 1955, Stevenson-Hamilton – one of the most diligent record-keepers imaginable who had left everything in its correct place in 1946 – was asked to supply records of past history of the park, all of which he had carefully handed over to Sandenbergh but who had them destroyed 'as he was starting a new era'. Although James learnt eventually to live with the new era in the Kruger National Park, he never could put it totally out of his mind.

Many of the rumours about the fate of the Kruger National Park which were communicated to Stevenson-Hamilton during the 1950s did not mater-ialise as facts, but they upset him greatly. There was, however, absolutely nothing that he could do. He no longer had friends in government. In fact, in his view, the whole country had changed with its political dispensation.

*A sketch of Gibraltar by Hilda Stevenson-Hamilton.*

He felt alienated from South Africa, and found government intervention, such as passes for Africans, distasteful. He thought that the country was becoming much like Germany of the 1930s. He foresaw some kind of African backlash against apartheid and when Hilda interrupted an all-night African Zionist church service, he recognised that it was 'fundamentally probably political – as in Kenya'.

After leaving Skukuza the family moved to 'Gibraltar' as they called the property they had bought from Willis. It was a small farm, well away from neighbours, and the lawn which led down from the house ended at the bank of Longmere Dam, an irrigation lake which had been constructed some years before. A spit of rock jutted into the water, hence the name 'Gibraltar'. White River, the nearest village where shops and other amenities were located, was just a short drive away. For major purchases, Nelspruit was just a little further. Many friends lived in the neighbourhood and Stevenson-

Hamilton's journal records the many, many visitors he and Hilda entertained at Gibraltar. Every day there was someone around, and while these visitors stimulated and interested Hilda (who was then in her forties), they were often too much for her husband, who took refuge 'resting' in his room. Occasionally he wrote a relieved entry in his journal that it had been a day without guests.

After settling into Gibraltar, the family left South Africa for Fairholm, where they spent long periods from July 1946 to October 1949, returning to South Africa at intervals. These were years of crisis and decision for them all because finally the time had come to choose where they would live for the rest of their lives. At last, the long-held dream of making Fairholm a permanent home could be realised. But while political and economic circumstances in South Africa had changed for the worse, so had they in Britain, and the matter required considerable thought and debate. Stevenson-Hamilton had never been good at making a decision, and in the trauma of retirement he found it even harder to make up his mind.

In 1946 he went to Britain in advance of Hilda and thus arrived at Fairholm without her. Once more the burden of his history descended on him:

> Fairholm welcomes me as usual in spite of the way I abandoned and ignored it. All my childhood comes back. While the inside is different, the outside is the same. But what to do? Were it possible to live here, I wouldn't hesitate. But there is no domestic help and with taxation and the threat of appropriation, it seems impracticable.

When Hilda arrived with Anne and Jamie in October 1946, they were thrilled with Fairholm. The ugly mining paraphernalia had disappeared, for the local mines had been worked out, and the decline of Scotland as an industrial power had been all to the good for Fairholm's surroundings. Hilda was particularly charmed; she did not even mind the household chores and her husband seemed to think that she was content to 'chuck Africa'. Certainly Fairholm would need attention, trespassers had used the grounds and the woods, fences were broken and the gardener's lodge was a ruin. But James, Hilda and the children explored their Scottish heritage with delight. Stevenson-Hamilton took his 'ain folk' to Hamilton church. They sat in the Fairholm seat and he told them what he remembered about his childhood. There was a sense of rightness in an almost primaeval sense, in returning to end his life in a place to which he really belonged and which, unlike the Kruger National Park, could never be wrested from him.

But by Christmas that year the enthusiasm with Fairholm and Scotland had palled. Perhaps the weather had much to do with it, because it was cold and frosty and they all had coughs and colds. James became anxious about the high cost of living in Britain. He was, after all, an elderly father with children in their early teens, and as 1946 became 1947 he began to be depressed by it all: 'Change and decay is all around, I see.'

The family returned to South Africa in March 1947 and soon Gibraltar was alive with the sounds of building construction and workers and the house was made comfortable and habitable. But still, the questions would not go away. Was he British or was he South African?

> What to do? Fairholm or Gibraltar? . . . Much het up about what to do . . . God knows what would be best . . . Did not leave the place. Gloomed all day . . . 80th birthday. Presents and lots of visitors. My problems have become an obsession, Hilda in tears . . . Depressed and bored, did all the wrong things to Jamie. Hilda openly miserable.

What Stevenson-Hamilton's personal crisis at retirement was doing to his wife can only be imagined. Her version is lacking, but from her husband's journals we obtain an inkling of how seriously she was affected. She, who had made him so happy on his birthdays since their marriage, was in tears on his eightieth. She loved the sun and fresh air of Africa, and had married James to share it with him. She would have lived anywhere with him, but she needed the sunshine, the light and sights of Africa, which she could convey so well in her paintings and sculptures.

The year 1948 started no better: 'Fairholm and Jamie on mind. Nothing to occupy me.' As can be imagined, the intensity of the internal conflict affected Stevenson-Hamilton's health, and in November 1949 he suffered a stroke. From 26 November until 10 December the journal is blank, and then in a very peculiar hand is the message, 'First day I have been able to write intelligently. Am still very dizzy.' A month later he was still affected, 'Wish my right hand would become unpalsied and that I could write.' Stevenson-Hamilton never typed out his handwritten journals of 1947, 1948 and 1949. It may well be that he could not bear to relive the agony of separation from the Kruger National Park and his inability to cope with retirement and its demands. By contrast, 1950 is typed and its tone is far less bleak than those before, even though not all was settled. But he commented on the children more than before, he played chess with Jamie, they hunted for Easter eggs, and he thought Anne 'charming with her pigtails and green frock'. Altogether a happier routine was established. At last, he was content with the

*James Stevenson-Hamilton next to the trophy of his first lion in the hall at Fairholm.*

decision to live in South Africa; perhaps also, his period of grieving for the Kruger National Park had ended. In April 1952 he spoke of going to Britain again, but the tone of the visit was different. Clearly he felt that this would be his last visit and he spent time putting things in order.

Because of his increasing infirmity – he could hardly walk – while at Fairholm he lived mostly in the library, clad in a dressing gown and deriving considerable amusement and interest from reading his old journals. Unlike many other old people, James was able to relive his life in the most immediate way, looking at its vagaries, rewards and disappointments through his own eyes, unclouded even by memory. He read the journal of his voyage to South Africa in 1888 to Hilda, telling her all about his first love, Hilda Browne. He read his father's journals, he went through the library safe, filled with family records, dating back to 1496 and 1554, and had an expert decipher the Latin inscriptions on the old vellum documents. He told Jamie every detail he could recall and took him around Braidwood and the other family properties of the past.

Just as his active working life had wider value, so did his inner life of old age. He remained critical, intelligent and his commentary on the process of ageing shows both wisdom and brutal accuracy. He saw his regimental friend, 'Ernest Holland, crippled from arthritis, stone deaf. Have to write everything for him. Pathetic. Family seem to make fun of him.' Jack Roberton 'my oldest friend from Ardenlee, Helensburgh. He also had to be written to. All the others are dead.' In September 1951 Smuts died, 'I had known him since 1907. Always a good friend . . .' The list grew ever longer. Even the King died and James Stevenson-Hamilton had lived in six reigns. In South Africa he lost Charlie Sanderson from the earliest days of the game reserve and Ranger Tomlinson died too. De Laporte was the next to go. And what of 'La Belle Helene', who wrote in 1942 'It is nice to have such a dear friend as you in my long life'? He saw her last in August 1952, and her daughter wrote to him of her death in 1955. His other interesting woman friend had been Princess Marie Louise who died in 1956. Of those friends who were alive, none were happy. Most were ill, some were blind, others lived in great poverty, another was 'helpless and had two nurses look after him all the time'. Some longed for death.

If there were big changes in the social landscape, they were matched by those in the natural. 'Visiting where Bill Sanderson must have been, about 1.5 miles, but country now so tree-covered and altered so one cannot get one's bearings . . . Went to Mtimba. Buildings pulled down and reverted to a jungle. Seen the complete circle from jungle to jungle. Jamie at Fairholm I am glad to think.' Only Fairholm was safe.

It was as well that Hilda was young and healthy, because James was a considerable physical liability. At the end of 1953 he had a fall and cracked a rib. Moreover, the doctor advised a prostate operation, but he did not see much point in that, knowing that he had only a year or two left to him. He was often giddy and had to be supported when he walked and his memory began to fail him. He felt he had 'disgraced' himself, because he 'fell and slipped while people were there'. He remarked that it was 'lucky that Hilda knows everything for I cannot get around any more'. For a man who was once extolled for killing lions so courageously, who had survived numerous attacks of fever, who had lived alone in tropical and dangerous places, these were humiliating years.

The children provided a strong interest. He often wrote to them while they were at school, their replies were treasured and kept, and Anne's competent drawings were an especial delight. In 1954 Anne found herself a partner, Peter Doyle, and they were engaged that November. Stevenson-Hamilton did not attend the wedding, but Hilda did. Afterwards the just-married couple came to South Africa and much merriment attended the showing of the wedding cine. James was devoted to his son Jamie, his male heir, determined to give him the happy childhood which he had, himself, been denied and Jamie's visits are recorded with extreme warmth and delight. He wrote regularly to his son, as he and Hilda did to Anne, giving advice and comment. But Jamie was soon burdened with the care of his father, rather than the other way around, for the old man needed advice and attention.

On Old Year's Night 1956, James wondered 'if I shall last another. I don't care for myself, but the longer I can live the better for Hilda financially and otherwise.' He did not quite make it. His journals record 'becoming worse and worse on my legs', 'very weak', 'nothing is wrong, only senile decay', 'voice going'. His journals are confused, the typing is bad, the incisive comment is no more. His ninetieth birthday on 2 October was cause for great celebration. There was a party, telegrams and letters poured in:

> Today I attained the unexpected age of 90 years. Two years older than my father when he died in 1926 [of] – as our doctor then said, 'Nothing but old age.' So, I have beaten him, but don't expect to see another. In fact, for the past two months, I have been pretty ill, and on my back a lot, which I recognise as purely senile decay. My hearing is poor, my voice suffers from chronic laryngitis and I can barely hobble on two sticks and usually take Hilda's arm. In fact, I depend on her now for almost everything, and must give her a lot of trouble with my slow ways.

A few days later, he detailed all his assets, protested that he could not start the generator any longer (it was his daily chore), had happy letters from both Jamie and Anne, and went to White River with Hilda. By 2 December he had realised that he was getting 'Feebler every day. I don't think I would last long without Hilda to help me, but what a drag I must be on her.' He sat in the sun and on 3 December wrote his last journal entry. It is almost illegible and is very confused. He became ill again and died one week later, on 10 December 1957.

Hilda, James and Anne received an enormous number of letters and tributes when James Stevenson-Hamilton died. There was no sense of tragedy in his death, for his work had ended and he was ninety years old. One sensitive letter noted that the atmosphere at Gibraltar at the time that Stevenson-Hamilton died was 'filled with a deep sense of human dignity and the "rightness" of death'. All the South African newspapers reviewed his career, many in considerable detail.

Many people who had known him wrote to the family offering their condolences: 'He did such great work for his country, and left something so valuable and lasting and real . . . he was someone who really lived . . . he understood values and I often think that is the whole art of living'. He was 'yet another of South Africa's great pioneers' who had done such a great deal with his life. 'The result of his life's work remains as a heritage to future generations . . .' 'His outstanding humanity will be remembered as well as his life's work, by all who were fortunate enough to know him . . . He was indeed blessed that he could achieve so much.' 'His life was filled with purpose and achievement.'[6]

Indeed it was. His tangible monuments are two landscapes: Fairholm and the Kruger National Park. The first he had inherited, in a long tradition of handing over from generation to generation not only a house and a family, but a piece of the earth. Over the many centuries of Hamilton habitation, that landscape had fluctuated. In many respects it was an artificial environment, a house had been built, and it had been altered by the planting of trees and crops, by mining and by industrial development. It had been invaded by people, by agriculture, and by industrialisation. In no sense could Fairholm be called wild, at times certainly rural, but throughout the centuries that the Hamiltons had been there it was never a wilderness. But it was an ecological whole, it had integrity, and the built, natural and intellectual environments meshed together in one.

While Stevenson-Hamilton could hardly bear to leave Fairholm because of what it meant to him, he found another landscape which entranced him just as much. Fairholm was an inheritance of land and history, but also of a military career. This took him to theatres of imperial wars, but it did not earn him the same acclaim as it did for his soldier forebears. Instead, it introduced him to the wilderness of Africa – Zululand, Barotseland, the Sudan and the Kruger National Park. It was there that he found his moments to make his greatest contribution. Sometimes he was held in the thrall of Fairholm, sometimes in the thrall of the Transvaal lowveld. The landscapes were both his, the one he had been given, the other he had created. The Kruger National Park also had ecological integrity. People and wildlife had lived there for aeons, themselves also in a symbiotic relationship as between the Hamiltons and Fairholm, simply on a larger scale. Just as he wished to preserve Fairholm for his family forever, so Stevenson-Hamilton laboured physically and intellectually to preserve the eastern Transvaal lowveld for the future. Although this destiny was not always clear to him and at times he groped for direction, it lay at the core of his life. The personal price was high. As an adult, he never lived permanently at Fairholm, seldom saw the seasons change or the Avon River rise and fall. But it was his, and he held on to it. By contrast, he lived for many years at Sabi Bridge, came to know every landmark, every creature and the history of the precolonial people who lived there. As with Fairholm, there was not one aspect of the landscape which dominated: people, wildlife and the veld were inextricably locked together. It was for this reason that he resented scientists who put one factor higher than others, and for that reason also that he was not involved in 'national parks' as a general concept. His interest was the Kruger National Park alone, for he had made it a part of his very being. But, unlike Fairholm, it was not his, and he was forced to leave it. The equality of meaning of both these places in his life and his burning ambition to protect both can be seen in the intense inner conflict which occurred when he had to leave Skukuza in 1946. Its resolution was difficult and it came only at the price of his health. Environmentalism has been defined as a 'sense of place'. This James Stevenson-Hamilton undoubtedly had to an extreme degree, and was able to use it to lasting effect.

# Notes

## Chapter 1
### 'A Good Family': Family Background and School Days, 1867–1883

1. The Ministers of the Respective Parishes, comp., *The Statistical Account of Lanarkshire* (Edinburgh and London, 1841), p. 269. 'The Hamiltons of Fairholm, descendants of the fourth son of Thomas Hamilton of Darngaber, are still a good family in the south-east side of this parish.'
2. Fairholm Archives, Newspaper cutting.
3. Ministers of Respective Parishes, comp., *The Statistical Account of Lanarkshire*, pp. 254–255.
4. For details of the Hamilton lineage, see *Burke's Genealogical and Heraldic History of the Landed Gentry*, 18th ed. (London, 1965–1969).
5. Born 6 November 1838.
6. G. Costigan, *A History of Modern Ireland with a Sketch of Earlier Times* (New York, 1969).
7. For an analysis of female deaths at this time and the social impact, see P. Jalland, *Death in the Victorian Family* (New York, 1996).
8. Fairholm Archives, Journal entry, 22 January 1957.
9. Fairholm Archives, *The Liberal Review* 12 July 1881, Frederick R. Leyland. Also L. Merrill, *The Peacock Room* (New Haven, 1997). The room has been reconstructed in the Freer Gallery, Washington DC.
10. *Dictionary of National Biography, 1912–1921* (Oxford, 1964), pp. 298–299.
11. The entire contents of the Duke of Hamilton's Palace were sold for the then unprecedented sum of £397 562; D. Cannadine, *The Decline and Fall of the British Aristocracy* (New Haven and London, 1990), p. 113. For an evaluation of the landed gentry at this time of social and political change, see also G. Best, *Mid-Victorian Britain, 1851–1875* (London, 1979).

## Chapter 2
### 'Brought up with Military Ideas': Army Training and First Commission in Pietermaritzburg, 1883–1890

1. Fairholm Archives, James Stevenson-Hamilton, 'Tabloid sketch of my life'.
2. For details, see H.S. Stevenson, *The Stevenson Family, A Record of the Descendants of James Stevenson, Burgess of Paisley in 1753* (Richmond, Yorks, 1965), and Fairholm Archives, James Stevenson-Hamilton's description of family members, 1885.
3. For army details, see E.M. Spiers, *The Late Victorian Army, 1868–1902* (Manchester,

1992); B. Bond, *The Victorian Army and the Staff College, 1854–1914* (London, 1972); E. Spiers, 'The late Victorian army, 1864–1914', in D. Chandler, ed., *The Oxford Illustrated History of the British Army* (Oxford and New York, 1994); A.R. Godwin-Austen, *The Staff and the Staff College* (London, 1927); J.M. MacKenzie, ed., *Popular Imperialism and the Military, 1850–1950* (Manchester, 1992); A. Shepperd, *Sandhurst: The Royal Military Academy Sandhurst and its Predecessors* (London, 1980).
4. Cannadine, *Decline and Fall*, pp. 264–274. Also, R.R. James, *The British Revolution: British Politics 1880–1939* (London, 1977); H. Perkin, *The Rise of Professional Society: England since 1880* (London and New York, 1989).
5. W.S. Churchill, *My Early Life: A Roving Commission* (London, 1947), p. 56.
6. Cannadine, *Decline and Fall*.
7. Ibid., pp. 9–27; Perkin, *Rise of Professional Society*, pp. 65–73.
8. Field-Marshall Viscount Wavell, *Allenby: Soldier and Statesman* (London, 1974), pp. 24–27.
9. The Royal Military College certificate of 16 January 1888 records that, out of a possible total of 3 100 marks, he obtained 2 019. He only did really well in drill (with 171 points out of a possible 200), while in other subjects he scored exactly 50 per cent.
10. W.Y. Carman, *British Military Uniforms from Contemporary Pictures; Henry VII to the Present Day* (Feltham, Middlesex, 1968), p. 105; E.S. Jackson, *The Inniskilling Dragoons: The Records of an Old Heavy Cavalry Regiment* (London, 1909).
11. For details of the history of Natal at this time, see C.T. Binns, *Dinizulu: The Death of the House of Shaka* (London, 1968); E.H. Brookes and C. de B. Webb, *A History of Natal* (Pietermaritzburg, 1965); A. Duminy and B. Guest, eds., *Natal and Zululand from Earliest Times to 1910: A New History* (Pietermaritzburg, 1989); B. Guest and J.M. Sellers, *Enterprise and Exploitation in a Victorian Colony* (Pietermaritzburg, 1985); J. Guy, *The Destruction of the Zulu Kingdom: The Civil War in Zululand, 1879–1884* (Johannesburg, 1982); A.F. Hattersley, *Portrait of a Colony: The Story of Natal* (Cambridge, 1940); A.F. Hattersley, *The Natalians: Further Annals of Natal* (Pietermaritzburg, 1940): G. Dominy, 'The Imperial garrison in Natal with special reference to Fort Napier 1843–1914: Its social, cultural and economic impact', Ph.D. (London, 1995); J. Laband and R. Haswell, *Pietermaritzburg 1838–1988: A New Portrait of an African City* (Pietermaritzburg, 1988).
12. The gravestone at Fort Napier records that Sgt W.J. Godwin died on 19 July 1889 aged 30.
13. Spiers, *The Late Victorian Army*, pp. 104–105.
14. The full account of this visit was published in 1986 in J. Carruthers, ed., 'Journal of a visit to the goldfields in 1889', *Africana Notes and News*, vol. 27, no. 3, September 1986, pp. 93–103.

## Chapter 3
### 'No Goal or Object': Regimental Life in Britain, 1890–1898

1. Fairholm Archives, Journal entry, 24 April 1894.

## Notes

2. T. Carder, *The Encyclopaedia of Brighton* (Lewes, 1990), item 87f.
3. Spiers, *Late Victorian Army*, pp. 255–265.
4. Wavell, *Allenby*, pp. 43–44.
5. G. Harries-Jenkins, *The Army in Victorian Society* (London, 1977).
6. Churchill, *My Early Life*, pp. 164–165.
7. Spiers, *Late Victorian Army*, pp. 255–256.
8. H.N. Cole, *The Story of Aldershot: A History of the Civil War and Military Towns* (Aldershot, 1980), p. 109.
9. Churchill, *My Early Life*, p. 65.
10. See W. Ferguson, *Scotland 1689 to the Present* (Edinburgh, 1968).
11. Cannadine, *Decline and Fall*, p. 101; M. Girouard, *Life in the English Country House: A Social and Architectural History* (New Haven and London, 1978), pp. 268–301.
12. When the family finally sold the house in 1984, these treasures went to the British Museum.
13. M. Girouard, *The Victorian Country House* (New Haven, 1979). Ashfold had been built of local material by George Devey for Eric C. Smith between 1875 and 1878. The house no longer exists, having been later converted into a school (it had fifty bedrooms) and then later destroyed by fire. The dower house, however, still stands and it was here that Helen lived in her old age.
14. M.R. Booth, *Theatre in the Victorian Age* (Cambridge, 1991), pp. 12–113.
15. Fairholm Archives, Gibbons to Yardley, 30 September 1897.
16. Ibid., 10 October 1897.
17. Fairholm Archives, Yardley to Stevenson-Hamilton, 22 November 1897.
18. The contract was signed on 15 March 1898.

## Chapter 4
### 'This Life Just Suits Me': Barotseland, 1898–1899

1. Fairholm Archives, Journal entry, 2 October 1898.
2. A. St H. Gibbons, *Africa from South to North through Marotseland* (London, 1904).
3. Fairholm Archives, Gibbons to Stevenson-Hamilton, 4 January 1897.
4. J.P.R. Wallis, ed., *The Barotseland Journals of James Stevenson-Hamilton, 1898–1899* (London, 1953), p. xxiii.
5. Gibbons, *Africa from South to North*, vol. 1, p. 109.
6. Ibid.
7. See J.M. MacKenzie, ed., *Imperialism and the Natural World* (Manchester, 1990) and J.M. MacKenzie, ed., *The Empire of Nature: Hunting, Conservation and British Imperialism* (Manchester, 1988).
8. Wallis, *Barotseland Journals*, p. 179.
9. Ibid., p. 272.
10. Ibid., p. 203.
11. Ibid., p. 150.
12. Gibbons, *Africa from South to North*, vol. 1, p. 14.

13. Wallis, *Barotseland Journals*, pp. 49, 207.
14. Ibid., p. 92.
15. Ibid., p. 103.
16. Ibid., p. 74.
17. Ibid., p. 44.
18. Ibid., p. 98.
19. Boyd-Alexander was murdered in 1910 while on a birding trip to central Africa.
20. Wallis, *Barotseland Journals*, p. 10.
21. Ibid., p. 138.
22. The Barotse are also referred to as the Lozi, Bulozi, Rozi or Luyi.
23. L.H. Gann, *A History of Northern Rhodesia: Early Days to 1953* (London, 1964), pp. 20–21.
24. Ibid., p. 21.
25. R. Hall, *Zambia* (London, 1965), p. 92; Wallis, *Barotseland Journals*, p. xxii.
26. Fairholm Archives, James Stevenson-Hamilton, 'Tabloid sketch of my life'.
27. Wallis, *Barotseland Journals*, p. 234.
28. Ibid., pp. 133, 179.
29. Gibbons, *Africa from South to North*, vol. 1, pp. 67, 75.
30. Wallis, *Barotseland Journals*, p. 208.
31. Ibid., p. 135.
32. Fairholm Archives, Stevenson-Hamilton to Moral, 23 February 1951.
33. Wallis, *Barotseland Journals*, p. 99.
34. Ibid., p. 202.
35. Ibid., pp. 207–208.
36. Ibid., p. 132.
37. Ibid., p. 158.
38. Ibid., p. 162.
39. Ibid., pp. 172–173.
40. Ibid., p. 119.
41. Ibid., p. 44.
42. Ibid., p. 103.
43. Ibid., pp. 108–109.
44. Ibid., p. 148.
45. Ibid., p. 168.
46. Ibid., p. 144.
47. Ibid., p. 183.

# Chapter 5
## 'My Regiment was in South Africa': The South African War, 1899–1902

1. Fairholm Archives, James Stevenson-Hamilton, 'Tabloid sketch of my life'.
2. J.W. Yardley, *With the Inniskilling Dragoons: The Record of a Cavalry Regiment During the Boer War, 1899–1902* (London, 1904), pp. 1–2.

3. L.M. Phillipps, *With Rimington* (London, 1902), pp. 2–3.
4. L.S. Amery, *The Times History of the War in South Africa*, vol. 3 (London, 1905), p. 460; R.L. Wallace, *The Australians at the Boer War* (Canberra, 1976), p. 108.
5. See Amery, *Times History of the War*, vol. 3, pp. 466–471.
6. Wavell, *Allenby*, p. 63.
7. H.H.S. Pearse, ed., *The History of Lumsden's Horse: A Complete Record of the Corps from its Formation to its Disbandment* (London, 1903).
8. Yardley, *With the Inniskilling Dragoons*, p. 54.
9. Ibid., pp. 60–61.
10. Spiers, *Late Victorian Army*, pp. 318–319.
11. Australian war correspondent and poet A.B. 'Banjo' Paterson, quoted in Yardley, p. 113.
12. Spiers, *Late Victorian Army*, p. 317.
13. Wavell, *Allenby*, pp. 40–41, 78–79.
14. Spiers, *Late Victorian Army*, p. 316.
15. In a letter to his father (26 February 1900) Stevenson-Hamilton complained about the behaviour of some troops – not his own regiment – being drunk, raping local women and allowing prisoners to escape while rounding up harmless women and children. By contrast, he described the Boers he met as having 'natural savvy' and of being a formidable enemy for whom he was having a 'growing respect and admiration'.
16. Swanston and Gibbs only joined the regiment in May 1900; see Yardley, *With the Inniskilling Dragoons*, pp. 54, 70. Terrot was made new subaltern on 1 August 1900.
17. Yardley, *With the Inniskilling Dragoons*, pp. 208–211.
18. Ibid., p. 209.
19. Ibid., pp. 236–237.
20. Ibid., Chapter 19.
21. Ibid., p. 259.
22. Ibid., p. 316.
23. On the journal page, James wrote a later footnote: 'He lasted for two years and then [was] compulsorily retired (1904) owing to bad report on him by Inspector-General of Cavalry.'
24. Kruger National Park Archives, Skukuza (KNP) Opsieners Jaarverslae 1, Lagden to Stevenson-Hamilton, 21 June 1902.
25. Fairholm Archives, Lagden to W. Parker, 5 February 1929.

## Chapter 6
### 'My Own Creation': Sabi Game Reserve, 1902–1914

1. Fairholm Archives, Journal entry, 30 August 1904.
2. Transvaal Archives: Executive Council Resolution 258, 2 July 1902.
3. For detailed source references see E.J. Carruthers, *Game Protection in the Transvaal, 1846 to 1926* (Pretoria, 1995) and for the history of the Kruger National Park see

E.J. Carruthers, *The Kruger National Park: A Social and Political History* (Pietermaritzburg, 1995).
4. For the full story of this game reserve, see E.J. Carruthers, 'The Pongola Game Reserve: An eco-political study', *Koedoe* 28, 1985, pp. 1–16.
5. Transvaal Archives (TA) CS43 5820/01, Undated note on file cover. TA CS66 1176/02, McInerney to Assistant Secretary, 3 February 1902; TA CS58 182/01, Walker to Assistant Secretary, 30 November 1901; TA CS63 722/02, McInerney to Assistant Secretary, 20 January 1902; TA CS31 4159/01, Casement to Controller of the Treasury, 30 August 1901.
6. TA SNA52 NA1904/02, Stevenson-Hamilton to Lagden, 4 September 1902.
7. TA SNA188 NA3112/03, Johannesburg Public Library (JPL), Transvaal Land Owners Archives (TLOA) Report for year ending 31 October 1903.
8. JPL TLOA, vol. 1, Report for year ending 31 October 1904.
9. TA Executive Council Resolution 365, 4/5 May 1903.
10. TA SNA178 NA2536/03, Report on Singwitsi Game Reserve, 13 October 1903.
11. TA Executive Council, Resolution 302, 21 April 1903; Proclamation 17 of 1903, 26 May 1903.
12. Annual Report of the Government Game Reserves 1903–1904, in *Transvaal Administration Reports, 1904*; TA SNA189 NA3226/03, Report on the Pongola Game Reserve, December 1903.
13. TA SNA15 295/02, Secretary of the Transvaal Administration to Secretary for Native Affairs, 18 June 1900.
14. TA SNA136 NA1303/03, Stevenson-Hamilton to Hogge, 7 July 1903.
15. TA LtG65 73/2, Colonial Secretary to Lieutenant-Governor, 26 August 1903.
16. TA LD453 AG2805/03, H.J. Tennant to Bourke, 6 January 1904. TA LD463 AG2805/03, Chief Staff Officer South African Constabulary to Lieutenant-Governor, 9 October 1903; TA LD463 AG2805/03, Military Secretary to Secretary of Law Department, 28 December 1903.
17. TA SNA300 NA3647/05, Lagden to Colonial Secretary, 30 November 1905.
18. Cape Archives (CA) A848, Stratford Caldecott Collection, 4(6), Stevenson-Hamilton to Caldecott, 19 July 1929.
19. TA SNA138 1390/03, Hogge to Secretary for Native Affairs, 18 January 1904.
20. Fairholm Archives, Journal entry, 22 June 1905.
21. TA SNA158 NA1702/03, Lagden to Fraser, 3 April 1905.
22. TA SNA243 2831/04, Stevenson-Hamilton to Acting Secretary for Native Affairs, 2 December 1904.
23. TA SNA63 NA2206/02, Hogge to Secretary for Native Affairs, 6 October 1902.
24. Fairholm Archives, Journal entry, 13 December 1902.
25. TA SNA52 NA1904/02, Stevenson-Hamilton to Lagden, 4 September 1902.
26. TA SNA50 NA1751/02, Stevenson-Hamilton to McInerney, 18 August 1902; Native Commissioner Lydenburg to Secretary for Native Affairs, 18 November 1902.
27. TA SNA169 NA2063/03, Report on the Sabi Game Reserve for the year ending August 1903.

28. TA SNA321 1321/06, F. Steinaecker to Secretary for Native Affairs, 4 April 1906.
29. J. Stevenson-Hamilton, *Animal Life in Africa* (London, 1912), p. 27.
30. TA SNA178 NA2536/03, Report on Singwitsi Game Reserve, 13 October 1903.
31. Fairholm Archives, Journal entry, 18 January 1909.
32. Ibid., 6 June 1912.
33. TA *Debates of the Legislative Assembly*, A. Woolls-Sampson, cols 1425–1426, 24 July 1907.
34. TA TPS8 3075, Annual Report of the Government Game Reserves, 1908–1909.

## Chapter 7
## 'Puzzling are the Ways of Wild Animals': Sabi Game Reserve, 1902–1914

1. J. Stevenson-Hamilton, *Wild Life in South Africa* (London, 1947), p. 8.
2. For details see Carruthers, *Game Protection*.
3. A. Duminy and B. Guest, *Interfering in Politics: A Biography of Sir Percy Fitzpatrick* (Johannesburg, 1987); A.P. Cartwright, *The First South African: The Life and Times of Sir Percy Fitzpatrick* (Cape Town, 1971).
4. Translations of the resolutions of this convention can be found in the Public Record Office, London: Cd3189, *Correspondence Relating to the Preservation of Wild Animals in Africa* (1906), pp. 86–91 and Public Record Office FO2/818.
5. See, for example, H.A. Bryden, *Nature and Sport in South Africa* (London, 1897), p. 299.
6. D. Hammond and A. Jablow, *The Africa That Never Was: Four Centuries of British Writing about Africa* (New York, 1970), pp. 89–90.
7. E.N. Buxton, *Two African Trips; With Notes and Suggestions on Big Game Preservation in Africa* (London, 1902), p. 116.
8. This society is still in existence but has twice altered its name: in 1919 it became the Society for the Preservation of the Fauna of the Empire and in 1950, the Fauna Protection Society. In 1904 the society began publication of a journal which continues today under the name of *Oryx*.
9. The establishment of this body took place in October 1902, and seems to have been at the instigation of C. Bramley of the Market Estates Company; see TA CS108 7277/02, C. Bramley to Colonial Secretary, 12 July 1902. The Association was formed as a completely new organisation.
10. TA Executive Council Resolution 1065, 5 October 1904; Executive Council Resolution 940, 10 June 1905.
11. *The Low-veld: Its Wild Life and its People* (London, 1934).
12. Stevenson-Hamilton, *Animal Life*, pp. 20, 27.
13. TA TPB785 TA3070, Report by Stevenson-Hamilton, undated.
14. KNP K11, Stevenson-Hamilton to Secretary, National Parks Board, 4 October 1944.
15. Elephant, rhinoceros, lion, leopard and buffalo.
16. A.B. Percival, *A Game Ranger on Safari* (London, 1928), pp. 214–215; H.A. Bryden, *Gun and Camera in Southern Africa* (London, 1893), p. 59.
17. R.C.F. Maugham, *Zambezia* (London, 1910).
18. Fairholm Archives, Hornaday to Stevenson-Hamilton, 22 August 1912.

## Chapter 8
### 'Biggest War in 100 Years': England and Gallipoli, 1914–1917

1. Fairholm Archives, Journal entry, early August 1914.
2. Sir O'Moore Creagh and E.H. Humphris, *The Victoria Cross, 1856–1920* (Polstead, 1920).
3. B. Bond, ed., *The First World War and British Military History* (Oxford, 1991), p. 166.
4. These should have reached Gallipoli early in June, but the replacement men were delayed at Gretna Green by the worst railway accident in British history, see R.R. James, *Gallipoli* (London, 1965), pp. 210–211.
5. James, *Gallipoli*, pp. 221–222.

## Chapter 9
### 'Truculent Dinka Clans': The Sudan, 1917–1919

1. Fairholm Archives, James Stevenson-Hamilton, 'Tabloid sketch of my life'. Stevenson-Hamilton realised that they were more properly the Jeng – the name they called themselves.
2. Vol. 46 no. 5, pp. 389–400.
3. P.M. Holt and M.W. Daly, *A History of the Sudan: From the Coming of Islam to the Present Day* (London, 1988), p. 3; K.M. Barbour, *The Republic of the Sudan: A Regional Geography* (London, 1961), pp. 237–247; D.H. Johnson, 'Reconstructing a history of local floods in the Upper Nile region of the Sudan', *The International Journal of African Historical Studies* 25(3), 1992.
4. J. Stevenson-Hamilton, 'The Dinka country east of the Bahr-el-Gebel', *The Geographical Journal* 46(5), 1920, p. 393.
5. R.O. Collins, *Land Beyond the Rivers: The Southern Sudan, 1898–1918* (New Haven, 1971), p. 53; Holt and Daly, *History of the Sudan*, p. 3; Barbour, *Republic of the Sudan*, pp. 84, 238–239; D.H. Johnson, 'Tribal boundaries and border wars: Nuer-Dinka relations in the Sobat and Zaraf valleys, c.1860–1976', *Journal of African History* 23, 1982, pp. 183–203.
6. Collins, *Land Beyond the Rivers*, pp. 180–185. M.W. Daly, *Empire on the Nile: The Anglo-Egyptian Sudan, 1898–1934* (Cambridge, 1986), pp. 145, 404.
7. D.H. Johnson, 'The Sudan under the British', *Journal of African History* 23, 1982, p. 545.
8. Johnson, 'Reconstructing a history of local floods'.
9. Buxton, *Two African Trips*, pp. 153–169.
10. A.L. Butler never gained an international reputation. His only publication was *Brief Notes for Identifying the Game Animals of the Sudan* (Khartoum, n.d.); Daly, *Empire on the Nile*, p. 68.
11. Fairholm Archives, Coryndon to Stevenson-Hamilton, 20 October 1919.

## Chapter 10
## 'An Imperishable Monument': Founding the Kruger National Park, 1920–1930

1. *South African Eden*, quotation from Dr W.T. Hornaday well known for his campaigns on behalf of wildlife in the United States of America. He wrote, *inter alia*:

   I do hope to Heaven you will gain your great objective in the nationalizing as a Park of the Sabi reserve. Stick to it! The stake is a great one. When it is really done, it will be an imperishable monument to each and all of you who have worked and fought for it. I am sure you will none of you give up until you get it.

2. TA *Debates of the Legislative Assembly*, cols 1425–1426, 24 July 1907.
3. TA TPS11 TA3087, vols 1, 2 and 3.
4. See, for example, Stevenson-Hamilton, 'The relation between game and tsetse-flies', *Bulletin of Entomological Research* 2, 1911, pp. 113–118; Stevenson-Hamilton, 'Tsetse fly and the rinderpest epidemic of 1896', *South African Journal of Science* 53(8), 1957, pp. 216–218.
5. *Votes and Proceedings of the Provincial Council*, 14 and 15 June 1911.
6. TA TPS7 TA3054, Stevenson-Hamilton to Provincial Secretary, 12 February 1913; Provincial Secretary to Secretary for Lands, 11 June 1913.
7. Central Archives, Pretoria (Cent.) LDE288 3081, vol. 2, Secretary for Lands to Provincial Secretary, 10 August 1916.
8. TA TPB513 TA1232, Minute of the Acting Under-Secretary for Mines, undated.
9. Proclamation 48 of 1914 made provision for the area between the Groot Letaba and Olifants Rivers to be added to the Sabi Game Reserve, but the land was later transferred from the Sabi to the Singwitsi Game Reserve.
10. TA TPS7 TA3054, Stevenson-Hamilton to Provincial Secretary, 12 February 1913.
11. Cent. LDE26 44/1, Smuts to Minister of Lands, 29 May 1914.
12. TA TPS7 TA3054, Smuts to Rissik, 26 May 1914.
13. *Votes and Proceedings of the Provincial Council*, 17 March 1916.
14. Transvaal Province, *Report of the Game Reserves Commission* TP5-18 (Pretoria, 1918), pp. 9–10.
15. TA TPS8 TA3075, Stevenson-Hamilton to Provincial Secretary, 3 May 1920.
16. JPL TLOA Sub-Committee Minute Book, Minutes of 13 February 1913 and 17 October 1916.
17. JPL TLOA Sub-Committee Minute Book, Minutes of 26 September 1916.
18. Cent. LDE537 7748/1, vol. 1, Minute of Department of Lands, 11 October 1921.
19. TA TPS7 TA3054, vol. 3, Approval of memorandum by Executive Committee, 21 December 1920; Notes on Departmental Conference, 25 February 1921; Cent. LDE537 7748/1, vol. 1, Report on the conference of 25 February 1921, 4 March 1921.
20. Cent. LDE537 7748/1, vol. 1, Secretary to the Prime Minister to Secretary for Lands, 6 November 1922.
21. Cent. LDE 537 7748/1, vol. 1.
22. This is stressed in R. Nash, *Wilderness and the American Mind*, 3rd ed. (New Haven,

1982) and A. Runte, *National Parks: The American Experience* (Lincoln, Nebraska, 1979).
23. Wildlife and Environment Society of Southern Africa (WLS) H.B. Papenfus file, Stevenson-Hamilton to Grobler, 5 October 1925; D. O'Meara, *Volkskapitalisme: Class, Capital and Ideology in the Development of Afrikaner Nationalism, 1934–1948* (Johannesburg, 1983), p. 34. Details of these land exchanges can be found in Cent. LDE563-570; R.G. Morrell, 'Rural transformations in the Transvaal; the Middelburg district, 1919 to 1930', M.A. thesis (University of the Witwatersrand, 1983), pp. 238–239.
24. CA A848, Stratford Caldecott Collection, 2(4), Stevenson-Hamilton to Caldecott, 9 January 1926; Stevenson-Hamilton, Journal entry, 22 March 1926.
25. WLS H.B. Papenfus file, Stevenson-Hamilton to Papenfus, 29 December 1925.
26. CA A848, Stratford Caldecott Collection, 2(4), Stevenson-Hamilton to Caldecott, 3 April 1926.
27. Fairholm Archives, Chapman to Stevenson-Hamilton, 13 September 1928.
28. *The Senate of South Africa: Debates*, col. 1079, 3 June 1926.
29. Fairholm Archives, Gill to Stevenson-Hamilton, 25 October 1926.
30. Personal comment from Mr James McClurg, prominent South African journalist.

## Chapter 11
### 'The Guardian Spirit of the Low-veld': The Kruger National Park and Retirement, 1930–1946

1. This is the dedication to Stevenson-Hamilton's book *The Low-veld*.
2. National Parks Act, No. 56, 1926; *Senate Debates*, cols 1081, 1083, 3 June 1926; *House of Assembly Debates*, col. 4369, 31 May 1926.
3. Fairholm Archives, Pirow to Stevenson-Hamilton, 30 October 1941.
4. KNP Stevenson-Hamilton documents in trust, Reitz to Stevenson-Hamilton, 10 October 1941.
5. J. Carruthers, 'Dissecting the myth: Paul Kruger and the Kruger National Park', *Journal of Southern African Studies* 20(2), June 1994, pp. 263–283.
6. O. Pirow, *Ashambeni* (Johannesburg, n.d.).
7. CA A848, Stratford Caldecott Collection, 2(4), Caldecott to Stevenson-Hamilton, 22 June 1926.
8. *The Star* 5, 7, 11, 17, 21, 25 August 1937; KNP *Veldwagters Dagboek*, Bowling to National Parks Board, January 1946.
9. Annual Report of the National Parks Board, 1940.
10. This was published in London in 1905.
11. TA TPB784 TA3006, Stevenson-Hamilton to Secretary to the Administrator, 15 February 1911.
12. J. Carruthers, ' "Police boys" and poachers: Africans, wildlife protection and national parks, the Transvaal 1902 to 1950', *Koedoe* 36(2), 1993, pp. 11–22.
13. KNP Minutes of the National Parks Board, 4 April 1934, item 24.

14. WLS H.B. Papenfus file, National Parks Board meeting 16 August 1937; KNP K1/11(II) KNP5/6, Warden to all rangers, 22 June 1937.
15. KNP K11, Stevenson-Hamilton to Secretary of the National Parks Board, 4 October 1944.
16. Annual Report of the National Parks Board, 1931.
17. National Parks Board meeting, 21–22 June 1932.
18. National Parks Board meeting, 15 August 1936.
19. KNP K1/11(I) K29, W.A. Campbell to Secretary of the National Parks Board, 27 February 1939.
20. Fairholm Archives, Stevenson-Hamilton to Mary Harrison, 6 February 1931.
21. J. Carruthers, 'The Dongola Wild Life Sanctuary: "psychological blunder, economic folly and political monstrosity" or "more valuable than rubies and gold"?', *Kleio* 24, 1992, pp. 82–100.
22. Fairholm Archives, Hon. LLD from the University of the Witwatersrand, 23 March 1935; Hon. LLD from the University of Cape Town, 13 December 1945.
23. *Debates of the House of Assembly*, 24 February 1925. I am grateful to my colleague, Prof. Japie Brits for finding this reference for me.

## Chapter 12
### 'Little Benefit to Living after One's Work is Done': After Retirement, 1946–1957

1. Fairholm Archives, Journal entry, 10 March 1955.
2. R.J. Labuschagne, comp., *60 Years Kruger Park* (Pretoria, 1958), p. 104. This book was published in 1958, thus commemorating the Sabi Game Reserve's proclamation rather than the national park.
3. P. Meiring, *Kruger Park Saga* (n.p., n.p., 1976), p. 25.
4. For full details of this process see Carruthers, 'Dissecting the myth'.
5. *Rand Daily Mail*, 27 October 1952, 1 November 1952.
6. Fairholm Archives contains these letters.

# Selected Sources

## OFFICIAL MANUSCRIPTS

**1. Transvaal Archives, Pretoria (TA)**
Barberton Resident Magistrate (BN)
Colonial Secretary (CS)
Executive Council of the Transvaal (ECO)
Lieutenant Governor (LtG)
Prime Minister (PM)
Secretary for Mines (MM)
Secretary for Native Affairs (SNA)
Transvaal Law Department (LD)
Transvaal Agricultural Department (TAD)
Transvaal Department of Local Government (TPB)
Transvaal Provincial Secretary (TPS)

**2. Central Archives, Pretoria (Cent.)**
Department of Justice (JUS)
Department of Lands (LDE)
Department of Mines and Industries (MNW)
Entomology Department (CEN)
Native Affairs Department (NTS)
Prime Minister (PM)

**3. Kruger National Park, Skukuza and Pretoria**
Diaries of Rangers: 1923 to 1942
Files: K1–K52
Minutes and Annual Reports
Opsienersjaarverslae: Assorted Early Correspondence and Annual Reports

## PRIVATE MANUSCRIPTS

**1. Cape Archives, Cape Town (CA)**
A848: Stratford Caldecott Collection

**2. Johannesburg Public Library (JPL)**
333.3 (06) (682): Transvaal Land Owners Association Archives (TLOA)

### 3. Kruger National Park, Skukuza (KNP)
Newspaper cuttings
Photograph albums
Stevenson-Hamilton documents in Trust
Miscellaneous unpublished manuscripts

### 4. Transvaal Archives, Pretoria
J.C. Smuts Archive: Private papers

### 5. University of the Witwatersrand, Johannesburg, Manuscript Collection
A839: H.E. Schoch Papers
A1403/1: F.C. Selous Papers

### 6. Wildlife and Environment Society of Southern Africa (WLS)
Minutes: Transvaal Game Protection Association, 1902–1920
Minutes: Wildlife Society Council, 1926–1945
Minutes: Annual General Meetings, 1927–1961
General Correspondence: 1926–1928
Correspondence: Transvaal Game Protection Association, 1925
H.B. Papenfus File: Correspondence, 1925–1937

### 7. Fairholm Archives, Fairholm, Larkhall, Lanarkshire, and Gibraltar, White River
Assorted MSS: James Stevenson-Hamilton
Folder: Hamilton of Fairholm
Journals: 1879–1957

## PRINTED OFFICIAL AND SEMI-OFFICIAL SOURCES

### 1. Transvaal
Bigalke, R.C. *Nature conservation in the Transvaal*. Bulletin no. 2. Pretoria: Transvaal Provincial Administration, Nature Conservation Branch, 1968.
*Transvaal Administration Reports*, 1902–1909.
Transvaal Colony, *Government Gazette*, 1900–1910.
Transvaal Colony, *Debates of the Legislative Assembly*, 1907–1909.
Transvaal Colony, *Debates of the Legislative Council*, 1903–1906.
Transvaal Colony, *Debates of the Legislative Council*, 1907–1910.
Transvaal Colony, *Minutes of the Executive Council*, 1901–1906.
Transvaal Colony, *Minutes of the Legislative Council*, 1902–1906.
Transvaal Colony, *Minutes and Proceedings of the Legislative Council of the Transvaal*, 1907–1910.
Transvaal Colony, *Votes and Proceedings of the Legislative Assembly*, 1907–1910.
Transvaal Province, *Official Gazette*, 1910–1930.

*Selected Sources*

Transvaal Province, *Votes and Proceedings of the Provincial Council*, 1910–1930.
Transvaal Province, *Report of the Game Reserves Commission*, TP5-18. Pretoria: Government Printer, 1918.

## 2. Union of South Africa

Acocks, J.P.H. *Veld Types of South Africa*. 2d ed. Memoirs of the Botanical Survey of South Africa No. 40. Pretoria: Botanical Research Institute, 1975.
Fuller, C. *Tsetse in the Transvaal and Surrounding Territories: An Historical Review*. Entomology Memoir No. 1. Pretoria: Department of Agriculture, 1923.
Union of South Africa, *Government Gazette*, 1910 to 1930.
Union of South Africa, *House of Assembly Debates*, 1926.
Union of South Africa, *The Senate of South Africa: Debates*, 1926.
Union of South Africa, *Majority Report of the Eastern Transvaal Natives Land Committee, 1918*, UG 31-18. Cape Town: Government Printer, 1918.

## 3. Britain

A. Foreign Office Confidential Print, FO 403:

7322 *Correspondence relating to the preservation of wild animals in Africa 1896–1900* Parts I and II (1901).
8384 *Further correspondence respecting the preservation of wild game in Africa 1902–1904* (1904).
8991 *Further correspondence respecting the preservation of wild game in Africa 1905* (1905).

B. Parliamentary Papers published by Command of the Government:

Cd3189 *Correspondence relating to the preservation of wild animals in Africa* (1906).
Cd4472 *Further correspondence relating to the preservation of wild animals in Africa* (1909).
Cd5136 *Further correspondence relating to the preservation of wild animals in Africa* (1910).
Cd5775 *Further correspondence relating to the preservation of wild animals in Africa* (1911).
Cd6671 *Further correspondence relating to the preservation of wild animals in Africa* (1913).
Cmd4453 *Agreement respecting the protection of the fauna and flora of Africa* (1933).
Cmd5280 *International Convention for the protection of the fauna and flora of Africa* (1936).

## BOOKS AND ARTICLES

Adam-Smith, P. *The Anzacs*. London: Hamish Hamilton, 1978.
Adland, D. *Brighton's Music Halls*. N.p.: Baron Birch, 1964.
Amery, L.S. *The Times History of the War in South Africa*. 7 vols. London: Sampson Low, Marsten, 1900–1909.
Barbour, K.M. *The Republic of the Sudan: A Regional Geography*. London: University of London Press, 1961.
Behrens, H.P.H. 'His name is Skukuza', *African Wild Life* vol. 1, no. 2, 1947, pp. 46–66.

———. '"Oom Paul's" great fight to preserve game', *African Wild Life* vol. 1, no. 1, 1946, pp. 12–22.

———. 'Paul Kruger – wildbeskermer: aspek van president se lewe wat selfs sy biograwe vergeet', *Huisgenoot* vol. 37, series 1542, 12 October 1951, pp. 6–7.

Bertrand, A. *The Kingdom of the Barotsi, Upper Zambezia*. Cape Town: Juta, 1899.

Best, G. *Mid-Victorian Britain, 1851–1875*. London: Fontana Press, 1979.

Bigalke, R.C.H. *National Parks and their Functions, with Special Reference to South Africa*. Pamphlet no. 10. Pretoria: South African Biological Society, 1939.

———. 'Our National Parks: past and future', *South African Journal of Science* vol. 40, 1943, pp. 248–253.

Binns, C.T. *Dinizulu: The Death of the House of Shaka*. London: Longmans Green, 1968.

Bond, B., ed. *The First World War and British Military History*. Oxford: Clarendon Press, 1991.

Bond, B. *The Victorian Army and the Staff College, 1854–1914*. London: Eyre Metheun, 1972.

Booth, M.R. *Theatre in the Victorian Age*. Cambridge: Cambridge University Press, 1991.

Brantlinger, P. 'Victorians and Africans: The genealogy of the myth of the dark continent', *Critical Inquiry* 12, Autumn 1985, pp. 166–203.

Brits, J.P., ed. *Diary of a National Scout: P.J. du Toit, 1900–1902*. Pretoria: Human Sciences Research Council, 1974.

Brookes, E.H. and C. de B. Webb. *A History of Natal*. Pietermaritzburg: University of Natal Press, 1965.

Bryden, H.A. *Gun and Camera in Southern Africa*. London: Edward Stanford, 1893.

———. *Nature and Sport in South Africa*. London: Chapman and Hall, 1897.

———. *Wildlife in South Africa*. London: Harrap, 1936.

Buchan, J. *Episodes of the Great War*. London: Thomas Nelson, 1936.

Bufton, J. *Tasmanians in the Transvaal War*. Launceston, Tasmania: S.G. Loone, 1905.

Buxton, E.N. 'The preservation of big game in Africa', *Journal of the Society of Arts* 2 (634), 15 May 1903, pp. 566–578.

———. *Two African Trips; With Notes and Suggestions on Big Game Preservation in Africa*. London: Edward Stanford, 1902.

Caldecott, S. 'Create a national park!', *South African Nation* vol. 2, no. 85, 21 November 1925, pp. 7–8.

———. 'Sabi Bushman Paintings', *South African Nation* vol. 3, no. 113, 5 June 1926, p. 17.

Caldwell, K. 'The commercialisation of game', *Journal of the Society for the Preservation of the Fauna of the Empire* part 7, 1927, pp. 83–90.

———. 'Game preservation: its aims and objects', *Journal of the Society for the Preservation of the Fauna of the Empire* part 4, 1924, pp. 45–56.

Campbell, R.H. *Scotland Since 1707: The Rise of an Industrial Society*. 2d ed. Edinburgh: John Donald, 1985.

Cannadine, D. *The Decline and Fall of the British Aristocracy*. New Haven and London: Yale University Press, 1990.

Caplan, G.L. *The Elites of Barotseland, 1878–1969: A Political History of Zambia's Western Province*. London: Hurst, 1970.

Carder, T. *The Encyclopaedia of Brighton*. Lewes: East Sussex County Libraries, 1990.

Carey, H.R. 'Saving the animal life of Africa: a new method and a last chance', *Journal of Mammalogy* vol. 7, no. 2, 1926, pp. 73–85.

Carruthers, E.J. 'Creating a national park, 1910 to 1926', *Journal of Southern African Studies* vol. 5, no. 2, 1989, pp. 188–216.

———. 'Dissecting the myth: Paul Kruger and the Kruger National Park', *Journal of Southern African Studies* vol. 20, no. 2, June 1994, pp. 263–283.

———. 'The Dongola Wild Life Sanctuary: "psychological blunder, economic folly and political monstrosity", or "more valuable than rubies and gold"?', *Kleio* no. 24, 1992, pp. 82–100.

———. *Game Protection in the Transvaal, 1846 to 1926*. Pretoria: State Archives Service, 1995.

———. 'Game protectionism in the Transvaal, 1900 to 1910', *South African Historical Journal* no. 28, 1988, pp. 33–56.

———., ed. 'Journal of a visit to the goldfields in 1889', *Africana Notes and News* vol. 27, no. 3, September 1986, pp. 93–103.

———. *The Kruger National Park: A Social and Political History*. Pietermaritzburg: University of Natal Press, 1995.

———. '"Police boys" and poachers: Africans, wildlife protection and national parks, the Transvaal 1902 to 1950', *Koedoe* vol. 36, no. 2, 1993, pp. 11–22.

———. 'The Pongola Game Reserve: An eco-political study', *Koedoe* no. 28, 1985, pp. 1–16.

Cattrick, A. *Spoor of Blood*. Cape Town: Timmins, 1959.

Chandler, D., ed. *The Oxford Illustrated History of the British Army*. Oxford and New York: Oxford University Press, 1994.

Chapman, A. *Retrospect: Reminiscences of a Hunter-Naturalist in Three Continents*. London: Gurney and Jackson, 1928.

Charter, A.E. 'Game preservation in Zululand', *Southern African Museums Association Bulletin* September 1943, pp. 69–76.

Churchill, W.S. *My Early Life: A Roving Commission*. London: Odmans Press, 1947.

Clay, G. *Your Friend Lewanika: The Life and Times of Lubosi Lewanika, Litunga of Barotseland, 1842 to 1916*. London: Chatto and Windus, 1968.

Cole, H.N. *The Story of Aldershot: A History of the Civil and Military Towns*. Aldershot: Southern Books, 1980.

Collins, R.O. and F.M. Deng, eds. *The British in the Sudan, 1898–1956: The Sweetness and the Sorrow*. Stanford: Hoover Institution Press, 1984.

Collins, R.O. *Land Beyond the Rivers: The Southern Sudan, 1898–1918*. New Haven: Yale University Press, 1971.

Coppinger, M. and J. Williams. *Zambezi: River of Africa*. Cape Town: Struik, 1991.

Costigan, G. *A History of Modern Ireland with a Sketch of Earlier Times*. New York: Pegasus, 1969.

Creagh, Sir O'Moore and E.H. Humphris. *The Victoria Cross, 1856–1920*. Polstead, Suffolk: J.B. Hayward, 1920.

Cubbin, A.E. 'An outline of game legislation in Natal, 1866–1912 (i.e. until the promulgation of the Mkhuze Game Reserve)', *Journal of Natal and Zulu History* vol. 14, 1992, pp. 37–47.

Curson, H.H. and J.M. Hugo. 'Preservation of game in South Africa', *South African Journal of Science* vol. 21, 1924, pp. 400–424.

Daly, M.W. *Empire on the Nile: The Anglo-Egyptian Sudan, 1898–1934*. Cambridge: Cambridge University Press, 1986.

Dicke, B.H. 'The tsetse fly's influence on South African history', *South African Journal of Science* vol. 29, 1932, pp. 792–796.

*Dictionary of South African Biography*. 6 vols to date. Pretoria: H.S.R.C., 1968–1987.

Dominy, G. 'The Imperial garrison in Natal with special reference to Fort Napier 1843–1914: Its social, cultural and economic impact'. Ph.D. London, 1995.

Drummond, A.L. and J. Bulloch. *The Church in Late Victorian Scotland, 1874–1900*. Edinburgh: The Saint Andrew Press, 1978.

Dubow, S. *Scientific Racism in Modern South Africa*. Cambridge: Cambridge University Press, 1995.

Duminy, A. and B. Guest, eds. *Natal and Zululand from Earliest Times to 1910: A New History*. Pietermaritzburg: University of Natal Press and Shuter & Shooter, 1989.

Duncan, R. *Steelopolis: The Making of Motherwell, c.1750–1939*. Motherwell: Motherwell District Council, Department of Leisure Services, 1991.

———. *Wishaw: Life and Labour in a Lanarkshire Industrial Community, 1790–1914*. Motherwell: Motherwell District Council, Department of Leisure Services, 1986.

Elgood, P.G. *Egypt and the Army*. Oxford: Oxford University Press, 1924.

Ferguson, W. *Scotland 1689 to the Present*. Edinburgh: Oliver and Boyd, 1968.

Fitter, R. and P. Scott. *The Penitent Butchers: The Fauna Preservation Society, 1903–1978*. London: Fauna Preservation Society, 1978.

Gann, L.H. *A History of Northern Rhodesia: Early Days to 1953*. London: Chatto and Windus, 1964.

Gibb, A. *Glasgow: The Making of a City*. London: Croom Helm, 1983.

Gibbons, A. St H. 'A journey in the Marotse and Mashikolumbwe countries', *The Geographical Journal* vol. 9, no. 2. Feb. 1898, pp. 121–143.

———. *Africa from South to North through Marotseland*. 2 vols. London: John Lane, 1904.

———. *Exploration and Hunting in Central Africa, 1895–96*. London: Methuen, 1898.

Gilbert, M. *The First World War*. London: Weidenfeld and Nicolson, 1994.

Gillett, F. 'Game reserves', *Journal of the Society for the Preservation of the Wild Fauna of the Empire* vol. 4, 1908, pp. 42–45.

Girouard, M. *Life in the English Country House: A Social and Architectural History*. New Haven and London: Yale University Press, 1978.

———. *The Victorian Country House*. New Haven: Yale University Press, 1979.

Godwin-Austen, A.R. *The Staff and the Staff College*. London: Constable, 1927.

Guest, B. and J.M. Sellers. *Enterprise and Exploitation in a Victorian Colony*. Pietermaritzburg: University of Natal Press, 1985.

Haagner, A.K. 'The conservation of wild life in South Africa', *South African Journal of Industries* December 1925, pp. 761–775.

Hall, R. *Zambia*. London: Pall Mall Press, 1965.
Harries-Jenkins, G. *The Army in Victorian Society*. London: Routledge, 1977.
Hattersley, A.F. *Portrait of a Colony: The Story of Natal*. Cambridge: Cambridge University Press, 1940.
———. *The Natalians: Further Annals of Natal*. Pietermaritzburg: Shuter & Shooter, 1940.
Henderson, K.D.D. *Sudan Republic*. London: Ernest Benn, 1965.
Hingston, R.W.G. 'The only way of saving African fauna', *The Illustrated London News* 13 December 1930, p. 1062.
Hobley, C.W. 'The conservation of wildlife', *Journal of the Society for the Preservation of the Fauna of the Empire* Section I, in part 32, 1937, pp. 38–43; Section II, in part 33, 1938, pp. 39–49.
———. 'The London Convention of 1900', *Journal of the Society for the Preservation of the Fauna of the Empire* part 20, 1933, pp. 33–49.
Hobsbawm, E. and T. Ranger, eds. *The Invention of Tradition*. Cambridge: Cambridge University Press, 1983.
Holt, P.M. and M.W. Daly. *A History of the Sudan: From the Coming of Islam to the Present Day*. London: Longman, 1988.
Hornaday, W.T. and A.K. Haagner. *The Vanishing Game of Southern Africa*. New York: Permanent Wildlife Protection Fund, Bulletin No. 10, September 1922.
Jackson, E.S. *The Inniskilling Dragoons: The Records of an Old Heavy Cavalry Regiment*. London: Arthur L. Humphreys, 1909.
James, R.R. *The British Revolution: British Politics 1880–1939*. London: Methuen, 1977.
———. *Gallipoli*. London: Batsford, 1965.
Jeal, T. *Livingstone*. London: Pimlico, 1993.
Johnson, D.H. 'Tribal boundaries and border wars: Nuer-Dinka relations in the Sobat and Zaraf valleys, c.1860–1976', *Journal of African History* no. 23, 1982.
———. 'Reconstructing a history of local floods in the Upper Nile region of the Sudan', *The International Journal of African Historical Studies* vol. 25, no. 3, 1992.
———. 'The Sudan under the British', *Journal of African History* no. 23, 1982.
Kloppers, H. *Game Ranger*. Cape Town: Juta, n.d.
Laband, J. and R. Haswell, eds. *Pietermaritzburg 1838–1988: A New Portrait of an African City*. Pietermaritzburg: University of Natal Press and Shuter & Shooter, 1988.
Labuschagne, R.J. *The Kruger Park and Other National Parks*. Johannesburg: Da Gama, n.d.
———., comp. *60 Years Kruger Park*. Pretoria: National Parks Board of Trustees, 1958.
Lyell, D.D., ed. *African Adventure: Letters from Famous Big-Game Hunters*. London: John Murray, 1935.
MacKenzie, J.M. *The Empire of Nature: Hunting, Conservation and British Imperialism*. Manchester: Manchester University Press, 1988.
———. *Empires of Nature and the Nature of Empires*. East Linton: Tuckwell Press, 1997.
———., ed. *Imperialism and the Natural World*. Manchester: Manchester University Press, 1990.
———. *Popular Imperialism and the Military, 1850–1950*. Manchester: Manchester University Press, 1992.

Maugham, R.C.F. *Africa as I have known it*. London: John Murray, 1929.
———. *Wild Game in Zambezia*. London: John Murray, 1914.
———. *Zambezia*. London: John Murray, 1910.
'Minutes of proceedings at a deputation from the Society for the Preservation of the Wild Fauna of the Empire to the Right Hon. Alfred Lyttelton (His Majesty's Secretary for the Colonies)', *Journal of the Society for the Preservation of the Wild Fauna of the Empire* vol. 1, 1905, pp. 9–18.
'Minutes of proceedings at a deputation from the Society for the Preservation of the Wild Fauna of the Empire to the Rt. Hon. the Earl of Elgin, His Majesty's Secretary of State for the Colonies', *Journal of the Society for the Preservation of the Wild Fauna of the Empire* vol. 2, 1906, pp. 20–32.
'Minutes of proceedings at a deputation from the Society for the Preservation of the Wild Fauna of the Empire received by the Right Hon. the Earl of Crewe K.G. (Principal Secretary of State for the Colonies), at the Colonial Office', *Journal of the Society for the Preservation of the Wild Fauna of the Empire* vol. 5, 1909, pp. 11–27.
Montgomery, J. *Brighton in Old Picture Postcards*. Zalthommel, The Netherlands: European Library, 1995.
Morrell, R.G. 'Rural transformations in the Transvaal; the Middelburg district, 1919 to 1930', M.A. thesis. University of the Witwatersrand, 1983.
Muir, J. *Our National Parks*. 2d ed. Madison, Wisconsin: University of Wisconsin Press, 1981.
Pakenham, T. *The Boer War*. London: Weidenfeld and Nicolson; Johannesburg: Jonathan Ball, 1979.
Patterson, J.H. *The Man-Eaters of Tsavo and other East African Adventures*. London: Macmillan, 1907.
Payne, D.G. *Voices in the Wilderness: American Nature Writing and Environmental Politics*. Hanover and London: University Press of New England, 1996.
Pearse, H.H.S., ed. *The History of Lumsden's Horse: A Complete Record of the Corps from its Formation to its Disbandment*. London: Longmans Green, 1903.
Pease, A. 'Game and game reserves in the Transvaal', *Journal of the Society for the Preservation of the Wild Fauna of the Empire* vol. 4, 1908, pp. 29–34.
Percival, A.B. *A Game Ranger on Safari*. London: Nisbet and Co., 1928.
Perkin, H. *The Rise of Professional Society: England since 1880*. London and New York: Routledge, 1989.
Perkins, R., comp. *Regiments and Corps of the British Empire and Commonwealth, 1758–1993: A Critical Bibliography*. Newton Abbot: Roger Perkins, 1994.
Phillipps, L.M. *With Rimington*. London: Edward Arnold, 1902.
Pirow, O. *Ashambeni*. Johannesburg: Dagbreek Book Store, n.d.
Pitman, C.R.S. *A Game Warden among his Charges*. London: Nisbet and Co., 1931.
———. *A Game Warden Takes Stock*. London: Nisbet and Co., 1942.
Prance, E.L. *Three Weeks in Wonderland: The Kruger National Park*. Cape Town: Juta, n.d.
Pratt, M.L. *Imperial Eyes: Travel Writing and Transculturation*. London: Routledge, 1992.
Pringle, J.A. *The Conservationists and the Killers*. Cape Town: T.V. Bulpin, 1982.

## Selected Sources

Reitz, D. *Commando*. London: Faber and Faber, 1929.
Robinson, R. and J. Gallagher (with Alice Denny). *Africa and the Victorians: The Official Mind of Imperialism*. 2d ed. London: Macmillan, 1981.
Roosevelt, T. *African Game Trails*. London: John Murray, 1910.
*Saturday Review*, 'The dying fauna of an Empire', *Journal of the Society for the Preservation of the Wild Fauna of the Empire* vol. 3, 1907, pp. 75–79.
Schikkerling, R.W. *Commando Courageous: A Boer's Diary*. Johannesburg: Hugh Keartland, 1964.
Scholtz, J. du P. *Strat Caldecott, 1886–1929*. Cape Town: Balkema, 1970.
Seaman, L.C.B. *Life in Victorian London*. London: Batsford, 1973.
Selous, F.C. *African Nature Notes and Reminiscences*. London: Macmillan, 1908. Repr. Salisbury: Pioneer Head, 1969.
———. *A Hunter's Wanderings in Africa*. London: Richard Bentley, 1881. Repr. Bulawayo: Books of Zimbabwe, 1981.
Shepperd, A. *Sandhurst: The Royal Military Academy Sandhurst and its Predecessors*. London: Country House Books, 1980.
Sillery, A. *Founding a Protectorate: History of Bechuanaland, 1885–1895*. The Hague: Mouton, 1965.
Smout, T.C. *A Century of the Scottish People, 1830–1950*. London: Fontana Press, 1987.
Spiers, E.M. *The Late Victorian Army, 1868–1902*. Manchester: Manchester University Press, 1992.
———. 'The late Victorian army, 1864–1914', in D. Chandler, ed., *The Oxford Illustrated History of the British Army*. Oxford and New York: Oxford University Press, 1994, pp. 189–214.
Spurr, D. *The Rhetoric of Empire: Colonial Discourse in Journalism, Travel Writing and Imperial Administration*. Durham and London: Duke University Press, 1993.
*The Statistical Account of Lanarkshire*. Compiled by the Ministers of the Respective Parishes. Edinburgh and London: William Blackwood and Sons, 1841.
Stevenson, H.S. *The Stevenson Family, A Record of the Descendants of James Stevenson, Burgess of Paisley in 1753*. Richmond, Yorks: The Author, 1965.
Stevenson-Hamilton, H. 'Preserving wildlife in South Africa', *Optima* vol. 2, no. 5, 1962, pp. 121–128.
Stevenson-Hamilton, J. 'Aantekeningen omtrent de wild-reserve aan de Sabi', *Het Transvaalsche Landbouw Journaal* vol. 4, 1906, pp. 636–650.
———. 'Address at Rotary Club luncheon, Pretoria, 17th November 1938', *Journal of the Society for the Preservation of the Fauna of the Empire* part 36, 1939, pp. 18–24.
———. *Animal Life in Africa*. London: Heinemann, 1912.
———. 'The coloration of the African hunting dog', *Proceedings of the Zoological Society of London* no. 27, 1914, pp. 403–405.
———. 'The Dinka country east of the Bahr-el-Gebel', *The Geographical Journal* vol. 46, no. 5, 1920, p. 393.
———. 'Empire fauna in 1922', *Journal of the Society for the Preservation of the Fauna of the Empire* part 2, 1922, pp. 38–43.

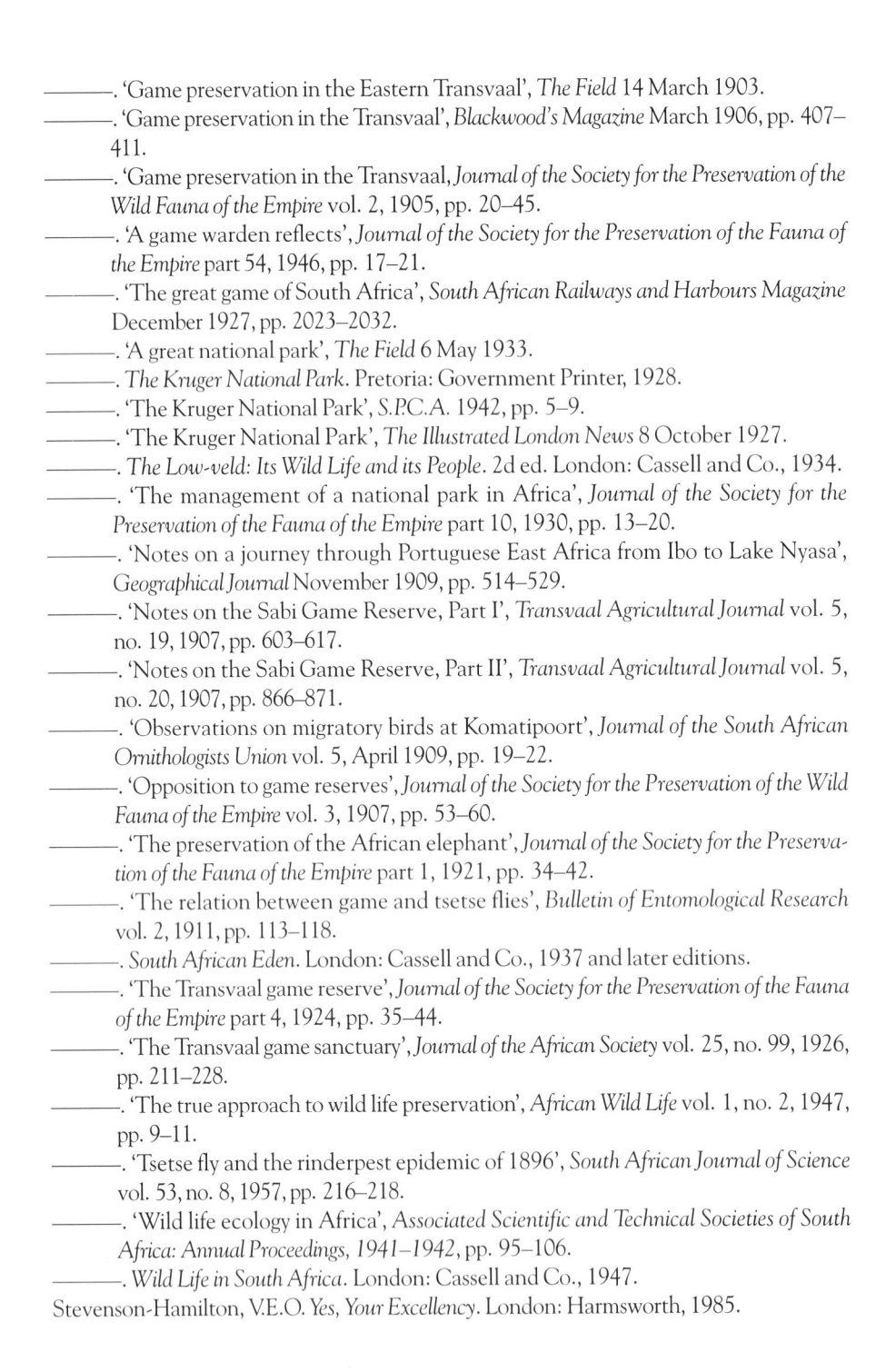

———. 'Game preservation in the Eastern Transvaal', *The Field* 14 March 1903.
———. 'Game preservation in the Transvaal', *Blackwood's Magazine* March 1906, pp. 407–411.
———. 'Game preservation in the Transvaal, *Journal of the Society for the Preservation of the Wild Fauna of the Empire* vol. 2, 1905, pp. 20–45.
———. 'A game warden reflects', *Journal of the Society for the Preservation of the Fauna of the Empire* part 54, 1946, pp. 17–21.
———. 'The great game of South Africa', *South African Railways and Harbours Magazine* December 1927, pp. 2023–2032.
———. 'A great national park', *The Field* 6 May 1933.
———. *The Kruger National Park*. Pretoria: Government Printer, 1928.
———. 'The Kruger National Park', *S.P.C.A.* 1942, pp. 5–9.
———. 'The Kruger National Park', *The Illustrated London News* 8 October 1927.
———. *The Low-veld: Its Wild Life and its People*. 2d ed. London: Cassell and Co., 1934.
———. 'The management of a national park in Africa', *Journal of the Society for the Preservation of the Fauna of the Empire* part 10, 1930, pp. 13–20.
———. 'Notes on a journey through Portuguese East Africa from Ibo to Lake Nyasa', *Geographical Journal* November 1909, pp. 514–529.
———. 'Notes on the Sabi Game Reserve, Part I', *Transvaal Agricultural Journal* vol. 5, no. 19, 1907, pp. 603–617.
———. 'Notes on the Sabi Game Reserve, Part II', *Transvaal Agricultural Journal* vol. 5, no. 20, 1907, pp. 866–871.
———. 'Observations on migratory birds at Komatipoort', *Journal of the South African Ornithologists Union* vol. 5, April 1909, pp. 19–22.
———. 'Opposition to game reserves', *Journal of the Society for the Preservation of the Wild Fauna of the Empire* vol. 3, 1907, pp. 53–60.
———. 'The preservation of the African elephant', *Journal of the Society for the Preservation of the Fauna of the Empire* part 1, 1921, pp. 34–42.
———. 'The relation between game and tsetse flies', *Bulletin of Entomological Research* vol. 2, 1911, pp. 113–118.
———. *South African Eden*. London: Cassell and Co., 1937 and later editions.
———. 'The Transvaal game reserve', *Journal of the Society for the Preservation of the Fauna of the Empire* part 4, 1924, pp. 35–44.
———. 'The Transvaal game sanctuary', *Journal of the African Society* vol. 25, no. 99, 1926, pp. 211–228.
———. 'The true approach to wild life preservation', *African Wild Life* vol. 1, no. 2, 1947, pp. 9–11.
———. 'Tsetse fly and the rinderpest epidemic of 1896', *South African Journal of Science* vol. 53, no. 8, 1957, pp. 216–218.
———. 'Wild life ecology in Africa', *Associated Scientific and Technical Societies of South Africa: Annual Proceedings, 1941–1942*, pp. 95–106.
———. *Wild Life in South Africa*. London: Cassell and Co., 1947.
Stevenson-Hamilton, V.E.O. *Yes, Your Excellency*. London: Harmsworth, 1985.

## Selected Sources

Stokes, C.S. *Sanctuary*. 2d ed. Cape Town: Maskew Miller Longman, 1953.

Struben, F.E.B. 'A history of the Kruger National Park', *African Wild Life* vol. 7, no. 3, 1953, pp. 209–228.

Tabler, E.C. *Trade and Travel in Early Barotseland: The Diaries of George Westbeech, 1885–188 and Captain Norman MacLeod, 1875–1876*. London: Chatto and Windus, 1963.

Tattersall, D. *Skukuza*. Cape Town: Tafelberg, 1972.

Troup, F., ed. *Physician and Friend: James MacDonald Troup*. Glasgow: Glasgow University Press, 1947.

Vaughan-Kirby, F. 'Game and game preservation in Zululand', *South African Journal of Science* vol. 13, 1916, pp. 375–396.

———. *In Haunts of Wild Game*. Edinburgh: Blackwoods, 1896.

Wallace, R.L. *The Australians at the Boer War*. Canberra: Australian War Memorial/Australian Government Publishing Service, 1976.

Wallis, J.P.R., ed. *The Barotseland Journals of James Stevenson-Hamilton, 1898–1899*. London: Chatto and Windus, 1953.

Wavell, Field-Marshal Viscount. *Allenby: Soldier and Statesman*. 2d ed. London: White Lion Publishers, 1974.

Wilson, M. and L. Thompson, eds. *The Oxford History of South Africa*. 2 vols. Oxford: Clarendon Press, 1969–1975.

Wolhuter, H. *Memories of a Game Ranger*. 12th ed. Johannesburg: Wild Life Protection and Conservation Society of South Africa, 1976.

Yardley, J.W. *With the Inniskilling Dragoons: The Record of a Cavalry Regiment During the Boer War, 1899–1902*. London: Longmans Green, 1904.

Yates, C.A. *The Kruger National Park*. London: Allen and Unwin, 1935.

# Index

Africa  24, 44–45, 49–50, 52–54, 60, 62, 81, 104, 108, 116–117, 135, 142, 171, 190, 204
*Africa from South to North through Marotseland*  58
Africans
  Ashanti  37
  Barotse  53, 61, 214 n.22
  Basotho  26
  collaboration with whites  53, 56–57, 60
  control of  135–139, 143
  as convict labour  185
  evictions from game reserves  93, 185–186
  as game rangers/police  87–88, 93–94, 97–98, 110, 152–153, 183–185, 187, 189
  hunting  105, 109–110, 139, 183
  labour  186
  land needs  150, 156, 185
  Lou (Lau)  134, 136
  Makuleke  185
  Marotse  45
  Mhinga  185
  Ndebele  60
  resistance by  135–136, 138–139, 143
  settlements within game reserves  92–93, 95, 185
  Swahili  94
  Swazi  83
  as tourists  186
  Tsonga  185
  Westernisation of  60
  Zulu  25–27, 83
Aldershot  34–36, 75, 122

Alexandria  128
Allenby, Field Marshall Edmund  27, 67–68, 70–71, 74, 76–77, 144
anarchism  17
Anglo-Boer War *see* South African War
Anglo-Zulu War  25–26
Angola  53–54, 56
*Animal Life in Africa*  115, 117, 171, 190
antelope  26, 49, 63, 91, 105, 107, 109, 116, 143, 156, 187
Ardagh, Sir John  47
Astor, Waldorf  112
Australia  7, 37, 41, 70, 77, 122, 163, 215 n.11

Baber, Ruth  169
Baden-Powell, Robert  112
Bahr-el-Gebel  131
Barberton  83–84, 196
Barotseland  1, 2, 44–45, 47, 53–54, 56–58, 61, 63, 69, 73, 80, 110, 113, 122, 208
  *see also* Stevenson-Hamilton, James: Gibbons expedition
*Barotseland Journal*  58
Basutoland  131
Battle of Diamond Hill  73
bats  143
Bechuanaland/Botswana  51, 80, 103
Beira  111
Belfast  78
Bethel  76
Bigalke, Dr R.A.  189, 199
*Blackwood's Magazine*  108
blesbuck  189

Bloemfontein 67–68, 70–71
Blood, General Sir Bindon 78
Boer/Afrikaner 25, 65, 67–70, 72–73, 75–77, 79–80, 92, 101–102, 142, 147, 149, 154–155, 163, 178, 200–201, 215 n.15
   Afrikaner nationalism 142, 147, 149, 154–156, 163, 178
   Broederbond 178
   Het Volk 101–102, 147
   Voortrekker 163
Bor 133, 136–139, 143
Botha, Louis 148, 155
Boyd-Alexander, Lieutenant A. 52, 55–56, 214 n.19
Brake, Ranger 154
Bramble, Major 136
Brent, Ranger 154
Brighton 31, 33–35
Britain/England/British 3, 25, 38, 49–50, 54, 68, 70, 75, 80, 83, 101, 103–105, 111, 113, 119, 121, 126, 133, 135–136, 138, 142–144, 146–147, 155, 159, 161, 163, 178–179
   class system 7, 17–18, 22–23, 38–42, 44, 90, 111, 170, 178
British South Africa Company 47, 54, 80
Broadhurst, Margaret 145, 170–172
Bryden, H.A. 112
buffalo 95, 217 n.15
Bulawayo 45
Bulgaria 122
Buller, General Sir Redvers 67, 75
Bushveld Carbineers 154
Butler, A.L. 139, 141, 218 n.10
Buxton, Edward North 104, 111–112, 144, 162

Cairo 111, 122, 128, 144, 157
Caldecott, Harry Stratford 164–166, 180
Cameron, Captain Cyril St C. 69
Campbell, W.A. 189
Cannadine, David 18

Cape Colony 65, 67, 83, 111
Cape Helles *see* Gallipoli campaign
Cape Town 24, 68, 115, 148, 155, 161, 169, 195
Caprivi Strip 54
Cardwell, Lord 16
Carlisle 145, 170
Carolina 76
Casement, Tom 84
Central African Archives 58
Cetshwayo 25
Ceylon 76
Chalmers Mitchell, Dr R. 111, 113
Chapman, Abel 84, 166
cheetah 107
Chikoa 54, 57
Childers, Erskine 74
Chinde 54
Chobe River 53, 56, 62
Churchill, Winston 17, 35, 37
Clements, Major-General R.A.P. 67–68, 70
Coetzee, S.H. 151
Coetzer, J.J. 154
Colenso 65
Colesberg 65, 67, 74, 171
colonialism/colonisation 3, 53–54, 57, 68, 97, 101, 111, 119, 134, 142, 154
Comores 94, 111
Connaught, Duke and Duchess of 115
Constantinople 122
Corydon, Robert 97, 110, 122, 131, 133
Coutts, Reverend C. 16
Crimean War 42
crocodile 49, 107, 117
Crocodile River 83–84, 91, 152, 184
Cronje, General Piet 70
Crosby, A.J. 159
Curzon, Lord 112

Darwinism 57
Dauncey, Major Thursby 68, 71–72, 74–80, 100, 121, 215 n.23

De Jager, Piet  154
Delagoa Bay  73, 75, 78, 110
De Laporte, Dick  88, 153, 184, 206
Department of Lands  90, 102, 150, 156, 160, 162, 175, 200
Department of Native Affairs  87, 90–91, 93, 150, 154, 156, 161, 185
Dinka  131–132, 134–137, 139–140, 142, 218 ch.9 n.1
Dinuzulu  25
Dorset  173, 175
Drakensberg  159
Dublin  1, 8, 100
duiker  95
Duke, Thomas  88, 152, 180
Dullstroom  78
Dundalk  34, 46
Durban  24–25, 65, 79

Eastern Cape  159
East London  24, 148
Edinburgh  8, 34
Egypt  2, 21, 111, 122, 129–130, 137, 143
eland  49, 63, 95
Elandsfontein  79
elephant  88, 95, 116, 137–138, 140–142, 188, 217 n.15
Ermelo  76
Esselen, Louis  178
Ethiopia  139
Europe/European  49, 54, 60, 104, 121, 155, 193–194
*Exploration and Hunting in Central Africa*  51

Fairholm *see* Larkhall, Lanarkshire/ Fairholm/Kirkton
*The Field*  108
First World War  1, 119, 122, 131, 147
  *see also* Flanders; Gallipoli campaign; Treaty of Versailles
Fitzgerald, Colonel  121
Fitzpatrick, Sir Percy  103

Fitzroy Hart, Major-General  75
Flanders  126
France  7, 128–129
Francis, Captain H.F.  84
francolin  157
Fraser, Major A.A.  86–88, 108, 142, 152, 154
French, Major-General  69, 74
Froom, Lieutenant-Colonel  27

Gallipoli campaign  1, 2, 119–128, 130, 133, 218 n.4
  Achi Baba  124
  Anzac Cove  125, 127
  Cape Helles  122–124, 127
  Chanuk Bair  125
  Koja Chemen Tepe  125
  Mediterranean Expeditionary Force  122, 128
  Mudros  128
  Suvla Bay  122, 125, 127
game reserves/national parks  47, 80–81, 83–84, 86–88, 90–91, 93, 95, 97, 101–102, 104–106, 109, 116, 119, 139, 143, 147–156, 159, 161, 165–166, 168, 175, 177–178, 199
  Addo  159
  Dongola  195
  game rangers  86–89, 93, 108, 131, 154, 179–180, 188–189, 194
  game wardens  84, 86–89, 116, 139, 148, 180, 188
  Kalahari Gemsbok National Park  159, 179
  Kruger National Park *see* Stevenson-Hamilton, James: career: game warden
  National Parks Bill/Act (1926)  166, 175, 177
  Pafuri Game Reserve  185–186
    *see also* Africans: evictions from game reserves

poaching 84, 87–88, 91, 93–94, 116–117, 152–153
  *see also* Stevenson-Hamilton, James: views on poachers
Pongola Game Reserve 83, 86–87, 149
Rustenburg Game Reserve 103, 149
Sabi Game Reserve/Sabi Bridge *see* Stevenson-Hamilton, James: career: game warden
Singwitsi Game Reserve 82, 86–88, 93, 97, 108, 148, 150–152, 154, 185, 219 n.9
  under threat/Commission of Inquiry 148–152, 155–156, 159–160, 162
  *see also* Stevenson-Hamilton, James: career: game warden
gazelle 140
*Geographical Journal* 110, 131
Germany/German 54, 121, 179, 194, 202
Gibbons, Major Alfred 44–47, 49–58, 60, 62
Gibbs, Florence 19–20, 22–23, 39–40
Gibbs, Lieutenant 76, 215 n.15
Gibraltar 7
Gill, Leonard 169
giraffe 63, 90, 95
Gladstone, W.E. 18
Glasgow 1, 7, 12, 17, 39
Gordonia-Kuruman 149
*Government Gazette* 102
Graham, Claude 170–171
Greathead, Percy 162
Grobler, Piet 162–163, 165–167, 200
Guadeloupe 7
guinea fowl 63, 158
Gwai River 55

Hamilton, Eliza 7–10, 168
Hamilton, Ian 127
Hardie, James Kier 7, 38
Harris, Lieutenant J. 76
hartebeest 140
Healy, G.R. 89, 153

Heidelberg 76
Heilbron 78–79
Hertzog, J.B.M. 155, 160, 177–179, 184
Hindlip, Lord 112
hippopotamus 95
Hitler, Adolf 179
Hobley, C.R. 111, 170
Hoek Commission 201
Holland, Ernest 206
Holt, Norfolk 121–122
Hornaday, Dr William 116, 147, 219 n.1
Howe, Elliott 169, 172
hyaena 9, 107

Ibo 110
*Illustrated London News* 36
impala 95, 189, 196
imperialism 3, 17, 21, 34, 53–54, 83, 101, 104, 119, 155, 179, 200
  hegemony 25
India 31, 51–52, 70, 78, 112, 122, 145
(Inniskilling) Dragoons
  6th (Inniskilling) Dragoons 23–24, 30, 34, 65, 80, 115
International Arbitration Court 54
Ireland/Irish 1, 7, 12, 15, 34, 38
  Irish nationalism 8, 18
Ismailia 128

jackal 99, 107, 189
Jameson Raid 37
*Jock of the Bushveld* 103
Johannesburg 29–30, 72, 80, 86, 148, 172
Jonglei 140
*Journal of the Society for the Preservation of the Wild Fauna of the Empire* 108, 111, 142

Kafue Falls 57, 59
Kafue River 55
Karoo 67
Kazangula 56

# Index

Kenna, Brigadier Paul  121–122
Kenya  189, 202
Kenyan Game Department  189
Khartoum  56, 130, 143, 158
Kimberley  53, 65, 67, 70
King Charles III  7
King George V  113, 115, 121, 206
King James VI  7
Kirkton *see* Larkhall, Lanarkshire/ Fairholm/Kirkton
Kitchener, Lord  76, 121
Kleinenberg, T.J.  151
Kruger National Park *see* Stevenson-Hamilton, James: career: game warden
Kruger, Paul  37, 73, 75, 101, 165–167
kudu  95
Kwando River  53, 56, 62

labour in England
  industrialisation  7, 9–10, 17, 112–113, 208
  organised  7, 17, 38, 143
  rise of professionalism  18
labour in South Africa
  industrialisation  148
  organised  160
    Bondelswarts Rebellion  160
    Bulhoek  160
    Rand Strike  160
Ladysmith  65
Lagden, Sir Godfrey  80–81, 84, 86–87, 90–92, 104–105
Lake Nyasa  110
land companies/private consortiums
  Henderson Consolidated Lands  86
  Oceana  86
  Sabi Sand  201
  Transvaal Consolidated Lands Company  159, 165, 201
  Transvaal Land and Exploration Company  86
  Transvaal Land Owners Association  155

Larkhall, Lanarkshire/Fairholm/Kirkton  5, 7–9, 12, 19–20, 22–23, 29, 33, 38–40, 42, 62, 80, 103, 113, 145–146, 148, 159, 162, 168, 171, 173, 190, 192–195, 203–206, 208–209
League of Nations  155
Lebanon  136
Lebombo Mountains  87
lechwe  63, 140, 189
Ledeboer, L.H.  86, 154
Legogote  85, 88
leopard  107, 217 n.15
Leopold, Aldo  187
Letaba River  86, 97, 150, 219 n.9
Levubu River  185
Lewanika  53–57, 60
Leyland, Frances  10
Lialui  55–56
Limpopo River  185, 195
lion  91–92, 99, 107–109, 117, 123, 156–157, 171, 179–181, 187, 190, 207, 217 n.15
Lisbon  24
Livingstone, David  47, 49–51
Lloyd, William  154
London  10–12, 17–20, 22–23, 27, 31, 34, 39–41, 111–114, 129, 143, 145, 147, 159, 161, 169
Lou (Lau) *see* Africans
Loveday, Richard  83, 102, 166
*The Low-veld: Its Wild Life and its People*  190
Luck, General Sir George  37, 46
Ludorf, J.G.  189
Lugard, Lord  112
Luxor  137
Lydenburg  92, 151

MacMillan, W.M.  111
Madeira  24
Mafeking  65
Magaliesberg  72
Magersfontein  65

Malan, D.F. 200
malaria 45, 49, 57, 113, 134, 143, 150, 169, 207
Mamili 56
*The Man-Eaters of Tsavo* 112
Marico River 103
Mary Queen of Scots 7
Matlabas River 103
Maugham, R.C.F. 110
McDonald, Hector 184
McKean, Lieutenant-Colonel A.C. 37
Meek, Lieutenant G. 72
Middelburg 75, 78
Milner, Lord Alfred 101
mining 30, 72, 91–92, 95, 106, 148, 150, 184–185
Mnyamana 25
Mongalla 130–131, 134, 136, 138, 140
Mosley, Captain A.R. 68
Mozambique/Portuguese East Africa 75, 82, 86, 110, 185, 194
Mpumalanga 1, 2
Mtimba 88, 191, 206
Muller, Theodore 52, 55–56
Munro, General 127

Nairobi 111
Namaqualand 149
Natal 1, 24–25, 28, 30, 65, 67, 74–75, 77, 115, 149
National Zoological Gardens 189, 199
*The Native Races of South Africa* 183
Natives Land Act (1913) 150
nature conservation/protection 3, 103–107, 116–117, 131, 139, 141–142, 144, 148–152, 156, 175–176, 187, 209
　Convention for the Preservation of Wild Animals, Birds, and Fish in Africa 104
　Preservation of Wild Animals Ordinance 139

Society for the Preservation of the Wild Fauna of the Empire 104–105, 111–112, 139, 162, 217 n.8
Transvaal Game Protection Association 90, 92, 105, 217 n.9
*see also* Stevenson-Hamilton, James: influence on nature conservation; philosophy of nature conservation
Ndlovu, Njinja 184
Ndlovu, Sergeant Judas 153
Nelspruit 201–202
New York Zoological Society 116
New Zealand 7, 122, 125
Ngonye Falls 53
Nile River 130, 133, 136, 139
Nkonjeni, Natal 25–26
Northcote, Major C.S. 138
Northern Cape 179
Northern Province 1
Nuer 134–139, 142
Nyalunga, Sinias 184
Nyasaland/Malawi 30, 54, 97

Okavango swamps 56
Olifants River 85, 97, 150, 219 n.9
Orange Free State 24, 65, 70, 78, 159
Orange River 65, 67
ostrich 95
Owen, Governor 136–137

Paardeberg 70, 72
Pafuri Game Reserve *see* game reserves/national parks
Pafuri River 86
Page-Henderson, Lieutenant-Colonel H.C. 67–71
Palestine 128
Papenfus, H.B. 166, 182
Paterson, Lieutenant E.S. 35, 76
Patterson, J.H. 112
Pease, Sir Alfred 112
Pennefather, Edward 144

# Index

Pietermaritzburg 15, 24–25, 27–29, 35, 115, 144
Pirie, F.D. 45
Pirow, Oswald 179, 194
Pongola Game Reserve *see* game reserves/national parks
Port Elizabeth 65
Port Said 129
Portugal/Portuguese 54, 57, 88, 110, 186
Preller, Gustav 186, 189
Pretoria 67, 71–74, 76–78, 80, 86, 119, 148, 156, 192

Quicke, Captain F.C. 51–52, 55–56

race 178
    black/African 57, 60, 76, 80, 87–88, 105, 137, 180, 183, 185–186, 202
    Indian 57, 186
    racial prejudice/segregation/apartheid 57–58, 60, 88, 92, 105, 110, 137, 139, 178, 180, 184–186, 202
    white 21, 49, 55, 60, 61, 87–88, 91, 95, 101, 109, 133, 136, 150, 152, 163, 180, 183, 186
reedbuck 95
Reitz, Deneys 156, 160, 163
rhinoceros 95, 217 n.15
Rhodes, Cecil John 47, 53–54, 67
Rhodesia 80, 119
Riekert, P.J. 149
Rimington, Mike 68, 74, 77–79
Rimington's Guides 68–70, 88
rinderpest 55, 62, 109, 149
Rissik, Johann 102, 149–151
roan antelope 62–63, 95
Roberts, Lord 67, 70–71, 74
Roland Ward 111, 144
Roosevelt, Theodore 111–112, 115–116
Roos Senekal 78
Rooth, Edward 102, 119, 147
Rothschild, Lord 112, 144
Royal Academy 36
Royal Colonial Institute 51
Royal Geographical Society 1, 44, 46–47, 111, 144
Royal Humane Society 121, 184
Russia 122
Rustenburg Game Reserve *see* game reserves/national parks

Sabi Game Reserve/Sabi Bridge *see* Stevenson-Hamilton, James: career: game warden
Sabi River 83–85, 89
sable antelope 95
San Bushmen 183
Sandenbergh, J.A.B. 196, 199–201
Sanderson, Charles 206
Schoch, Dr Arnold 177
scops owl 99
Scotland/Scottish 1, 5–8, 17, 20, 24, 38–39, 158, 170–171, 191–192, 203–204
    *see also* Larkhall, Lanarkshire/Fairholm/Kirkton
*The Scotsman* 22
Sebituane 53
Second World War 35, 183, 194–195
Sekeletu 53
Selous, Frederick Courteney 45, 112, 167
Sesheke 56
Shaka 25
Sharif, Ali 94, 111
Sharpe, Sir Alfred 97, 112
Singwitsi Game Reserve *see* game reserves/national parks
Sioma 53
sitatunga 63
Skukuza 192–193, 195, 202, 209
Slingersfontein 69
Smillie, Robert 7
Smith, Dr 52, 55–56
Smuts, Jan Christiaan 102–103, 115, 121, 147–149, 151–152, 155, 159–160, 163, 165, 169, 177–178, 190, 197, 200, 206

Sobat River  139
socialism  7, 17, 39, 112–113
Society for the Preservation of the Wild Fauna of the Empire *see* nature conservation/protection
Somaliland  51
South Africa  1–3, 24, 35, 57, 65, 80, 101–103, 113, 116, 121, 130, 136–137, 139, 141–142, 144–148, 152, 155, 158–160, 162–163, 169, 171–172, 175, 177–178, 183–185, 190–191, 193–197, 200, 202–205, 208
South African Constabulary  89–90
*South African Eden*  81, 88, 97, 163, 165, 189–190, 200
South African Museum  169
South African Railways  160–161, 165
South African War  1, 34, 37–38, 63, 65–80, 83–84, 100, 119, 127, 148, 154, 156, 178
South West Africa  121
Soutpansberg  86, 151
Spiers, E.M.  72
springbuck  189
Stack, Sir Lee  143
Standerton  77
*The Star*  30
steenbok  95
Stevenson, Andrew  16, 41
Stevenson, Gwladys  41, 112, 122, 130, 145
Stevenson, Nathaniel  11, 15
Stevenson, Robert  15
Stevenson, Tom  12, 15–16
Stevenson-Hamilton, Eliza 'Cissy'  8, 19–20, 22, 39–40, 70, 77, 115, 129, 145–146, 162, 194
Stevenson-Hamilton, James
  ancestry  5–8, 15, 17, 103, 208, 211 n.11
  awards
    Coronation Medal  196
    Fauna Society Medal  196
    Honorary Doctorate: University of Cape Town  196
    Honorary Doctorate: University of the Witwatersrand  196
    Order of the Nile  131
    Warden Emeritus of the Kruger National Park  199
  career
    agent for London Zoo  113–114
    army  1, 2, 99–101, 119, 121–130
      in Britain  33–38, 42–43, 46, 63
      in Gallipoli *see* Gallipoli campaign
      Sandhurst  16–17, 20, 22–24, 27, 40, 69, 212 n.9
      in South Africa  15, 18, 22–31, 65, 67–80
      in the Sudan *see* Sudan
      Woolwich  16–17
    game warden  57, 80–95, 97–109, 111–112, 115–116, 121, 142, 148–157, 159–162, 165
      Kruger National Park  1–2, 82, 147, 152, 155–157, 159–163, 164–170, 172, 175–177, 179–190, 192–196, 199–201, 203–205, 208–209
      Sabi Game Reserve/Sabi Bridge  1, 80–95, 97–99, 102–103, 105, 107, 113, 115, 119, 131, 146, 148–152, 156–157, 159, 161, 165, 168, 172, 177, 183, 209, 219 n.9
    Secretary of the Fauna Society/London Zoo  162, 169–171
    Sudanese civil service  130–144 *see also* Sudan
  death of  208
  educational and social milieux  5–13, 15–17, 22, 27
    Rugby  11–12, 15
  family life/relationships  1–2, 5–6, 8–13, 15–20, 24, 37, 39–41, 103, 112, 115, 119, 129–130, 145–146, 157–158, 162, 168, 173, 175, 190–197, 202–204, 206–208
    associations with women  22, 24, 41–

44, 112, 129, 137, 161, 170, 148, 157–158, 161
Helen Lindsay-Smith 42, 113, 122, 131, 144, 206, 213 n.13
Hilda Browne 24, 148, 206
Hilda Stevenson-Hamilton (née Cholmondeley) 167, 170–173, 175, 179–180, 189–196, 202–204, 206–208
Princess Marie Louise 161, 206
relationship with father 10, 12–13, 17, 22, 27–29, 33, 37, 39, 43, 46, 100, 112–113, 121, 129, 144–146, 158, 162, 168–169, 171, 205, 215 n.15
Gibbons expedition 44–52, 54–57, 62–63, 69, 110
historical context 1, 3, 12, 17–18, 21
influence on nature conservation 62, 94–95, 97, 102–103, 105–106, 108–110, 112, 116–117, 141–142, 165, 167–168, 189, 195–196, 201, 208–209
philosophy of nature conservation 62, 93, 95, 99, 102, 105–106, 108–110, 117, 142, 150–151, 186–190, 196, 199
powers of/authority 95, 150, 188
publications of 1, 58, 81, 88, 97, 106, 108–110, 115–117, 131, 165, 179, 189–190, 196, 200
  illustrations/photographs 2, 109, 131, 190
  journals 1–3, 10–11, 23, 26–28, 30, 33, 35–36, 38, 43, 58, 61, 73–74, 79, 94, 110, 113, 121, 124–126, 133, 140–141, 143, 147–148, 157, 161, 169, 171, 176, 190, 193, 203–204, 207–208
relationship with/attitude to Africans 57–58, 60–61, 92–95, 109–110, 134–139, 183–186, 190
relationship with National Parks Board 166, 169, 172, 175–179, 182, 185–187, 189, 191–196, 199–201
reputation denigrated 200
retirement 1, 2, 103, 147, 161, 169–170, 172, 177–178, 195–196, 199–209
travels in east Africa, Egypt and Sudan *see* Egypt; Sudan
views on British politics 38, 101, 113
views on poachers 183
views on/relationship with rangers 87–88, 179–185, 188–189
views on scientists 106, 187–189, 200, 209
views on tourists 91, 105–106, 175, 180–183, 186–187, 195
Stevenson-Hamilton, Leyland 10, 12, 168
Stevenson-Hamilton, Olmar 9, 39–41, 70, 77, 112–113, 122, 130, 144–145, 158
Stevenson-Hamilton, Vivian 145, 158, 162, 170, 193
Steyn, Louis 180
Stormberg 65
Stowe, G.W. 183
Sudan 2, 16, 21, 47, 111, 130–144, 147–148, 156–159, 208
  *see also* Lou (Lau); Bor; Khartoum; Mongalla; Nile River
Sudd 133
Suez Canal 128
Swanston, Lieutenant A.W. 76, 215 n.16
Swaziland 86–87, 149, 187
Syria 128

Tasmania 69–70
Terrot, Lieutenant 76, 215 n.16
Tete 52, 54, 57, 63
Thukela River 25
tiang/topi 140
*Times Literary Supplement* 116
Tomlinson, Ranger 184, 206
Transvaal 2, 37, 65, 75, 77, 80, 83–85, 91, 95, 101–106, 109, 116, 141–142, 147, 149–151, 155, 158, 165–167

*Transvaal Agricultural Journal* 108–109
Transvaal Consolidated Lands Company
　　*see* land companies/private
　　consortiums
Transvaal Game Protection Association
　　*see* nature conservation/protection
Transvaal Progressive Association 102
Treaty of Vereeniging 80
Treaty of Versailles 155
Tring 112, 144
Tsavo National Park 188
tsessebe 63, 95
tsetse fly 106, 109, 149, 187
Tshokwane 99–100
Turkey 122, 125–126, 128

Uganda 97, 131
Ulundi 25–26
Umfolozi 149
United States of America 95, 116, 147, 160, 163
Upper Nile Province 134, 136
Usan 12, 17

Vaal River 71
Van Graan, H.J. 185–186
Veëiro, Antonio J. 54
'vermin' 107–108
Victoria Falls 49, 55
Victorian 11, 17–18, 20, 27, 35, 39, 58, 62, 63, 106
Viljoen, General Ben 78
Vryheid 25
vulture 52–53

Walker, W.M. 84
Wallis, J.P.R. 58
Ware, Harry 53
Warmbaths 83
Warren, Dr 115
waterbuck 63, 95
Wavell, Field-Marshall 34, 74
Weller, C.L. 52, 55–56, 63
Whistler, J. 10
white-eared kob 140
White River 170–171, 191, 196, 202, 207
wild dog 107
wildebeest 62, 95
wildlife management, scientific 199–200
Witwatersrand 72
Wolhuter, Harry 88, 93, 142, 152–154, 180–181, 191, 195, 201
Wood, Sir Evelyn 35
Woodville, Richard Caton 36
World War I *see* First World War
World War II *see* Second World War

Yardley, John Watkins 44–45, 76
Yellowstone National Park, USA 95, 147, 160, 168

Zambezi River 47–49, 51–55, 57, 63
Zambia 53
Zanzibar 111
zebra 63, 90
Zoological Society of London/London Zoo 111, 114–115, 142, 144, 159, 162, 171
　　*Proceedings of the Zoological Society of London* 131
　　*see also* Stevenson-Hamilton, James: career
Zululand 25–26, 30, 86–87, 105, 149, 159, 187, 208
Zumbo 57, 63